AF701471

DUTCH TRANSATLANTIC MEDICINE TRADE

A.M.G. Ruttten

DUTCH TRANSATLANTIC MEDICINE TRADE IN THE EIGHTEENTH CENTURY UNDER THE COVER OF THE WEST INDIA COMPANY

ERASMUS PUBLISHING
Rotterdam 2000

© 2000 A.M.G. Rutten, Erasmus Publishing, Rotterdam
Alle rechten voorbehouden. Niets uit deze uitgave mag worden verveelvoudigd, opgeslagen in een geautomatiseerd gegevensbestand, of openbaar gemaakt, in enige vorm of op enige wijze, hetzij elektronisch, mechanisch, door fotokopieën, opnamen, of enige andere manier, zonder voorafgaande schriftelijke toestemming van de uitgever.

Voorzover het maken van kopieën uit deze uitgave is toegestaan op grond van artikel 16b Auteurswet 1912 j° het Besluit van 20 juni 1974, *Stb.* 351, zoals gewijzigd bij Besluit van 23 augustus 1985, *Stb.* 471 en artikel 17 Auteurswet 1912, dient men de daarvoor verschuldigde vergoedingen te voldoen aan de Stichting Reprorecht (Postbus 882, 1180 AW Amstelveen). Voor het overnemen van (een) gedeelte(n) uit deze uitgave in bloemlezingen, readers en andere compilatiewerken (artikel 16 Auteurswet 1912) dient men zich tot de uitgever te wenden.

ISBN 90 5235 148 1
D / 2000 / 41 / 6
NUGI 730

Boekvormgeving: Designworks, Chris Geurts

Erasmus Publishing
Glashaven 14-A
3011 XH Rotterdam

Keywords: Medicines, trade, traffic and Netherlands history; European expansion; West India Company; Health care Caribbean, Guiana and West Africa.

Cover picture: Keelhaul (kielhalen) of a surgeon. The surgeon was hauled under the keel of a Dutch naval vessel from bow to stern by ropes in punishment. Oil painting by Lieve Verschuier (1630-1686). Courtesy of the Rijksmuseum Amsterdam.

CONTENTS

PREFACE

'An apple a day keeps the doctor away'. This observation (or is it just wishful thinking?) might apply in Europe; it certainly did not apply to the history of European expansion in the Atlantic. In order to survive as a European in West Africa or as an African in the Caribbean more than an apple was required and the odds were that the mortality among the migrants was much higher than among those who stayed at home.

There is no area or period in human history where medicines were so important as on the plantations, settlement colonies and trading forts in the Atlantic during the period between 1500 and 1800. In spite of a very limited understanding of the medical problems involved, Europeans risked their lives in the completely different disease environments of other continents and they made African slaves do the same. The human costs were enormous: European mortality on the West Coast of Africa was as high as 600 per 1000 per year, the mortality aboard slave ships could come to 50 per 1000 per month and the mortality among Europeans and African slaves on the plantations in the Caribbean and Northeastern Brazil could not be reduced to less than 50 per 1000 per year. As an aside I should mention that the highest mortality in the expansion of Europe anywhere occured between 1500 and 1650 among the Amerindians in the New World killing perhaps as much as half of the original population of the Americas.

All this explains why physicians and their medicines were so important in the history of the Atlantic. Unfortunately, little is known about this vital aspect. Much is written on the economic, demographic and social consequences of the expansion of Europe, but to date only a few studies exist regarding the role of physicians and healers, be they European, African or Amerindian. Equally absent are studies regarding the medicines used in the treatment of diseases encountered by voluntary and forced migrants in the Atlantic.

In view of this it is more than fortunate that Dr. A.M.G. Rutten has produced the first comprehensive survey of the trade in medicines in the Dutch Atlantic between 1600 and 1800. His scholarship is unique in that he combines his expertise as a pharmacologist with an extensive knowledge of the relevant historical literature. His book shows that physicians and other medical practitioners were trying to cope with the various Atlantic disease environments. Over time their efforts resulted in a considerable decline in mortality. Before the breakthrough in medical knowledge at the end of the 19th century, Rutten's analysis of the trade in medicines shows that trial and error could achieve stunning results.

Ut prosit!

P.C. Emmer.

ACKNOWLEDGEMENTS

As is the case with everyone who has written a book, I have become indebted to many individuals along the way and would like to take this opportunity to express my gratitude. First of all I want to thank Peter Verhoef (Erasmus Publishing Rotterdam) who has offered me the chance to publish my book.

Thanks also go to Professor P.C. Emmer (Institute for the History of European Expansion, Leiden University) for his careful reading and valuable suggestions. I would like to extend my thanks to the staff of the Koninklijke Bibliotheek and the Algemeen Rijksarchief at The Hague, and the Rijksmuseum Amsterdam. My thanks are due to Dr. Renate Wilson (Johns Hopkins University, Baltimore) for information on the traffic in Halle medications. I am grateful to Dr. C. Baggerman (Farma Consult BV Eindhoven) for checking the pharmaceutical part of the text, to Mrs. José Koelman (Librarian of the Eindhoven University of Technology) for assistance and to Mrs. Jenny Wormer, who translated part of my book and improved my English. The errors which remain, of course, are mine.

Most particularly I am grateful to my wife Marie Louise who has lived through the ordeal of writing this book and given me her usual wise counsel and cheerful support.

Alphons M.G. Rutten
Research Associate
Institute for the History of European Expansion
Leiden University
The Netherlands

Eindhoven, March 2000

INTRODUCTION

The art of being wise is the art of knowing what to overlook
William James (1842-1910)

From an early period of civilisation after man's search of his environment for food and vegetable drugs, he learned to recognise those beneficial to health and the ways to obtain remedies by trade. Cinnamon, dragon's blood, cassia, cardamom, ginger and turmeric were known and employed as drugs by Eastern people thousands of years ago. They became important items of commerce early in the evolutionary course of trade. Ancient herbals including those of Cathay (China), Sumer, Assyria, Egypt and Greece testify to the use of spices and herbs in the treatment of disease. The need for drugs that were not available forced the ancient peoples to develop international trading contacts. Part of the immense yearly income of King Solomon came from the traffic of the drug and spice merchants. Strabo (fl. 50 BC) in his *Geography* speaks of the extensive trade in spices and herbal drugs carried on by the Arabians. The role of herbal medicines and spices in shaping the course of the history of trade is a long and fascinating story. Traders from Europe, Asia and Africa passed in their track with raw drugs, fragrant woods and incense, hides, spices and pottery, exchanging the goods found in one area for the products in another.[1] Melegueta pepper, for example, obtained from the Grain- or Pepper Coast (Liberia) and carried from West Africa across the desert to the harbour of Mundibarca on the coast of Tripoli, appeared in 1214 AD at the Treviso market as Grains of Paradise, and physicians were apt to include it in their prescriptions.[2] The practitioner George Fordyce remarked that there always has been a tendency in mankind to employ almost everything in medicine.[3]

How did medicines that were found in a small part of the world find their way to another part in the transatlantic drug traffic? In early times European traders made their crossings with large caravans, sometimes they had as many as 2000 camels. Whatever part the overland trade routes played, it was mainly by sea that the trade in vegetable drugs and spices grew. In the eighteenth century transatlantic traffic was a matter of sailing ships. For mariners this century was an age of adventure, risk, hardship, typhus, dysentery, yellow fever and death; for nations an age of struggle, smuggling, defeat or conquest.

The history of the Dutch transatlantic medicine traffic during the eighteenth century is a forgotten chapter in the broad frame of the historiography of Dutch expansion overseas. This book will focus the attention of specialists and laymen on the Dutch share in the Atlantic medicine traffic and will try to shed light on the volume, kind and target of medicines shipped to overseas possessions. It demonstrates the manifold functions, which the interdisciplinary history of pharmacy fulfils. Its factual material consists of a well-documented collection of letters found in the archives of the New Dutch West India Company (WIC) during the years 1700-1791.[4]

After the expiration of the twelve-year truce between the Netherlands and Spain in 1621, the Dutch prepared themselves for renewed conflict with Spain and the West India Company was founded. The Company was intended to present consolidated opposition to the Spanish and was granted the right to settle, build, administer and defend colonies on the coasts of West Africa and the Americas. Dutch enterprise continued to be characterised by interest in trading and raiding, rather than in establishing a colonial empire.[5] After the loss of the colonies New Holland (Dutch Brazil) and New Netherland (Dutch New York) in the middle of the seventeenth century, little was left of a Dutch territorial empire in the Atlantic world.[6] There remained however an interesting trading area covering the Caribbean islands, the colonies along the North Coast of South America and the factories and castles on the Gold Coast of West Africa. In the 18th century the WIC no longer had an effective trade monopoly but had to leave the trade function to private merchants, who committed smuggling with the foreign colonies via Curaçao or St. Eustatius.[7] These merchants had direct commission trade in colonial products for export to Amsterdam. Most trade across the North Atlantic had always been covered by private merchants.[8] As disease and mortality played such an important role in the Dutch overseas expansion, it is remarkable that so little attention has been paid to kind, volume and controle of the travelling materia medica. The history of early modern trade seldom focuses upon Atlantic drug trade with the exception of the studies of some English and American scholars.[9]

This study deals with the medicine traffic into the Dutch Antilles, the Guiana colonies Essequebo, Demerara, Pomeroon and the forts and lodges on the Gold Coast of West Africa, covered by the WIC. Berbice, although managed by the

Society of Berbice, is included because it had many links with the WIC. Surinam ruled by the Society of Surinam is not dealt with. A selected list of the archives, books and articles consulted is included at the end of the text. For readers who are not familiar with medical terms, a glossary of the principal medical indications, terms and diseases used in this publication has been appended.

Notes

1 Franck, *Trade and Travel Routes.*
2 Van Harten, 'Melegueta Pepper', 208-16.
3 Fordyce, *Dissertation*, 96.
4 Archival notes: The WIC Archives: Brieven en Papieren van Curaçao (Archief West-Indische Compagnie) class number and volumes are all found at the Algemeen Rijksarchief, Den Haag, The Netherlands.
5 Parry, *A short history*, 49.
6 Emmer, 'The Dutch Atlantic', 48-69.
7 Parry, *Trade and Dominion*, 31.
8 Emmer, *The Organization of Interoceanic Trade*, XXI.
9 Roberts, W.I., Samuel Storke' 147-170; See also Stander, S., 'Transatlantic trade', 326-343 and Steele, I.K., *Atlantic merchant-apothecary.*

Chapter I
FROM ARCHAIC MEDICINES TO MARKETABLE DRUGS

Full ready had his apothecaries
To send his drugges and his lectuaries
Chaucer, Geoffrey (1343?-1400): *The Canterbury Tales*

EARLY TRAFFIC IN REMEDIES

The search for medicines against disease and ailments is as old as mankind.[1] When the herbs searched for were not available in the direct vicinity, they had to be taken from foreign parts. Traders carried spices and drugs, exchanging the products in one area for commodities found in another. Trade by barter developed; rather than taking money for goods, they simply exchanged them for other goods. The knowledge of the road medicines had to travel from source to user is summarised by Tschirch in the concept of *Pharmako-emporia.*[2] A thousand years before recorded history the Persian Royal Road and the Great Desert Route were used to obtain drugs from western Asia.[3] Archaeological finds confirm the role of medicines, which were shipped from their original place to another warehouse. Sometimes they fell into the hands of the conqueror as war booty, sometimes they were purchased or they were sent as presents.

So, the Byzantine emperor Heraklius seized in AD 627 from the palace of the Persian king Chosroes II a party of aloe or eaglewood (*Aquilaria agallochum*), pepper, ginger and sugar. The Egyptian sultan Meleh Elmaydi sent the Venetian Doge in 1461 as a present a number of medicines such as benzoe, eaglewood, Mecca balsam, opium, sugar and civet. To be less dependent on the suppliers people soon started to grow medicinal plants and spices. King Merodak-Baladan

II (c.710 BC) possessed a herbal garden laid out in Babylon. Plinius secundus had a hortus botanicus, although it was not his property. The king of Pergamum, Attalus Philometor (c.150 BC) had a poisonous plants garden of his own for his toxicological research and Pope Urban IV (1261-1264) thought it necessary to warn Charles of Anjou that Manfred of Sicily had sent a large quantity of poisonous medicaments to France in order to kill Anjou.[4]

With the collected quantities of food, drugs and poisons people tried to defend themselves against hunger, disease, cold, bad spirits and enemies, and mankind has learnt to distinguish certain remedies or actions as good or bad. Diseases are as old as life, which is exposed to physical, chemical, biological and psychical harmful influences.[5] Man has always been forced to busy himself with the care of his wounded or sick fellow man. A task that was particularly awarded to the first healers, thc priest-magician-apothecary, who knew how to bring recovery and softening of suffering with hymns, incantations or drugs. The pharmacological knowledge that was gained by the use of drugs led to the conception of the medicament in the broadest sense. The experience gathered was not only passed on orally, but also sometimes registered in prescription books or pharmacopoeias. The oldest one is to be found in the Nippur table, a Sumerian tablet from the third century before Christ. Even then the assortment of medicines comprised a large number of simples (i.e., the crude uncompounded drugs), that were occasionally imported from foreign parts. Other documents from former times originate from Egypt, India and Persia. The Papyrus Ebers (c.1550 BC) shows that the Egyptians knew about 700 medicaments. The working of certain herbs and poisons was recognised by them and played a part in the support of their magic rites. Fragrant remedies were the central element in ancient medicine.[6] Precious stones and amber were prescribed by Mesopotamian practitioners as amulets against diseases.[7] Amulets beside herbs, roots and seeds, played an important part as preventive or curative aid. All through the Middle Ages they were given as relics in monasteries, together with vegetable drugs to passing sick and wounded people and they have not disappeared from contemporary traditional medicine either.

In Greece doctors were priests for a long time, judging by the mythological writings such as Homer's Iliad and Odyssey. Aesculapius was the god of physicians and the Asclepiads were priest-doctors. In the third millennium before Christ books of recipes must have existed in Mesopotamia that were free from magic and were compiled according to rational views.[8] Even then relations existed between India and Mesopotamia, as contacts were maintained over land and sea between Egypt and ancient India. Medicinal products were transported by caravans over roads that ran parallel to the Elburs Mountains in North Iran and from there turned off to the south, to Belutsjistan.[9] The 'Assyrian Herbal' published by R. Campbell Thompson, gives a correct impression of the drug trade and mentions nearly all herbs that used to be shipped massively from India to Egypt.[10] Mesopotamia too got its share of it with simples like cinnamon, sweet flag, ginger, pomegranate, sandalwood, cannabis and asa fetida (Devil's Dung). These examples make clear that nearly all exchange of goods was inextricably linked with social and sometimes political factors.

The Greek practitioner Hippocrates, born in Cos around 450 BC, is known as the founder of a medicine that was disposed of empiricism and founded on observation of symptoms. This father of medicine also had a vast knowledge of the qualities of medicines. In the Western Roman Empire, where Greek physicians practised, Dioscorides (fl. AD 60) wrote an extensive work in the Greek language on the effects of about 600 botanical and animal medicines. It was published in Latin in the 16th century under the title of *De Materia Medica*. He mentions the Egyptian origin of 80 vegetable drugs that he described. As a contemporary of Dioscorides, Plinius secundus published his work *Historia Naturalis*. These writings show how many medicaments were even then known and available.

Figure 1.1. Despatch of vegetable drugs under the supervision of King Arkesilas (6th century BC)

Many of the simples described had to be imported from other parts or countries, so that a lively trade developed. Especially in the first centuries after Ch. the Roman spices and drug trade was booming. Import and export were mostly in the hands of Greek, Etruscan or Punic traders for the Romans did not hold trade in high regard. A favourite product such as frankincense was obtained from Dzofar, the eastern province of the Hahdramut. Transport was expensive, as the costly gum resin had to be transported to the assembly point on camels. The building of Roman roads marked a new geographical and historical change within the Mediterranean and created a new political formation – the Roman Empire.

Through the world trade of the Roman Empire with almost all peoples known the assortment of botanical drugs expanded quickly. Rare balsams, resins, gums, colouring agents and animal products such as hartshorn, musk, Spanish flies, salamanders, snakes, civet, sea-hare and amber, were sent to Rome from all provinces. Every year shipments from Sicily, Africa and Crete arrived too, where emperor Marcus Aurelius had appointed his own herbalists, who carefully wrapped the simples harvested and provided them with a label with name and site of origin.[11] Opium and peganum came from Egypt and Syria, coriander from Africa, aconite from Galley or from the mountainous Danube area, helleborus from Anticyra (Ankara), worm wood from Mesopotamia; from Pontus beeswax was obtained, honey, mastic and Phu or Creticum, from Asia Minor marjoram and asa fetida. The colourful and fragrant harbours on the Somalian coast supplied cannabis, turmeric (curcuma) and cinnabar (dragon's blood). Bdellium resin, myrrh, sugar and pepper all came from Barugaza, volatile oils and perfumes were supplied by Egypt, sulphur was obtained from Sicily, rue (*Ruta spp.*) from Greece. From the East shiploads of cinnamon, myrrh, frankincense, precious stones, ivory, pepper and ginger arrived.[12] The *Periplus Maris Erythraei*, written about AD 120, shows again clearly how intensive the barter trade was with the harbours in the area bounding the Red Sea, Persian Sea and the Indian Ocean and mentions a number of medicines that were traded in Barugaza.[13] In AD 165 Emperor Marcus Aurelius sent delegates via Tonkin over the sea to China in order to get hold of aromatic drugs. Aromatic gums and resins had been popular from remote antiquity as herbal remedies. Galen (AD 130-200), the emperor's practitioner, too wanted to acquaint himself personally with the sites and qualities of drugs and travelled at the end of the third century to a large number of countries in search of exotic medicaments, such as bitumen, eaglewood and the Indian lycium. The Roman trade dwindled in the 6th century. During Galen's practice even more than 1000 simples were available. In his medical treatises it was accurately laid down what a medicament was, how preparation and delivery had to take place and which forms of administration, i.e. pills, ointments, infusions, plasters or syrups, were in use. Galen's *Opera omnia* comprises all that was known at that time about medicine. Nowadays people still speak about 'Galenic pharmacy'. A supplement to this was the *Grabadin* of Pseudo-Mesues (11-12th c. AD), a work on medicine and materia medica that laid the foundation of later pharmaco-therapeutic works and dispensaries.[14]

During and even long after the Justinian disaster in AD 536 when a large part of Asia and Europe was disrupted,[15] it was especially the monasteries that busied themselves with the study, preparation, barter trade and sale of medicines.[16] The monasteries moreover gave the opportunity to receive and take care of sick, poor, old and hungry passers-by. Through their isolated and protected position in the mountains and further inland and financial reserves the monks could maintain themselves better than ordinary citizens in the times following the volcanic eruption.[17] Although England had hardly recovered from the consequences of the disaster, the Benedictine monk the Venerable Bede (8th century) was able to write books on medical subjects and vegetable drugs and to keep in close touch with monks on the European continent.[18] As a result of the pilgrimages to Mecca a lively barter trade of medicaments both from Spain, India and China developed at the end of the 8th century. Mecca was not only the biggest pilgrim's town, but the world's largest market of medicinal and poisonous herbs as well. Constantinus Africanus (c.1050), an Islamite converted to Christianity, gave in South Italy an important impulse to the foundation of the University of Salerno. Of the many works of the Salernitan school especially the *Alphita* has to be mentioned i.e. a list of 1387 simples and synonyms that was highly important for practitioners and merchants in medicines.[19]

On the crossroads of Antiquity and the Modern Age Paracelsus made a name for himself with his struggle against old medical systems. He drew up his own rules for the use of mineral remedies and is sometimes called the father of iatro-chemists. His effort to use mercury against syphilis was not accepted with gratitude by the Fuggers, who traded profitably in the medicinal guaiac wood and sarsaparilla, used against venereal disease and rheumatism in Europe.[20]

In the fourteenth century Bruges became the most important trade centre, where Italians annually supplied herbs and spices from India and the Levant and collected products from Germany and the Balkan countries. Almost all English trade passed through Bruges. Thus a large party of the wax, almonds, rice, sugar, ginger, cassia, galangal, pepper, grains of paradise, saffron, cloves, cubebs, aniseed and liquorice went to the Bishop of Exeter, who died in 1307.[21] The wholesalers in vegetable drugs and spices held their Bruges market in the Cruythalle. In the 13th and 14th centuries Antwerp also had a flourishing herbal trade, but in 1585 Antwerp was conquered by the Spanish troops and the Dutch closed the Scheldt River. Yet it too has been able to keep its function in the world market of herbs and spices for a long time. All newly discovered drugs from America and East-India could be found there on the market. An important part of the trade of Antwerp moved to Amsterdam in the 16th and 17th centuries. This city soon became a trading metropolis and Dutch merchant ships not only sailed out to the Mediterranean but also to the East Indies, South America and Africa.

In Venice the fishing population concentrated from the 8th century on the salt production and the trade in Oriental goods. Alexandria where Venetian ships arrived as early as 820 was the junction of the herbal trade between Orient and Occident. From time immemorial, southern Arabia had been a trading centre for medicinal resins, gums and woods. Especially the Crusades promoted the Venetian trade and its naval supremacy. The Venetians brought the first sugar to Europe during the Crusades at which time is was so costly that is was used exclusively as a medicine. The republic of Venice became a great power once and for all when Marco Polo succeeded in reaching China. The discoveries of Marco Polo were neglected by the Venetians themselves, but they later became the means of depriving the republic of the exclusive trade in drugs and spices with the Orient which they lost to Portugal at the beginning of the 16th century. For three centuries, however, the republic kept in control of the trade in Oriental medicinal herbs. From 1317 there was a regular shipping service between Venice via Flanders and Brabant to Bruges and Antwerp and via Gibraltar with London and Southampton. Big consignments of aloe, benzoe, camphor, cinnamon, cloves, cubeb, ginger, nutmeg, nardus, opium, pepper and rhubarb left the Italian harbours every year.[22] A Dutch ship sailing for Venetians and captured by the Spaniards of Gibraltar carried currants, textile and a range of Near Eastern drugs.[23] Goods for Bruges were mainly meant for transit to the Hanseatic League and the Fuggers, who took care of further distribution. Spices and drugs meant for Germany went along the Alps route in heavily guarded transports.[24]

A fleet of Venetian galleys supplied Western Europe and England. Italian connections reached far and wide and by the 15th century Italy was a formidable power in Europe.

Venice was famous for its impressive ceremony and the care that was taken of the preparation of theriac, the wonder drug of polypharmacy. Theriacum Venetum (Venice Treacle) was globally a very eligible antidote and helpful remedy. It was known for its outstanding quality and acquired a supremacy over the theriacs as made by the rival cities of Genoa, Florence, Bologna and even Constantinople or Cairo, which led to extensive trade.[25]

Venice began to lose its lustre when the Turks conquered Constantinople (1453) and Egyptian trade gradually declined. The discovery of the route to India round the Cape of Good Hope by Vasco di Gama in 1498 was the deathblow to the Venetian monopoly on the import and resale of Oriental spices and drugs.

Portuguese who were to monopolise the trade in goods from India, did not unload their cargoes in Venice but in Lisbon; the Spanish their gold and silver in Seville. In the 16th century pharmacist Tomé Pires was sent to India by King Manuel the First to handle drug trade in the Orient. He reports to the Portuguese King on his mission and refers to an order of a series of medicines from the Orient, which were dispatched under his direct supervision.[26] By the 1550s these two great colonial powers had not only opened up the world but also created huge demands for investment in entirely new methods and institutions. If the Ophir were voyages of the Phoenicians, the voyages of the Romans and Arabs to China and those of the Chinese to the Persian Gulf and the Red Sea were commercial travels only without political background, with the Portuguese and the Spanish both trade and politics were at stake.

Italy was the traditional German area of trade, while in the North the Baltic trade was mainly a matter of the Hanseatic merchants. The Hansa was an association of German cities, which promoted trading monopolies. Between both areas of trade a lively distributive trade existed, in which especially Frankfurt played a part. In Nuremberg particularly the Imhof firm and the Behaim merchant house occupied themselves with the simples trade in the 14th century. Further German trade focused on France and the Iberian peninsula. Favourite bases in this were Geneva, Lyons and Barcelona.[27] An important part in the German spices and medicaments trade was played in the 15th and 16th centuries by the Fuggers mentioned above, a family from Augsburg that occupied themselves with international trade and banking. With saffron, pepper, guaiac wood and china root they gained an enormous turnover, in which the monopoly yielded such big profits, that in 1524 on the *Reichstag* in Nuremberg maximum prices were fixed with a *Reichsreglement.*[28] Beside the botanical drugs chemical products started to conquer a place in therapy too under the influence of Avicenna and Paracelsus, which led to an extensive traffic in medicinal minerals like lead, mercury and antimony. By the end of the 16th century medicine was divided into the warring camps of Paracelsians and Contra-Paracelsians and the alchemists began to penetrate into pharmacy.

With the discovery of America a large number of vegetable medicines unknown until then were added to the European assortment. Columbus had reached what he at first thought was India by sailing due west from Spain and his discovery opened unpreceded opportunities for the return traffic of Central American plants. In addition to the many New World herbs taken by the Europeans, the potent drug *Datura metel* (Thorn apple) is one example and occurs on many of the West Indian islands. Drugs like guaiac, Peruvian balsam, sarsaparilla, cocoa, tobacco, ipecac, copaiba balsam, jalap, Peruvian bark (cinchona), vanilla and quassia are some examples of this. In Frampton's (1577) translation of Monardes (1574) it is stated that '...afore saied Medicines are now by our Marchauntes and others brought out of the West Indies into Spaine, and from Spaine hether unto Englands, by such as dooeth daily trafficke thether'.[29] Herbal drugs were continually returned not only to Europe but also to Spanish and Portuguese colonies and factories like Calicut, Goa, Timor, Macau and Philippines. Extensive trade and shipment to Amsterdam developed in those products, an important part of which was shipped via the Caribbean Islands of Curaçao and St. Eustatius in the 17th and 18th centuries.

The discovery of the seaway to the East-Indies by the Portuguese by the end of the 15th century also brought on the market a number of medicines unknown or scarce until then, like benzoin, rhubarb, camphor, ginger, incense and myrrh. A Dutch fleet under the command of Cornelis Houtman sailed for the Spice Islands in 1595; another commanded by Jacob Cornelisz van Neck put to sea in 1598 and four ships returned home with rich cargoes of spices and medicinal herbs. The Dutch gained a monopoly on spices such as pepper, mace, nutmeg, cloves and finally cinnamon. Medicines from the East and West were often doomed to travel round the globe on the way to their final destination. East-Indian camphor, cinnamon, frankincense, cloves, turmeric and rhubarb were shipped via Amsterdam to the West-Indian colonies, while guaiac, sarsaparilla and gum anime as medicaments from the New World ended up in the territory of the East-India company. The physician Garcia da Orta, who was forced out of his native Portugal by the inquisition, took a bale of 500 pounds of Caribbean guaiac wood with him from Portugal on a sea voyage to Goa on the West coast of India in 1536 and wrote a valuable book on pharmacognosy and medicine trade *Coloquios dos simples e drogas da India* (1565-71).[30] In the 17th century, the Dutch shipped Western drugs and Western medicine to Japan and found their place in the Japanese armamentary.[31] Trade saw to a wide distribution of medicaments, trade supported health care and trade made formerly unknown drugs into fashionable articles. However, we do not intend to make this trade an object of economic study here.

PHARMACOPOEIAL GUIDANCE

The strong influx of new medicaments from the East and West forced the government to act regulatingly with regard to the processing and delivery of these remedies. The uniformity of the locally used prescription books was experienced by both doctors and pharmacists as bad. Prescription books and dispensatories that were used did not have any legal force, as was the case with pharmacopoeias, so therefore the directives were trifled with. There were a few Dutch editions of foreign pharmacopoeias or prescription books in circulation, but the wide variety promoted errors. Especially the epidemic of plague in Amsterdam many people fell victim to in 1635 led to this condition being changed. In that year Dr. Nicolaas Tulp (1593-1674) took the initiative to compile a shopping book for pharmacists, decided on by the law. As soon as the work was finished it was presented to the *Collegium Medicum* by the *Raad der Vroedschap* (The Amsterdam City Council) and in 1636 it was introduced by the Court as the first Dutch pharmacopoeia, the *Pharmacopoea Amstelredamensis.*[32] As its sources primarily served the *Pharmacopoea Augustana* (1622), further the *Dispensatorium Coloniensis* (1627) and the *Pharmacopoea Londinensis* (1627). A pharmacopoeia is a book containing a list of medicinal substances (drugs) and/or articles (devices) with descriptions and formulas for preparing the same, selected by some recognised authority.[33]

The Amsterdam pharmacopoeia in the Latin language went through many reprints and was revised twice.[34] The drawback that many surgeons and pharmacists did not have sufficient command of the Latin language, so that the chance of misunderstanding was not inconceivable, made the editor Jan ten Hoorn publish a Dutch version under the supervision of Dr.med. Pieter Bernagie. The same as did William Salmon (1644-1713), a London empiric who produced his famous translation of the *London Pharmacopoeia* in 1678. In 1686 a third edition of the Dutch translation was printed under the title of *Pharmacopaea Amstelredamensis* or d'Amsterdammer Apotheek (Ph.A) (figure 1.2).[35] It was this edition of Ph.A. that was best loved in the Dutch colonies and was considered binding on the basis of the rules that the fatherland employed and that relied on the *Ordre van Regieringe* from 1629.[36, 37]

The book was a guidance both for pharmacotherapy and the medicine trade. Physicians in the colonies were often insufficiently taught in the Latin language and this translated edition offered a welcome alternative, even more so because, contrary to the Latin edition, the effects and the measurement of the composites were mentioned. Composites or compounds are medicines with several ingredients. This Amsterdam pharmacopoeia also gives extensive instructions for the method of preparation, the distillation of waters, the confectionery of fruits and mentions in a register the diseases that can be treated with the medicaments described. Pharmacists were obliged to have the assortment of simples mentioned in the pharmacopoeia in store in their pharmacy: 'De medicamentis simplicibus in officinis asservandis'. It was succeeded in 1726 by the *Pharmacopoea Amstelaedamensis renovata.* The inclusion of 72 new simples in this edition resulted in an extensive trade, as the pharmacists had to supplement their stock with a large number of East and West-Indian medicines like ipecacuanha, ginseng, serpentaria, cascarilla, cinchona, winter's bark, colubrinum, tolu, catechu, copal, olibanum and cochineal. Besides a number of tinctures, balsams and elixirs were included for the first time. The version translated into Dutch of this pharmacopoeia did not contain instructions for use anymore as did its predecessor, to deprive unauthorised persons of the chance to get access to pharmacotherapy. For the use of medicaments that were not described in the Amsterdam pharmacopoeia one referred in the colonies also to other Dutch pharmacopoeias, like the *Pharmacopoea Harlemensis* (Haarlem 1702).[38] Pharmacopoeias were a major reason why the selft-taught in the colonies could function as apothecaries and a major determinant of what drugs they could know and prescribe.

THE DUTCH WEST INDIA COMPANY

In 1621 the West India Company (WIC) was founded at the insistence of a refugee from the Southern Netherlands, William Usselincx. It aimed to establish a commercial empire and not so much at exploiting colonial territories. This Dutch commercial enterprise received from the States-General the monopoly on all trade and shipping on the African coast between the Tropic of Cancer and the Cape of Good Hope and on the Americas. Private merchants were excluded

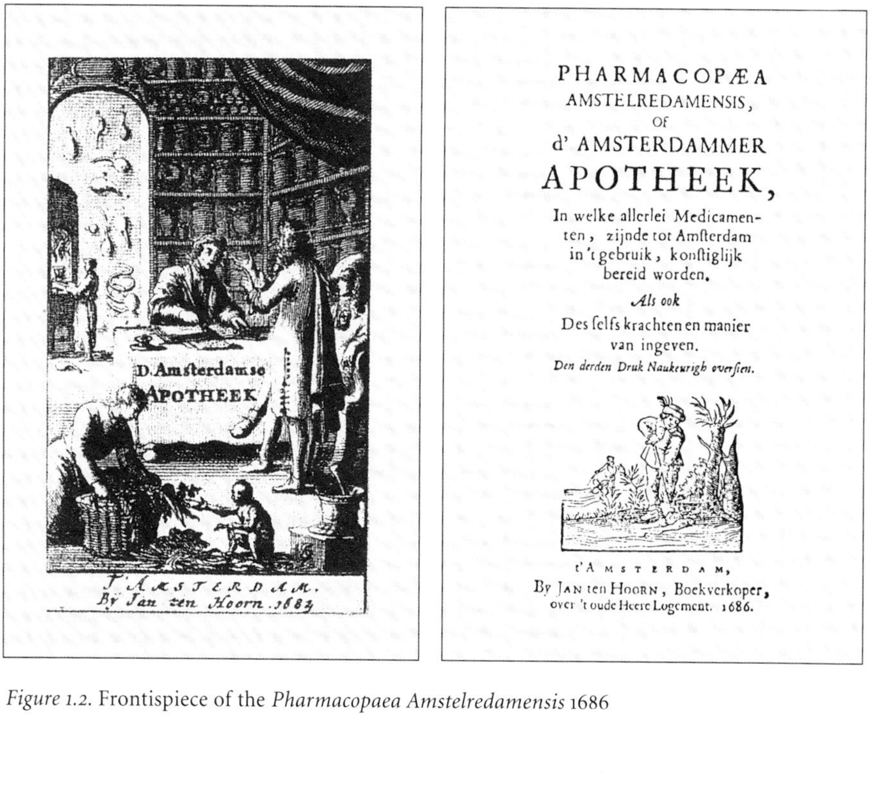

PHARMACOPÆA
AMSTELREDAMENSIS,
of
d' AMSTERDAMMER
APOTHEEK,
In welke allerlei Medicamenten, zijnde tot Amsterdam in 't gebruik, konstiglijk bereid worden.
Als ook
Des selfs krachten en manier van ingeven.
Den derden Druk Naukeurigh oversien.

t'AMSTERDAM,
By JAN ten HOORN, Boekverkoper, over 't oude Heere Logement. 1686.

Figure 1.2. Frontispiece of the *Pharmacopaea Amstelredamensis* 1686

from trade. The WIC hardly occupied itself with plantation economy, except in Guiana, not in the least because only with difficulty sufficient settlers could be found for inhabiting the overseas territories. The Company was more interested in trade than in colonisation and the most important motive at its founding really was causing damage to archenemy Spain. It was not true that trade was waiting for the birth of the Company. Even before the foundation of the WIC there was a lively trade with the New World. In 1620 Dutch freighters already took care of half to two-thirds of the sea shipments from Brazil to Europe. For the slave trade founding of the trading company had not been particularly necessary. Between 1620 and 1623 even in the capitania Pernambuco only, where the WIC was to get an important settlement, 15,340 black slaves were imported.[39]

In the 1640s the Company was at the height of its powers, when it disposed of New Holland (Dutch Brazil) and New Netherland (Dutch New York), further of territories on the West Coast of Africa, colonies in Guiana and in the Antilles.[40] Because of considerable losses the WIC suffered through bad management, corruption, the transfer of Brazil to Portugal in 1654 and of New Netherland to England in 1664, the Company was dissolved in 1674.[41] In that year a new WIC was founded on a more modest scale, receiving its income mainly from the monopoly on the trade in slaves, gold, melegueta-pepper and gum from Africa. In 1683 too it had given up one of its most important possessions, i.e. Surinam in Guiana, to the Geoctroyeerde Societeit of Surinam. The Company's charter was discontinued in december 1791, when the States-General took over the WIC possessions and debts.

THE MERCHANTS ELITE VAN EEGHEN

Trade in the territory of the New West India Company as it was conducted on the Caribbean Islands of Curaçao and St. Eustatius, further in Essequebo, Demerara and Berbice in Guiana and the trading stations on the African Gold Coast, was a monopoly of the WIC until 1730. After that private trade was permitted and the monopoly limited to the Guinea coast. A few years later this privilege went too and trade with the West-African coast, including the sixty-mile zone on the Gold Coast, was opened to all residents of the Republic. Private interlopers thereby came in a legal position, but did have to pay recognition. The WIC only kept the monopoly on the slave trade to Surinam, Essequebo and Berbice. Henceforth the income of the Company did no longer come from trade, but mainly from the collection of capitation and recognition money.

The most attractive possession of the reorganised WIC, the most important basis for trade with the New World and the most striking example of medicine traffic operations was Curaçao, one of the islands of the Netherlands Antilles. Together with Aruba and Bonaire it is part of the Leeward Islands that are situated right off the Venezuelan coast, the Costa Firme. The distinction of Windward and Leeward (in Spanish Islas de barlovento and Islas de sotavento) is connected with the Northeast trade wind, the prevailing wind in the Caribbean Sea. Windward are the Netherlands Antilles islands of St. Eustatius, St.Maarten and Saba between the Parian Gulf and Puerto Rico; leeward those between this gulf and the Paraguaná Peninsula.

Curaçao developed in the 17th and 18th centuries into an important West-Indian harbour and staple place for European trade with South and Middle America. In peacetime illicit trade was lucrative there, in case of friction of war privateering was. Privateers were tradesmen licensed by national governments to seize enemy ships. All trade of the Dutch outside the WIC's influence, either direct or transit trade via Curaçao and St. Eustatius was illicit trade.[42] This with the exception of the slave trade, in so far it was conducted under the auspices of the Spanish asiento. It was small private firms that transported the greatest number of slaves to and from the plantation areas in the New World during the 18th century.[43] However, traders were often more interested in the prospects of contraband for which slaving gave a cover, than in slaving itself. The prosperity of the island was due to the transit of products of others to Amsterdam and import of goods from Europe and North America that were in demand for miles around. Traders continually concluded contracts with Spanish merchants on the Costa Firme on conditions and kind of goods.[44] Dutch commercial ships took an important share of those transactions. The goods trade between Spain itself and its colonies was organised particularly badly in the late 17th and 18th centuries and flotas or galleones were sometimes absent for years. The Dutch tried to fill the gap. As early as the 17th century Colbert estimated the size of the European merchant fleet to be 20,000 ships, of which 16,000 were Dutch. England and France had agreed in 1686 that trade with or between the mutual colonies could not be allowed. Such mercantilism made legal traffic between English North America and the French Antilles impossible. The Dutch made grateful use of the ban by acting clandestinely as intermediary with Curaçao as operating base. The clandestine traffic with the Spanish colonies was so efficiently organised that cocoa from the Caracas coast via Curaçao was cheaper in Holland than in Spain.[45] Yet the trade proved to be not invulnerable. The outbreak of the War of the Spanish Succession (1702-1713) brought about a disruption of the trade system. The asiento passed into the hands of French slave traders. Felipe V, the Spanish king, decided that Dutch ships were no longer allowed to put into Spanish-American ports to deliver slaves or commodities. Both France and England tried to undermine the Dutch trade position in South America. In 1710 the prospects of Curaçao were grim and a letter from the Governor shows that the trade with the Spanish continent eased off to almost nothing.[46] Nevertheless Amsterdam merchants like Semah Ferro and Mendes da Costa increased their trading activities with the Caribbean. From 1720 however, a recovery was involved again, in spite of the competition of the strongly expanding British, French and Spanish transit trade and traffic.[47]

There was a highly important Amsterdam trade with Spain itself as well, worth 20 million Dutch guilders around 1720, that was almost entirely based on the needs of Spanish America. The 1715 treaty arranged this trade. New wars like the one that broke out in 1739 provided more prosperity. In 1746 Curaçao and St. Eustatius received permission for the trade with St. Domingue and Guadeloupe, as the French colonial authorities wanted to prevent that the sugar harvest was not shipped and a lack of foodstuffs and drugs would develop on account of the English blockade.

Medicine traffic into and from the Caribbean was situated in Amsterdam, which after the fall of Antwerp had taken up a controlling position as colonial goods depot. A much smaller part as staple market was reserved for Middelburg, which mainly profited from the trade in Guiana colonial products. The big business houses in Amsterdam, Jews as well as Gentiles, had their representatives and agents in Spanish colonial ports on the opposite shores.[48] Many Jews trading with Curaçao Jews were related to each other, so that Curaçao really was the commercial and religious centre of one big family.[49] Jewish New York merchants like Nathan Simson and Moses Michall or Mikal also traded extensively there and Michall stayed so often in Curaçao that this Yankee trader was regarded as a Curaçao-resident.[50]

In Amsterdam business houses like Reynier van Weert, the Weduwe (Widow) Fred. Bolmeyer, the Society of Vredenburgh, the merchant houses of Elias van Laar, Jan Westerburgh and Thomas Meyer, to mention a few, kept in close touch with Curaçao. Surgeons in Curaçao often acted in this as go-between in the medicine trade. Thus in 1724 civil physician Willem Columba sent a crate of elemi gum to Van Weert by the ship Vigilantia, chief surgeon Johan Rudeloff shipped to his brother in Amsterdam various vegetable drugs and doctor medicinae L.R. Horst shipped several barrels of lemon juice and orange peel to Jan Westerburgh in 1743.[51]

Among the many business houses that occupied themselves in Amsterdam with the trade in medicines and spices, especially the Van Eeghen firm played an important part as merchants and shipowners of vessels sailing to Curaçao, St. Eustatius and St. Thomas. The Van Eeghen family arrived in Amsterdam in 1662 from Flanders. In the early 18th century Jacob van Eeghen's business house was specialised in the sale of return cargoes arrived from West-India, including return commodities such as sugar, sarsaparilla, indigo, redwood, cochineal, tobacco, cocoa, lemon juice, divi-divi (the pods of *Caesalpinia coriaria*) and salt. These products came along as return freight after the supply of linen, East-Indian cloths, wooden articles, ceramics, beer and wine. Curaçao and St. Domingue were the most important places for reshipment. The business house owned several ships including the *Vrouwe Cornelia*, the *Anna Galey* and *De Curaçaose Visser*. The last mentioned ship was confiscated by the English in 1759 on its return voyage.[52] The ships sent were not particularly big and did not exceed a cargo of 300 tons.

The history of the Van Eeghen merchant house clearly shows that the exchange of goods is inseparable from social and political factors. In 1735 we see for the first time the name of Susanne Blok, Jacob's widow, mentioned in official documents on the trade on Curaçao.[53] After the WIC opened up the private trade on the West-Indies in the seventeen thirties, Van Eeghen was able, with the help of correspondents working on commission and shipowners-insurers like Jan van Lennep, Abraham de Levy Maduro and Abraham Henriques Moron, to extend his business relations with Curaçao further and establish a merchant's and shipping company there. Richter & Cresons was one of the trading partners in indigo, coffee and cocoa. For this clever use was made of the fact that all products of inter-regional and international trade came on the market in Curaçao and were forwarded from there to Amsterdam, which even though it was not the only European market town where these goods could be bought, it certainly was the most important one. For the trade between the Caribbean islands the governor at Curaçao issued passports making it possible to navigate and trade freely.[54]

From Amsterdam the Van Eeghens shipped linen cloth, cheese, sausage, oil, beer, ink, brandy and canvas to Curaçao and as return home goods the above mentioned products were taken along. The linen came from Silesia and France, indigo in its turn was redelivered again to Danzig, spices to the business associates Johan Felthusen and Peter Wickelhausen in Bremen. Through the mediation of surgeon Johan Rudeloff in Curaçao the Van Eeghens also received consignments of products to be sold on the Amsterdam market that were shipped by the vessel *Anna Galey*.[55] Rudeloff was appointed in 1740 as master surgeon in the service of the WIC and also acted as private merchant.[56] Unfortunately no specifications of the return wares are to be found, but it is clear that drugs like sarsaparilla, Peruvian bark (cinchona), tamarind and cassia were shipped to which Rudeloff would have contributed the necessary know-how. Council member Johannes Stuijlingh too traded in drugs and in 1737 sent about thirty seroons of Peruvian bark in all to the Amsterdam business house of Thomas Meyer and Van Bunschoten & Boulde.[57] This confirms that the servants of the WIC too occupied themselves with private trade. Political channels were tapped so as to take control of the trade.

The consignments increased in importance after 1740: cocoa, hides, sugar and tobacco were the main transit goods and private trade was yet to expand considerably in the years 1750 to 1784. Many bags of costly cinchona were shipped by Van Eeghen from Curaçao to the Amsterdam market and dispatched to Germany. In 1758 the ship the *Curaçao Visser* took a cargo of 354 seroons of cinchona, probably from Maracaibo, via Curaçao to Amsterdam.[58] A stumbling block for trade became the Seven-Year War, which broke out in 1757 between England, Prussia and France. The English confiscated several ships sailing home from the West, because they shipped goods that came from the French colonies and were regarded as contraband. A recovery was also brought about by the American War of Independence broken out in 1774, which caused a strong increase in trade between Holland and the West. Because of their favourable location Curaçao and St. Eustatius could function as big staple places, where American ships collected goods that were supplied by the Dutch. After 1781 trade declined because of the war between Great Britain and the Netherlands, but in 1782 another improvement was noticeable because of the increased trade with the USA. In 1783 more than 50 ships left the Curaçao harbour in convoy. In the 1790s each year 16 to 20 loaded ships came from the Netherlands, and returned home with West-Indian freight. The developments in the Netherlands in 1795 made the supply of trade goods come to a standstill. For Curaçao the war circumstances were disastrous. In 1798 a number of merchants alerted governor Lauffer (1753-1833) to 'the sad and most miserable condition the island is in' and insisted on an agreement to be made with the French governor Gabriel Hédouville (1755-1825) in Cap Français, so that all neutral nations allied with Curaçao would be permitted to call freely at the island with cargo. Moreover it was requested to forbid French privateers to take any further action.[59]

For more than a century the Dutch Republic had been able to control trade and shipping. Not only on account of its favourable location, but also because of the lack of energetic competitors. When England outstripped her, not only a privileged position was lost, but power and influence had also disappeared. This was not so much due to lack of energy, but a result of the fact that the Republic could not, like England, dispose of an industry of its own. Yet the Van Eeghen merchant house was able to carry on well in the years of recession and in 1807 we read about return freights from Curaçao of sugar, coffee, tobacco, potash, indigo and rice and of important medicaments like a party of 20 bags of jalap root that brought in *f* 5800,00 and further drugs like spermaceti, senega root, simaruba bark, cinchona bark and musk.[60]

The above gives no more than an impression of number, extent and kind of medicines that were shipped by the WIC and private persons from Amsterdam or arrived as return freight from Curaçao. A more detailed source is deposited with the lists of the drugs that were sent by order of the WIC from Amsterdam or Middelburg to the hospitals in the colonies in the Caribbean, Guiana and Guinea. They provide insight into the every-day medical practises of the eighteenth century that will be explored in more detail in later chapters.

Notes

1 Sonnedecker, *Kremers and Urdang*, 3.
2 Tschirch, *Handbuch*, 1.1., 145.
3 Franck, *Trade and Travel Routes*, 63-4.
4 Lewin, *Die Gifte*, 235.
5 Schmitz, *Geschichte der Pharmazie*, 3.
6 Parry, *The story of spices.*
7 Sigerist, *History of Medicine*, 478.
8 Thorwald, *Heelmeesters*, 176.
9 Thorwald, *Heelmeesters*, 169.
10 Thompson, *Assyrian Medical Text.*
11 Friedländer, *Sittengeschichte*, 181.
12 Rutten, *Ondergang in bedwelming*, 76.
13 Huntingford, *Periplus*, 30.
14 Vandewiele, *Grabadin.*
15 Stothers, 'Volcanic eruptions', 6357-6371.
16 Rutten, 'Het zwarte gat', 596-9.
17 Harrison, *Mountain and Plain.*
18 Haeser, *Leerboek*, 281.
19 Tschirch, *Handbuch*, 1.2, 639.
20 Crosby, *Columbian Exchange*, 145.
21 Matthews, *History of Pharmacy*, 23.
22 Tschirch, *Handbuch* 1.2., 713.
23 Israel, *Straatvaart*, 164.
24 LaWall, *Four thousand years*, 198.
25 LaWall, *Four thousand years*, 139.
26 Correia da Silva, *Exposição*, 82.
27 Lutz, *Rechtliche Struktur.*
28 Bauer, 'Conrad Peutingers Gutachten', 1-43 and 145-195.
29 Symon, 'Datura is a New World Genus', 203.
30 Tschirch, *Handbuch*, 1.2., 735.
31 Cowen, *Pharmacy*, 66.
32 Haver Droeze, *Collegium Medicum*, 4.
33 Gennaro, *Remington*, 55.
34 Daems, *Pharmacopeeën.*
35 *Pharmacopaea Amstelredamensis.*
36 Cau, *Ordre van Regieringe*, 1235.
37 Archives WIC 579/80 (1731) 157.
38 Doerffel, 'Berichten', 409.
39 Kunst, *Recht*, 62.
40 Emmer, *The Dutch in the Atlantic Economy.*
41 Emmer, 'The Dutch Atlantic', 48-69.
42 Klooster, *Illicit Riches.*
43 Emmer, *Organization of Interoceanic Trade*, XXII.
44 WIC 606 (1766) 210-11.
45 Emmanuel, *History of the Jews*, 216.
46 WIC 571 (1714) 733, 749-50.
47 Israel, *Dutch primacy*, 395.
48 Israel, *Empires and Entrepots.*
49 Bloom, *The economic activities.*
50 Emmanuel, *Precious stones*, 260-265.
51 WIC 578 (1724) 183; 1165 (1737) 39; 590 (1743) 41.
52 Old Archives Curaçao, (1759) 839.
53 Rogge, *Van Eeghen.*
54 WIC 597 (1749) 531 to Adriaan Jacob Pietersz.
55 Archives Notary Hermanus de Wolff, Amsterdam nr. 8933 fol. 596.
56 WIC 586 (1740) 525; 584 (1737) 150.
57 WIC 1156 (1737) 44.
58 A bale or package of vegetable drugs covered with hide or wood bound with hide. One seroon = about 130 pound.
59 Old Archives Curaçao 140 (1798) nr. 55 of 6 June.
60 Rogge, *Van Eeghen*, 134.

Chapter II
SOME EARLY OVERSEAS MEDICINE SHIPMENTS

Among the lists referring to the transatlantic traffic of medicaments, which the WIC did not bear responsibility for, several specimens are to be found that are interesting as reference material for the shipments under Company colours. This involves a list of one of the first transatlantic medicine shipments to America in 1496, a list of medicines that were intended for the Portuguese hospitals at Goa and Angola in 1519 and a list of a shipment to Greenland within the scope of the Dutch whale fishing in 1631. For comparison we will also go into a transatlantic medicine shipment from America to the Mediterranean at the end of the 18th century.

THE COLUMBUS MEDICINE CHEST

One of the earliest lists of medicines that Spain shipped to America is found in the papers of Columbus' second voyage made from 1493 to 1496. The list is present in the Archivos de la Casa de Contratación.[1]

The four voyages to the Western Hemisphere opened the way for European exploration and colonisation of the New World. During the first voyage Columbus founded the fort La Navidad, an establishment on Española, and chose 40 men to remain there.[2] He left food, medicines and stores for a year and sailed for Spain in February 1493. The second voyage was filled with misadventures. Columbus founded Isabella, the first European city in the New World and now a ruined settlement on the northern coast of the Dominican Republic. Then he left for Cibao, a region of the island, where he founded Santo Tomás and left 56 men under the command of a Catalan captain.

Medicines appear to have quickly become an important part of the luggage people took with them to the New World. The second voyage referred to 17 ships and 1500 men, who shipped 112 drugs, including 51 simples and 49 compounds. Of the simples 79% was herbal, 9% animal and 12% mineral/chemical. Two compounds, i.e. Philonium majoris and Philonium Romanum, contained opium and hyoscyamus seed. It is not known whether the drugs were intended for the health care on board or for the colonists left in America. Bénézet, who investigated the list of the second voyage, takes the first to be correct, but comparison with the Dutch colonial lists makes it likely that the medicines were intended for the colonists in La Navidad and Isabella settlements.Bénézet's statement that Confectio Hamech too is one of the opiates is incorrect. Theriac is absent in the Columbus list, which was probably drawn up by Dr. Chanca, the official physician on Columbus' second voyage. In table 2.1 the names of a number of drugs from the list have been translated into Latin nomenclature, thereby facilitating a comparison with the medicaments from the Dutch *Pharmacopaea Amstelredamensis.* This does not imply that the formulas of the Spanish compounds were the same as mentioned in the Dutch Ph.A.

The pharmacist appears to have provided himself well with the most necessary remedies. A large number of purgatives is present such as euphorbia, colocynt, diaprunum, diacarthamum, diasena, tamarind and pills containing rhubarb. For stomach complaints the expensive preserves with peppermint and violets, and herbs such as camomile, poppy and aromatics were available. Superficial pustules or inflammatory nodules on the skin could be treated with cantharis in blistering plaster or with aegyptiacum or fuscum ointment, whereas diachylon plaster and poultice substances such as fenugreek and cydonia served for the maturing of ulcers. Pulmonary disorders, cough and dyspnea asked for althea ointment, but for the rest remarkably few cough medicines are present. For scurvy lemon, grape and pomegranate juice was available, for seasickness gingerroot. Flux and dysentery could be treated with bolus (kaolin) and opium; mouth and throat affections with pyrethrum, camomile or rose-flowers. As antiphlogistics (relieving inflammation) olibanum and myrrh were used; as diuretic oxymel scillae. Finally analgesia and anaesthesia were obtained with Philonium. To speed up recovery the ingredients for a luxurious Hippocras wine like cloves, cinnamon, lemon and crocus were included. All together a well thought-out assortment.

Table 2.1. Drugs shipped from Spain to America in 1493

Adeps bovis	Lapis hematites	Radix rubiae
Adeps suillus	Mastix	Radix zingiberis
Aerugo	Mel rosarum	Saccharum rosado
Alumen rochae	Mercurius sublimatus	Sanguis draconis
Ammoniacum gummi	Myrrha	Sarcocollum
Aqua ardiente	Oleum absynthi	Sebum
Arsenicum album	Oleum juniperi	Semen foenugraeci
Asa foetida	Oleum nardinum	Semen cydoniae
Auripigmentum	Olibanum	Succus granatorum
Bolus armenia	Oxymel	Succus limonum
Cantharides	Oxymel scillae	Succus rosarum
Caryophylli	Oxysacra composita	Succus uvae
Colocynthis	Oxysacra simplex	Syrupus scolopendri
Confectio Hamech	Philonium maioris	Syrupus 5 radicibus
Conserva boraginis	Philonium Romanum	Syrupus absynthi
Conserva de alcosla?	Pilulae agregativae	Syrupus acetosa
Conserva menthae	Pilulae aloephanginae	Syrupus fumo terrae
Conserva violarum	Pilulae aureae	Syrupus menthae
Cortex cinnamomi	Pilulae cochiae	Syrupus rosarum
Crocus sativus	Pilulae communis Rhazi	Tamarindum
Diaprunum laxativum	Pilulae e fumo terrae	Trochisci scillitici
Electuarium diacarthamum	Pilulae rhabarbero	Trochisci camphorae
Electuarium diasena	Pulpa cydoniae	Trochisci diarrhodonis
Emplastrum diapalmae	Pulvis aromaticus rosaceus	Trochisci rhabarberi
Emplastrum diachylon	Pulvis diamargariton frig.	Turbithum
Euphorbium	Pulvis diarrhodon Abbatis	Unguentum aegyptiacum
Flores chamaemeli	Radix aristolochiae	Unguentum dialtheae
Flores rosarum	Radix asari	Unguentum fuscum
Flores violarum	Radix hermodactylorum	
Fructus pini nuclei	Radix iridis florentinae	
Fructus piperis	Radix pyrethri	
Galbanum	Radix rhabarberi	

PORTUGUESE DRUG TRAFFIC

During the reign of King John II (1481-1495) and his successor Emanuel I (1495-1521) the foundations were laid for a powerful Portuguese empire that was to include South-America, the Indian Ocean and West Africa. In 1482 the São Jorge da Mina castle was build on the Gold Coast, which was later to play an important role under the cover of the WIC. The castle also had accommodation for a hospital and pharmacy.[3] Until 1637 the health care and medicine supply of the about sixty strong staff of the castle were in the hands of the Portuguese. In order to guarantee an extensive assortment of medicaments on the Portuguese ships and in their factories, king Afonso V had already granted privileges and rights to master-pharmacist Ananias and to a group of pharmacists that had come along from Ceuta. Since 1492 the drugs for the overseas voyages were obtained from the Hospital de Todos los Santos at Lisbon, where king Emanuel appointed in 1502 pharmacist Alvaro Rodrigues as his private pharmacist, and also regulated by law the job of hospital pharmacist.[4]

After the conquest of the castle in 1637 the Dutch were to find the medicines there that the Portuguese took with them on all their voyages.[5] An impression of the stock is given by the list that boticario (pharmacist) João Fernandes drew up in 1519 for the hospitals in Goa.[6] Similar assortments can be found in other Portuguese settlements such as Angola and Brazil. Table 2.2 lists the shipped drugs.

The Portuguese list includes considerably fewer laxatives, about one third, than Columbus took with him. The Portuguese were also more than the Spaniards prepared on painkilling in emergencies. They disposed of opium, the seed capsules of the opium poppy and just like the Spaniards of Philonium. The latter drug was not much loved by the surgeons as it could easily provoke hallucinations which people on board were very wary of. Of healing ointments and plasters the Portuguese did have more than double the amount the Spaniards disposed of and they paid more attention to haemostasis with unguentum stypticum and antibacterial vulnerary covering with oleum rosarum. Both the Portuguese and the Spaniards treated ulcers and fistulas with plumbiferous ointments. Bolus with opium could have been of use in cases of diarrhea and dysentery. For belly and kidney suffering polypodium was present; for coughs and pulmonary diseases rob acaciae and liquiritia; as diuretics were used oxymel scillae, syrupus capilli veneri and electuarium diureticum. There is an ample choice of purgatives such as myrobalanum, cassia, tamarind, syrupus quinque radicibus and scammony. As tonic and cordial the drugs camphora and quassia could function. Polypodium is also an effective treatment for tape worms. Remedies for the treatment of syphilis are lacking, both on the Spanish and the Portuguese list.

Table 2.2 Some Portuguese medicines shipped to their trading stations early 16th century
Names of drugs translated in Latin nomenclature

Acetum rosaceum	Oxymel
Adeps capri	Oxymel scillae
Aqua portulaccae	Philonium maior
Aqua rosarum	Philonium Romanum
Bolus armena	Pulpa cassiae
Camphora	Pulpa tamarindorum
Electuarium de semences	Radix liquiritiae
Electuarium diureticum	Rhizoma polypodii
Emplastrum cerussae	Rob acaciae
Emplastrum confortativum	Sanguis draconis
Emplastrum stomachicum	Scammonium
Farina hordei	Semen cucurbitae
Flores chamaemeli	Syrupus acetosus
Fructus foeniculi	Syrupus capilli veneri
Fructus myrobalani	Syrupus 5 radicibus
Fructus myrtilli	Syrupus liquirittiae
Fructus papaveris	Syrupus myrtinus
Lignum quassiae	Stigmata croci
Lignum santalinum rubrum	Turbithum
Myrrha	Unguentum diachylon
Oleum chamaemelinum	Unguentum lithargyri
Oleum nymphae albae	Unguentum resumptativum
Oleum rosarum	Unguentum rorismarini
Oleum terebinthinae	Unguentum sambuci
Opium	Unguentum stypticum

WHALING TRADE

In 1631 the Schiedam pharmacist Pieter Maerlandt got ready a chest of medicines for surgeon Jan Jeronimus Mario at Delft. The latter had been appointed as surgeon on a whaler, which left for Greenland in April 1631 under the command of shipmaster Jan Bouwensz from Delfshaven. Probably the voyage was made with the same ship *De Eenhoorn* (The Unicorn) with which Bouwensz by order of the Delft Chamber of the Noordsche Compagnie (North Company) went whaling again in 1633. The invoice of pharmacist Maerlandt fills the gap in the knowledge of the drugs shipped to Greenland.[7] The medicines and prices are mentioned in table 2.3.

Comparison of the various lists shows striking differences. The chilled sailors of the Greenland vessel ran much more risk of receiving injuries and wounds than the Portuguese colonists in the Orient around 1520, or the Dutchmen on the tropical Arguin in 1674. Foodstuffs and drinking water were a much bigger problem on the whalers and in the Greenland settlements than in the tropics. Surgeon Mario therefore took with him unguentum dialtheae, succus liquiritiae and aniseed against pulmonary complaints; basilicon ointment against ulcers and boils; oleum hypericae for rubbing frozen limbs; theriac and bolus against diarrhoea. To treat constipation he used senna, pilulae aureus and pilulae cochiae, but figs and prunes too. Ginger was present for the stomach and to prevent seasickness.[8] In Mario's chest there were also a number of remedies to treat syphilis such as sarsaparilla and mercurials. Moreover he took a few pounds of laurel oil with him as liniment against muscle cramp and stiff limbs. The range of medicines for whale fishing has been determinedly chosen broadly, because one was far away from home for four to five months with a crew of about 40 men. Moreover, one had to reckon with passing through the winter. Scurvy and dysentery were in that case the most important threat to the sailors, as can be gathered from the account of an overwintering.[9] The 4½ pints of lemon juice were certainly inadequate to realise prevention of scurvy. Contrary to the assortment of the Portuguese and Spaniards theriac and mithridatium were present here as painkillers, but not the hyoscyamine containing Philonium or Requies Nicolai. The latter remedies gradually disappeared in the 18th century from the lists of medicines.

AMERICAN DRUGS SHIPPED TO SPAIN AND THE MEDITERRANEAN 1802

Roughly three hundred years after the documented medicine traffic on Columbus' second voyage to America, the frigate New York shipped a number of drugs to Spain and the Mediterranean. Several medicine lists of that period are available in professional literature, but we have chosen this transatlantic voyage as an arbitrary example to compare medicine lists of the 15th, 16th centuries and from the end of the age onwards. To guarantee protection from attacks on American shipping by those of the Barbary Coast, the George Washington administration in the 1790s signed peace treaties with Algiers, Tunis and Tripoli. In 1801, however, Tripoli declared war on the United States. The new president Thomas Jefferson ordered the navy to confront the pirating North African States with military force.

One of the war frigates was the 'New York.' which carried more than a hundred remedies. Table 2.4 specifies the shipped drugs. The designation of the drugs has been transferred to Latin nomenclature, to facilitate comparison with the descrip-

Table 2.3 List of drugs dispatched on a Dutch whaling ship in 1631 to Greenland
Prices expressed in gulden-stuiver-duit; amounts in pound (lb), ounce (u) and drachm (d)

Medicine	Amount	Price	Medicine	Amount	Price
Aqua plantaginis	2 lb	0-6-0	Oleum hypericae	¼ lb	0-28-0
Aqua rosarum	2 lb	0-10-0	Oleum laurinum	2 lb	2-4-0
Aqua vitae	?	1-0-0	Oleum liliorum	3 u	0-9-0
Argentum vivum	3 u	0-12-0	Oleum rosaceum	3 u	0-9-0
Bolus armenia	2 lb	0-5-0	Oleum terebinthinae	½ lb	0-6-0
Cortex cinnamomi	1 u	0-5-0	Pilulae aureus	6 d	0-12-0
Crocus sativus	1 u	0-6-4	Pilulae cochiae	6 d	0-12-0
Empl.diachyl.c.gum	¼ lb	0-8-0	Prunes	2 lb	0-5-8
Empl.diachyl.simple	½ lb	0-5-0	Pulvis algarothi	1 u	2-10-0
Empl.diapompholyg.	½ lb	0-6-0	Radix liquiritiae	½ lb	0-3-8
Emplastrum meliloti	¼ lb	0-12-0	Radix sarsaparillae	½ lb	2-10-0
Empl.mucilaginum	¼ lb	0-9-0	Resina pini	¼ lb	0-1-0
Empl.oxycroceum	¼ lb	0-18-0	Rhizoma zingiberis	2 u	0-1-8
Flores chamomillae	2 lb	0-10-0	Sanguis draconis	½ lb	1-10-0
Flores meliloti	1/2 lb	0-10-0	Sapo	1 lb	0 12 0
Flores rosarum	2 u	0-3-0	Sarcocollum	2 u	0-4-0
Folia sennae	4 u	0-8-0	Scammonium	3 u	3-0-0
Fructus carvi	2 d	0-12-0	Semen anisi	2 u	0 1 12
Fructus piperis	2 u	0-2-8	Semen foenugraeci	½ lb	0-6-0
Gummi elemi	2 u	0-6-0	Semen myristicae	1 u	0-5-8
Herba absinthii	3 u	0-6-0	Sirupus diamorum	3 u	0-9-0
Herba artemisiae	½ lb	0-4-0	Sirupus violarum	3 u	0-12-0
Lapis haematites	1 u	0-6-0	Spongia	?	0-5-0
Lignum quassiae	2 lb	0-10-0	Succus limonum	4½ pint	1-5-0
Lithargyrum aureum	¼ lb	0-1-0	Succus liquiritiae	6 tabulae	0-6-0
Macis	½ u	0-5-0	Sulphur	1 u	0-1-8
Mel commune	2 lb	0-3-0	Theriacum	1 lb	1-10-0
Mel rosarum	½ lb	0-19-8	Tutia	1 u	0-3-0
Mercurius praecipitat.	1 u	0-10-0	Unguentum basilicum	1 lb	0-10-0
Mercurius sublimatus	2 u	0-12-0	Unguent. defensivum	2 lb	2.0.0
Mithridatium	2 u	0-12-0	Unguent. dialtheae	½ lb	0-8-0
Myrrha	2 u	0-12-0	Unguent. populeum	1 lb	0-12-0
Oleum chamomillae	3 u	0-9-0	Vijgen (Ficus carica)	1 lb	0-4-1

tions in the Dutch pharmacopoeia of 1686 and following editions; the *Pharmacopoea Amstelaedamensis renovata* 1726 and the *Pharmacopoea Amstelodamensis nova* of 1792.[10]

Table 2.4 Medicines shipped with the frigate New York to the Mediterranean[11]

Absinthium herba	Emplastrum lithargyri	Oleum terebinthinae
Acidum vitrioli	Emplastrum mercuriale	Oleum vitrioli
Aether vitrioli	Extractum liquiritiae	Opium
Agaricus	Gallae quercinae	Quassia lignum
Aloe	Gambogia s.gummi guttae	Rhabarberum radix
Alumen	Gentiana radix	Saccharum saturni
Ammoniacum gum	Guajacum resina	Sal absinthii
Anisi semen	Huxham tinctura	Sal ammoniacus
Aqua s. liquor stypticus	Ipecacuanha radix	Sal mirabile Glauberi
Arabicum gummi	Jalappa radix	Sal tartari
Asa foetida	Kino resina	Saleb radix
Aurantium fructus cortex	Lapis infernalis	Sarsaparilla radix
Balsamum copaivae	Laudanum liquidum	Scilla radix
Balsamum traumaticum	Linimentum de sapone	Senega radix
Benzoe	Linum semen	Senna folia
Calamine lapis	Litharge oxide	Serpentaria radix
Camphora	Magnesia alba	Spermaceti
Cantharis	Manna	Spiritus lavendulae
Cera flava	Mel	Spiritus nitri
Chalybis s. rubigo martis	Mercurius dulcis s. calomelas	Spiritus salisammoniaci
Chamaemelum flores	Mercurius praecipitatus ruber	Spiritus vini rectificatus
China cortex flavus	Mercurius sublimatus corrosivus	Sulphur flores
China cortex ruber	Mixtura aloes cum rhei	Tartarus emeticus
Cinnamomi cortex	Nitrum depuratum	Terebinthina veneta
Columba radix	Nux moschata	Tinctura myrrhae
Conserva rosarum	Oleum anisi	Unguentum basilicum
Cremor tartari	Oleum cinnamomi	Unguentum hydragyri
Elixir stomachicum	Oleum lini	Unguentum simplex
Elixir proprietatis	Oleum menthae piperitae	Vinum antimoniale
Emplastrum adhesivum	Oleum olivae	Vitriolum album
Emplastrum diachylon	Oleum ricini	Vitriolum coeruleum
Emplastrum diachylon cum gummi	Oleum succini	Vitriolum viride
Emplastrum hydrargyri		

It is not impossible that medicines were exchanged with, or handed over to, the infirmaries in Malta or Gibraltar, where several American seamen were hospitalized. Frequently medicine trade took place during the interrelation of warships and local hospitals.[12]

Table 2.5 Drugs frequently prescribed in 1700 and omitted in 1800

Aqua alexipharmaca	Emplastrum opodeldoch	Mithridatium
Aqua antiepileptica	Emplastrum ranarum cum mercurio	Oleum caryophylli
Aqua antinephritica	Emplastrum betonicae	Oleum chamaemeli
Aqua antiparalytica	Emplastrum gratia dei	Oleum cinnamomi
Balsamum sulphuris anisata	Emplastrum meliloti	Oleum ligni rhodi
Cinnabar antimonii	Emplastrum mucilaginis	Oleum nardinum
Confectio hamech	Emplastrum stichticum	Oleum terebinthinae
Confectio hyacinthi	Fructus myrobalani	Philonium
Conserva rosarum	Fructus dactyli	Spiritus salis dulcis
Diacarthamum	Gummi anime	Syrupus 5 radicibus
Diacatholicum	Gummi bdellium	Syrupus capillaris veneri
Diascordium	Hiera picra	Tinctura bezoardi
Electuarium benedicti	Lignum santalinum album	Unguentum aureum

COMPARISON

Of the 93 Columbus medicines from table 2.1 only 9 remained by the end of the 18th century: alumen, ammoniacum, asa foetida, mercurius sublimatus, myrrh, cinnamon, camomile, rhubarb and diachylon. In the Portuguese and Greenland lists many drugs were left out as being obsolete; other medicines appeared to be so reliable and effective that doctors continued to prescribe them. Even though more than 60% of the drug range from the early 18th century passed out of use, still 273 products from the *Pharmacopoea Amstelodaemensis nova* (1792) were adopted in the 'Nederlandse Pharmacopee' (Dutch Pharmacopoeia) 4th edition 1905 a century later.[13]

Notes

1 Bénézet,'Pharmacie', 289-300.
2 Helps, *Spanish Conquest*, 126.
3 De Marees, *Beschryvinghe*, 226.
4 Correa da Silva, *Catálogo*, 78:83.
5 De Pina, 'A cura dos nautos', 3-42.

6 De Pina, 'Notas para a medicina', 12-26.

7 Rutten, 'Traan- en zouthandel', 123-8.

8 Jaspersen-Schib, 'Phytotherapie', 621.

9 Segersz van der Brugge, *Twee journalen.*

10 Haver Droeze, *Collegium Medicum*, 176-258.

11 Estes, *Naval surgeon*, 215-19.

12 WIC 584 (1737) 182.

13 Nederlandse Pharmacopee, (*Dutch pharmacopoea*) 1905.

Chapter III
THE TRAFFIC IN MEDICINES TO CURAÇAO

'The Dutch are notorious for their illegal trade'
(Lord Cornbury's letter 1701)[1]

'It seems as if the English cannot refrain from cheating'
(Storm van 's Gravesande, 1752)[2]

CARIBBEAN MEDICINE TRAFFIC

For centuries world trade was the backbone of the Dutch economic existence. The trade pattern of the Dutch included whaling and salt expeditions, the spices trade penetration into the Indonesian Archipelago and the transatlantic slave and commodities navigation under WIC auspices.[3]

The chief subject of this chapter is Curaçao, a small island of the Netherlands Antilles at about 40 miles off the coast of Venezuela (map 3.1). This former Spanish territory was captured in July 1634 by the Dutch West India Company and can serve as a good example to demonstrate the therapeutic orientation and medical resources that were available to the population of the Dutch possessions overseas.

Apart from a few works on the medicine chests shipped by the Dutch East India Company (VOC)[4] and on the materia medica that was shipped about 1645 to the Dutch Castle São Jorge da Mina on the African Gold Coast,[5] no publications are available relating to the Dutch traffic in medicines other than the author's preliminary studies on the slave trade.[6]

Atlantic activities were coordinated by the WIC, which was set up in 1621 on the model of the East India Company. The first act of the Newborn Company was to begin operations on a large scale in the northeast of Brazil, the world's largest sugar producer. In the year 1634 Curaçao and the neighbouring islands Aruba and Bonaire were occupied. Between 1616 and 1648 the Dutch conquered Guiana and the islands St. Eustatius, Saba and St. Martin and also strengthened their position in New Netherland. Factories and lodges of the Portuguese on the African West Coast were also occupied. In 1634 Arguin became a Dutch possession and Elmina followed in 1637. With these conquests distribution channels were opened for the regular shipping of drugs from Amsterdam to the colonies and vice versa. Several defeats in Brazil resulted in a withdrawal from that country in 1654 and at the Treaty of Breda in 1667 the English possession of New Netherland was confirmed. These events were disastrous for the financial position of the Company and in 1674 a New WIC with a more limited charter was established. Until the extension of its Charter in 1730 the WIC monopolized trade with its overseas territories, and the charter was renewed, though with some far-reaching changes. The most important change was to open trade in its Atlantic possessions and along the African Coast. However, the new Company was never especially successful and in the year 1791 it was abolished. The corruption and mismanagement by its employees accelerated the decline of the Company. The newly formed *Raad der Coloniën* subsequently took over responsibility for the possessions overseas.

The small island of Curaçao was primarily utilized as a naval refurbishing station. Soon after the conquest the Heren X (Assembly of Ten) planned to abandon the island because they found it worthless. It developed however into the most important smuggling and slave market for almost half a century. The Curaçaoan inhabitants were notorious for their clandestine trade with the neighbouring islands. There was a rigid application of certain monopolistic rights on the part of the WIC, but between the Company and the merchant's elite on the island a latent and open opposition was notable. Together with the other West Indian islands Curaçao formed a miniature world of maritime powers combating each other. Both English and French merchants tried to improve their profits from sugar cultivation. Sugar, tobacco and cocoa were initially not only expensive stimulants but also important medicines, sold by pharmacists. The Caribbean offered the shortest and easiest access to the drugs of Spanish America. In the Caribbean Dutch and British merchants traded illegally with the Spanish colonial area using Curaçao as a trading basis.[7] Dutch-Hispanic trade was predominantly the work of merchants in Curaçao. Around 1700 sugar had pushed tobacco and coffee from the market. Tobacco was by far the most important item carried to Amsterdam, but cocoa, indigo and hides formed an important part of the shipments too. Cultivation of sugar and indigo was technically difficult and appeared not viable in Curaçao. The fumes of the fermented indigo plants were believed poisonous to the plantation slaves who stirred the material in the dye vats.[8] The Curaçaoan plantations were mixed enterprises and their agricultural output was low, being too dependent on unfavourable climatic factors. The same can be said about cotton cultivation. Government land and plantations were meant to provide food and shelter for slaves in transit and private plantations were a status symbol for the elite families rather than real productive centers. Dividivi, civet, logwood and guaiac were some important semi-pharmaceutical export products.

In 1637 the West African Castle São Jorge da Mina was occupied by the WIC. It was gold and tusks that lured the Dutch there. But it was the slave trade that became increasingly important and pressed the WIC to a strategy of rapid conquests. The blacks were carried across the Atlantic to the West in exchange for European and colonial products. This trade was the exclusive monopoly of the Company, which exploited Curaçao with its natural harbour as an ideal depot for the black slaves. The slaves were sold to the Spanish Main, the southern states of America and Guiana. On their return voyage the slave ships carried dyewood, orlean, sugar, indigo, guaiac and other goods. It is impossible to discover if ships of the *Grote Vaart* or transatlantic navigation carried medicines to Curaçao. Medicines outside the WIC were classified as 'general goods' and no records of what was bought or sold are accessible. Many merchants and their heirs may well have considered business letterbooks as socially, if not morally, incriminating evidence, to be destroyed once their debt-collecting function had been served.

Less than four per cent of the total volume of the West African exports consisted of spices and medicinal products such as melegueta pepper, gum Arabic, beeswax, dyewood and lemon juice.[9] A menace to the Dutch WIC trade were rival nations and Dutch interlopers who ventured into the WIC territories at the risk of having their goods confiscated. Interloping was the direct trade between Europe and the West by private merchants in defiance of the Company's monopoly. The *Kleine Vaart* also carried along a lot of commodities and medicinal products to Curaçao. The term refers to the inter-insular shipping between the many Antilles of different nationalities in the Caribbean, the Spanish American mainland and the North American colonies, expanding its relations as far away as Rhode Island and Boston. Under the Company's reluctant auspices the *Kleine Vaart* of the island flourished. Most WIC crewmembers were involved in the *inter-insular shipping* and were allowed a certain amount of free trading. It was generally accepted, however, that they undermined the WIC monopoly through extensive smuggling and contraband trade. During the 1730s the Dutch West India possessions as well as the Gold Coast were opened up to private Dutch merchants. This resulted in an enhanced exchange of goods through Curaçao. There were commercial links between Barbados, Jamaica, Martinique and the

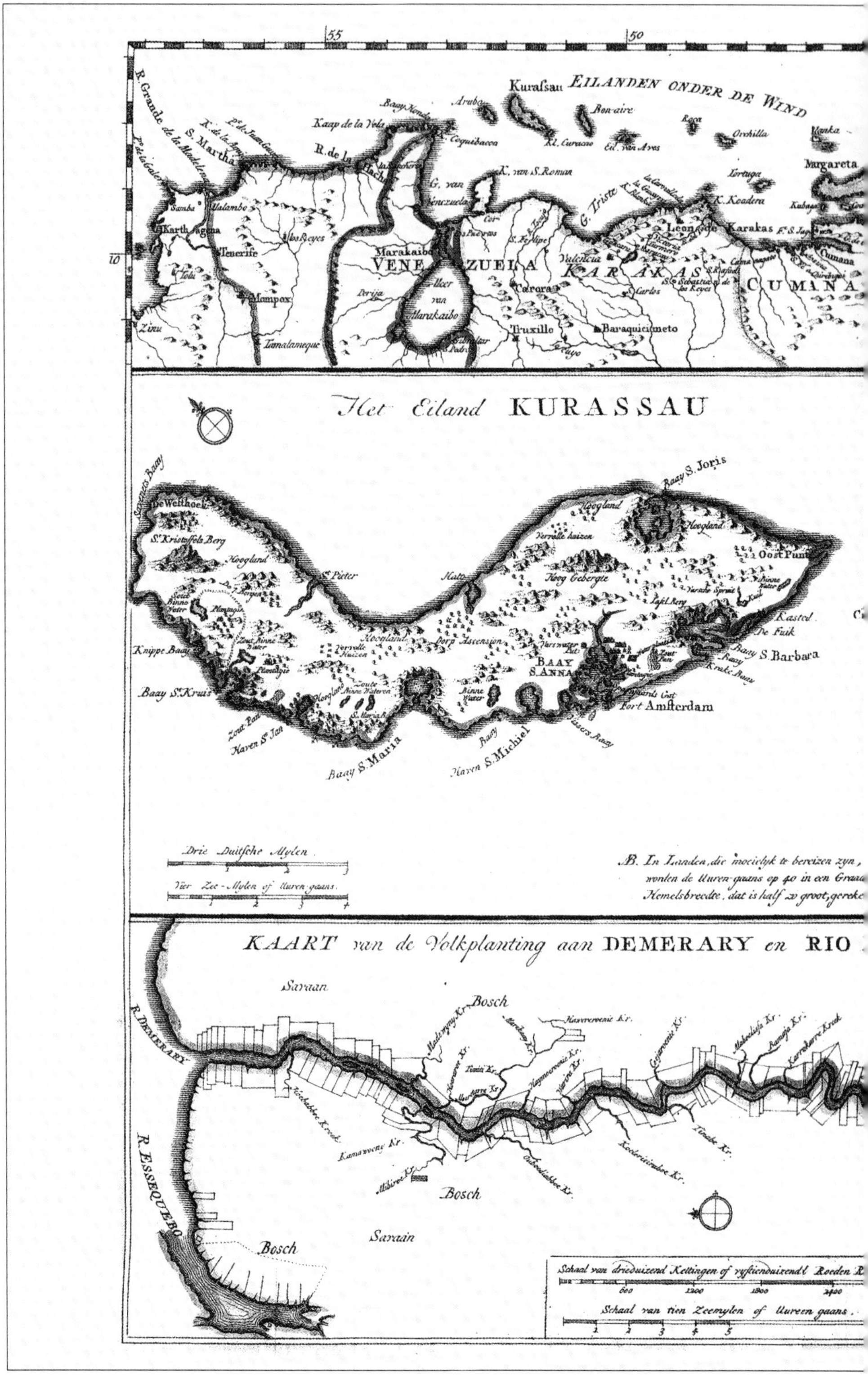

Map 3.1 of the Caribbean region by Isaac Tirion (1767)

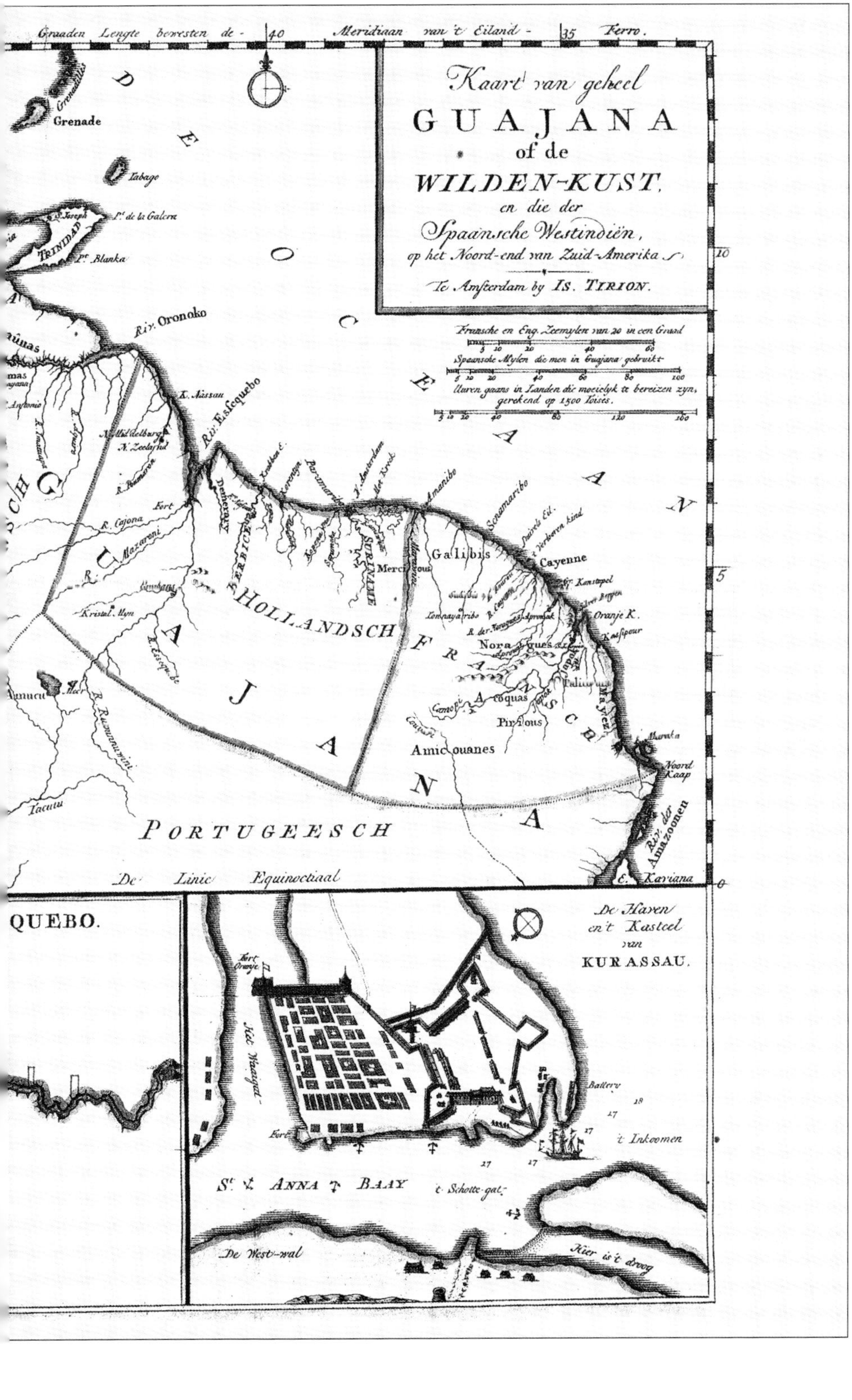
Kaart van geheel
GUAJANA
of de
WILDEN-KUST,
en die der
Spaansche Westindiën,
op het Noord-end van Zuid-Amerika
Te Amsteerdam by IS. TIRION.
Graaden Lengte bewesten de - 40 Meridiaan van 't Eiland - 35 Ferro.
Fransche en Eng. Zeemylen van 20 in een Graad
Spaansche Mylen die men in Guajana gebruikt
Uuren gaans in Landen die moeielyk te bereizen zyn, gerekend op 1500 Toises.
Grenade
Tabago
TRINIDAD
Pt. Blanka
Riv. Oronoko
Riv. Essequebo
K. Nassau
N. Middelburg
N. Zeeland
Fort
R. Cajona
R. Mazaroni
Demerary
BERBICE
SURINAME
Amanibo
Sonamaribo
Cayenne
Galibis
Oranje K.
Noord Kaap
Riv. der Amazoonen
Kariana
Amicouanes
Acoquas
Noraques
HOLLANDSCH
FRANSCH
PORTUGEESCH
GUAJANA
DE OCEAAN
De Linie Equinoctiaal
Tacutu
QUEBO.
De Haven en 't Kasteel van KURASSAU.
Fort Oranje
Batterÿ
't Inkoomen
St. Anna Baay
't Schotte-gat
De West-wal
Hier is 't droog

Dutch West Indies. Intensive traffic also existed between the Bermudas and Curaçao, which extended to the continental colonies from Carolina to New England.[10] Logwood, salt, tobacco, linen, molasses, rum, cocoa and important semi-pharmaceutical raw materials came from the British, French and Spanish colonies. The *Grote Vaart* often carried these colonial products to the United Provinces. Dutch vessels left homeward-bound with hundreds of thousands of pounds of logwood, stowed in bags immediately above the keel. There was an uncontrolled cutting of logwood and guaiac trees in the Curaçaoan islands (Curaçao, Bonaire and Aruba). In 1709 about 180,000 pounds of logwood were stored in the Curaçaoan warehouse.[11] The United Provinces not only shipped hats, soap, glass, paper, ink and gin as exchange goods, but also spices and flavourings such as East Indian pepper, cinnamon, rhubarb, nutmeg, mace, cloves, camphor and other medicines to Curaçao. Nutmeg was used in considerable quantities to provide the slave ships.[12] Slaves knew that nutmeg powder would relieve their weariness and bring euphoric sensations and pleasant visions, due to nutmeg's hallucinogenic active principles.[13] Dutch anise seed was exported to Martinique where it was processed to anise liqueur, which was spread across the Dutch Antilles. It is known that the apothecary-distiller in France and in its colonies was very skilled in the preparation of liqueurs.[14] The first public apothecary established in Curaçao was the 'distillateur' Simon Pradelle, born 1782 in Martinique.[15]

Curaçao was never a real plantation settlement and never an exploitation colony. It had no plantations of any importance due to unfavourable climatic factors. Surinam was the largest and most highly developed Dutch colony in the Guianas. Essequebo and Berbice plantations were languishing, despite the financial aid provided by the States of Zeeland. After 1650 the Dutch played only a modest role in shipping their own colonial goods, including medicinal products. In one field, however, the Dutch managed to obtain an important place in the Atlantic world with the Caribbean transit trade: smuggling. The principal market of the traders was the Spanish Main, which now comprises the coast of Venezuela and Colombia. Curaçao developed into one of the New World's major smuggling centres comparable with Rio de la Plata. From Caracas cocoa, tobacco and hides were imported, from St.Domingo indigo and from Portorico tobacco. The greater part of these products was re-exported to and processed in the mother country. There was an illegal commerce between Curaçao and the British plantations in America during the whole seventeenth and eighteenth centuries. In the 1660s New Netherland would furnish all foodstuffs in exchange for slaves from Curaçao, horses from Aruba and salt from Bonaire. The profits of this contraband trade enriched the Company's servants rather than the Company itself. From the English plantations and New England Curaçaoan merchants also obtained bread, butter, cheese, beans, rice, beef, pork and corn. From Pennsylvania and New York came strong and small beer; from Carolina and New England pitch and tar; from Virginia sassafras root, the attractive purifier of the blood. The Caribbean Islands also delivered sugar, kill-devil (West Indian rum), molasses, indigo, cotton and tobacco. These goods were bought or exchanged for slaves, linens, silks, anchors, gunpowder and shot. Both the English and the Dutch profited considerably from this illicit trade, but to the Spanish smugglers it was even more advantageous.[16] It was a public secret that in Curaçao and Sint Eustatius – just as in the Danish and Swedish Antilles – colonial products were exchanged in a lively illicit barter trade. It is feasible that in 1774, at the beginning of the American War of Independence, Curaçao and St. Eustatius were able to provide the rebels with almost everything they needed, including drugs.

Vegetable drugs constituted a small, but important part of the total trade goods the WIC shipped from Brazil, the Caribbean, Guiana and Western Africa through Curaçao. Dutch vessels came from Brazil with ipecac, tobacco and sugar. The Guiana's supplied orlean, cayenne pepper, simarouba (*Simaruba amara*) and vanilla, the Gold coast gum Arabic, tamarind (*Tamarindus indica*), melegueta pepper (*Aframomum melegueta*), beeswax of *Apis Adansonii*, redwood (*Pterocarpus tinctoria*), lemon juice and copal. The Caribbean islands exported dried ginger, pimento, indigo, anise liqueur, rum, cascarilla and the medicinal 'pokhout' (*Guaiacum officinale*).[17] The latter was shipped to Europe soon after the discovery of America and about 1502 it was used to treat venereal diseases. Syphilis was considered to be a cold poison, lodged in the blood. Guaiac was introduced as a hot antidote to replace the mercurial induction hitherto employed. Nicholas Pohl wrote in 1517 that 3000 Spaniards were cured with guaiacum and Uhlrich von Hutten further spread its reputation. Boerhaave (1668-1738) was an advocate of guaiac and thought that the drug could reach spots in the body where mercury could not penetrate.[18] After mid-century, however, medical enthousiasm for guaiacum waned.

The hope of the surgeons that guaiac, sassafras, chinaroot (smilax) and sarsaparilla could take the place of the elusive precious metals created a continuous commerce in these drugs. In addition logwood or heartwood (*Haematoxylon campechianum*) – mainly used as a black-chroman dyewood – had found with considerable advantage an application in medicine in the treatment of diarrhoeas and chronic dysentery.[19] Another dyestuff, indigo, was also prescribed as a medicine in the case of typhus, epilepsy, as an antiseptic, febrifuge and to heal sores and ulcers.[20] In 1701 the ship *Quinira* carried 36900 pounds of logwood from Curaçao and 20620 pounds from Bonaire at a total amount of 1725 pesos (c. 4300 guilders) to Amsterdam. There was also a lively traffic in lemon juice, which was used for the treatment of scurvy. The vessel *Rachel* dispatched six barrels of lemon juice with a declared value of 90 pesos to Amsterdam in 1739. Indigo seed needed for cultivation in Curaçao was furnished by Barbados and from 1702 to 1718 a total amount of 2186 pounds of indigo obtained from the Curaçaoan plantations was shipped to The Netherlands. Some years later, however, the culture collapsed.[21] Cocoa, tobacco and snuff, imported from Cumaná, Caracas, Trinidad and the coast of Guiana (northeastern Brazil), found their way through Curaçao and Amsterdam to continental Europe. Jean Nicot had already introduced tobacco into Europe in 1559 and it was looked upon as one of the wonders of the New World possessed of many medicinal virtues. Another stimulant imported from Venezuela and Guayaquil, cocoa, was employed to alleviate gastrointestinal disturbances and dysentery. West Africa provided the WIC with black slaves, gold, ivory, grains of paradise and resins. North America delivered butter, wheat, maize, meat and salted fish, but also herbal medicines such as senega and sassafras, which were re-exported by Dutch vessels, mainly sloops, to the planters in the sugar islands. South America formed the source of maté, Brazilian carnaubawax, fernambuco, quebracho, ipecac and cascarilla, which entered the port of Curaçao. Mexico furnished jalap, cochineal and vanilla, Bolivia and Peru delivered Peruvian bark (Cinchona) and ratanhy (*Krameria triandra*). Tar (*Pinus* spp.) from Carolina was used as a heating diuretic and sudorific remedy, but was not so powerful as Bishop George Berkeley represented it.[22] Externally it was applied in dermatological disorders. From Barbados also mineral tar was obtained that was used in disorders of the breast and lungs. The stimulant Pimento varieties and the pods of purging cassia (trommelstok) were obtained from Jamaica. Dutch private traders and WIC crewmembers shipped a huge part of these medicinal products and spices to Curaçao and re-exported it to Amsterdam.

COLONIAL MISSION AND DRUG TRAFFIC

A separate kind of medicine traffic was created by the enterprises of Pietist foundations such as the Labadists mission to Surinam and the Halle Orphanage commerce. In 1684 a group of Labadists, members of the radical Pietists from the Wieuwerd community in East Friesland, put into the port of the Dutch colony of Surinam and settled at the La Providence plantation.[23] Their aim was the conversion of 'the poor Indians' and spreading the word of God. Governor Van Sommelsdijck's sister was a member of this community. They were advanced in medicine, surgery and midwifery and we know they carried medicines into Surinam including basilicum ointment and plasters. The brothers also gathered medicinal products during their stay, including at least two pounds of some kind of a medicinal resin. The community collapsed about 1719.

The juncture of medical care and Christian teaching was also a remarkable activity of the German Francke Orphanage Foundations, as Dr. Renate Wilson clearly demonstrated.[24] Pietist missions abroad were used as a channel for the distribution of bibles and pharmaceutical products, but it is uncertain if this material reached Curaçao at any time. The influence of the success the German Halle Orphanage pharmaceuticals acquired in the early 1700s was a factor not to be underestimated, as the attempt to replicate the gold preparation by the Curaçaoan doctor medicinae Horst has shown.

TRADE FOR CARE

The Chamber of Amsterdam had the supervision of the Curaçao islands. The captains of WIC ships leaving for Curaçao had to buy their cargoes, take their men on board and fit out their ships on account of the WIC. An important part of their outfit was medicines. Compounding of drugs and delivering of the medicine chest was strictly the task of an apothecary.[25] The dispensing of drugs was always the backbone of pharmacy. The drugs for the hospital pharmacies of the WIC had as their main geographic destinations the Caribbean, Brazil, Guiana or the Wild Coast and the Gold Coast of Guinea. The activity of the WIC within the framework of preparation and shipping of the required armaments resulted in a lively international traffic in medicines and medical ideas to the West.

What medicines were carried overseas? The materia medica consisted of simples and compounds or composites. Simples such as herbs, roots, barks and chemicals were shipped unprocessed via Amsterdam to Curaçao. Compounds, medicines with several ingredients such as electuaries, ointments, pills, had first to be prepared in the 'Apotheek' (Pharmacy) of the *St. Pietersgasthuis* at Amsterdam, who furnished the medicines, the WIC ordered and paid for. After 1674 delivery of WIC drugs was also permitted to public pharmacists. These preparations were predominantly made according to the *Pharmacopaea Amstelredamensis* 1686. As a guide for the equipment of their chests the physicians or surgeons could refer to the *Lijst der Medicamenten van de Raad ter Admiraliteit te Rotterdam* of 1691[26] or to the nearly identical *Admiralty List* 1692 of Amsterdam.[27] These lists indicate the quantities and assortment of medicines that ships should carry on a journey of six months with a crew of 100-500 heads (see Appendix VI). In the year 1796 the *Commitee van Algemeen Welzijn, Koophandel en Zeevaart* at Amsterdam issued a new list of medicines and instruments to replace the old merchant navy regulations. Examination of this list reveals that during the whole 18th century there was only minor change in the composition of the drug equipment.[28] A couple of about 124 herbals played a significant role in Curaçaoan professional practice (see Appendix V).

In the area covered by the WIC there was a constant need for medicated care of the sick and wounded personnel and slaves. The bewindhebbers (directors) of the

Amsterdam Chamber had to get their teeth into this problem. Health conditions were often bad. Initially barbers performed medical service because doctors were not available. Besides at the small hospitals for the infectious diseases and the mentally ill, most care was provided at home, often with the help of outdoor relief. Medical supplies were always a source of anxiety to the Governors of the overseas colonies. Direct access to reputable and reliable medicines was indispensable. The Government had to trade in order to be able to provide care and to take proper precautions in protecting the health of their population. Curaçao in particular had to struggle for the provision of the necessary medicines during the heyday of the slave trade, because of the presence of a large number of slaves in depot. The local public health officer inspected all slaves before embarkation and after disembarkation. Since local medicinal plants were hardly used in therapy, it was taken for granted that Holland would send the required drugs. Moreover, the Government was often in desperate need of European practitioners. If they were lucky they could pick somebody out of the arrived crew of surgeons, soldiers and commanders, who appeared to be best qualified for merchandising and pen or for health service. Like the English sea-surgeons, these men were strictly prohibited from treating internal diseases when at home, yet they were required to do so on entering the Company's service. Military surgeons contracted by the WIC for the slaves and the garrison were often of German extraction and about 36% of the soldiers in the garrison were born in Germany.[29] The surgeons working under an apprenticeship system on board merchant ships or slave vessels received training in the diagnosis and treatment of diseases, luxations and fractures, cauterizations, cure of wounds, surgical repair of inguinal hernia, resection of cancers of the liver, withdrawing fluid from body cavity (ascites), removing urinary calculi, pharmaceutical preparation of compounds and the practice of phlebotomy, which was then the universally accepted way to eliminate the humours thought to cause disease. Throughout the territory of the WIC and into the nineteenth century we can encounter them. Both surgery and what we would call internal medicine were practised simultaneously by the WIC surgeons. In general they worked conscientiously and skilfully. In case of carelessness they risked severe punishment, such as keelhaul. On the Gold Coast the Dutch surgeon Gilbert Petri was captured and molested by a local tribe, because one of them had received bad attendance.[30] One could call this an early form of quality control of appalling brutality.

The surgeon in the Dutch Antilles was European trained and his medication and therapy were focused on West Europe. Bleeding, vomiting, purging and blistering were the most common forms of treatment for a wide range of diseases. Such plagues as smallpox, pleurisy, dracontiasis, venereal disease, leprosy, filariasis, typhoid, dysentery of every type, parasitism or the devastating yellow fever commonly brought to the city port by ships, caused victims to die by the hundreds and raised European drugs consumption. Interest in the native drugs or simples used by the Indian and African inhabitants was hardly stimulated, with the exception of the use of guaiac.

In the middle of the eighteenth century public health officer Carel Doerffel prescribed local phytotherapeutics such as Sentebibu (*Aloe vera*) and Tebink (*Pectis febrifuga*). Hering writes in 1779 that the people of Curaçao made use of certain balsams and resins (of Burseraceae trees) to cure injuries and wounds.[31] In the nineteenth century David Capriles MD stressed the importance and health potential of several herbal drugs such as Basora corra (*Melochia tomentosa*), Watapana chimaron (*Acacia villosa*) and Yerba di vruminga (*Chenopodium ambrosoides*).[32] The leaves of Welensali (*Croton flavens*) mixed with tobacco snuff were used to alleviate common cold.[33] These are a few examples of local plants prescribed by European physicians.

Since the conquest of Curaçao 'physicians' had to take care of the health of the servants, militia and slaves of the WIC. In the first decades this was the task of ship's surgeons or clergymen comforters-of-the-sick (ziekentroosters),[34] who arrived in Curaçao and were appointed by the WIC as public health officer. With a growing number of imported slaves the WIC bewindhebbers (directors) decided to appoint a medical doctor to care for the black slaves and white soldiers. In the first part of the seventeenth century the role of medical doctors in health care was negligible. From the end of the age onwards, however, the importance of physicians increased. During the climax of the slave trade four medical doctors were appointed successively. The first physician placed on probation was Dr. med. D. van der Sterre in 1688. He was succeeded from 1691 to 1693 by Dr. med. G. Schagen, a medical graduate from Utrecht and by Dr. med. J.P. Ewalt till 1699. The eighteenth century started with the German born Dr. med. L.R. Horst. Immigrated Company and civilian practitioners were educated in the European materia medica and this is what they continued to use in Curaçao and the other possessions. It appears that Curaçaoan doctors were well able to keep in touch with medical developments in Europe.

Horst was appointed in 1699 by the Amsterdam bewindhebbers as a slave doctor to examine imported African slaves, to prevent, care and alleviate many disorders of blacks and to improve the shipment and administration of drugs in Curaçao. Sick or wounded 'negotieslaven' (deliverable blacks in stock) were housed in the infirmary of fort Amsterdam and in large Negro houses to recuperate before they were sold. The hospital was a small building. This was supplemented by hiring sick-quarters elsewhere in the town. Horst did his own compounding and dispensing of pills, potions and ointments. Pharmaceutical practitioners were absent in Curaçao in the seventeenth and eighteenth century. In 1707 Horst established a pharmaceutical laboratory at Otrobanda where medicines could be compounded and surgeon chests of boarding merchant marine or slave ships were put up and replenished. This WIC laboratory should serve to prepare a lot of composites otherwise shipped through Amsterdam to Curaçao. Clearly Horst's practice indicates that he was a rather large practitioner of the art of the apothecary and had a great skill in the manipulation required. Backed by information on German proprietary medicines he demanded of Amsterdam to ship gold leaf to prepare more efficient and reliable drugs for 'the poor slaves and the white garrison soldiers, the most despised section of the colony's population'. His aim was to manufacture a potable tincture of gold similar to that of the highly profitable Halle Orphanage arcanum developed in 1702. The gold preparation was intended as a general tonic in the treatment of nervous disorders, lung ailments and arthritis.[35] Without doubt Horst was well aware of the medicine chests that were supplied by the Franckesche Waisenhaus Stiftung at Halle. There were current contacts between Antillean and German merchants through Amsterdam.[36] Colonial physicians learned from correspondents, from ship surgeons and from emigrating Dutch or German practitioners and customers. Some Dutch merchants personally purchased textiles and other products at their visit to the Leipzig fairs, with the express purpose of sending them to Curaçao.[37] It is uncertain if any Halle chests were imported into Curaçao, because the only sources we have on drug traffic are those supplied by the WIC archives. However it is possible that private medicine chests filled up with proprietary drugs reached the Curaçao population as some archival notes indicate. Printed medical directions must have informed the buyer, just as they did in the nineteenth century.[38] Table 3.1 deals with the first lists of medications ordered by the Curaçaoan WIC physician in the early 1700s.[39]

Often the shipped medicines – due to the great distance, wrong season, falsification or inefficient drying and packing – revealed no obvious medicinal value when finally employed.[40] Usually ships were eight weeks under way. Many complaints were received by the bewindhebbers at Amsterdam because of adulteration for greater commercial gain. This reliance on imported medicines was to cause great problems at the beginning of the French revolution when imports from Amsterdam were cut off.

Some local medicines traveled a triangular route. Gum anime, for example, a helpful drug against consumption (phthisis) and colds, first was shipped from Mexico, Surinam or the Caribbean islands to Europe, and then re-exported via Amsterdam as a component of the medicine chests to Curaçao. Other drugs, such as aloe resin, tamarind and jalap also indirectly reached the island. Only a limited number of the drugs available in the mother country and quoted in the Amsterdam pharmacopoeia were wanted by the Curaçaoan practitioners. Table 3.3. shows, which kinds of drugs were prescribed and which were omitted. This does not mean that those drugs were not used in their therapy. Gum caranna and guaiac, for example, were never ordered, as they existed abundantly in Curaçao. Sarsaparilla was only ordered in 1775, but it was always stocked in transit in Curaçaoan warehouses.[41]

THE IMPACT OF THE AMSTERDAM PHARMACOPOEIA ON THE DRUG ASSORTMENT

The medicine chests shipped by the Amsterdam Chamber to Curaçao and other Dutch overseas possessions were equipped with an assortment of drugs, for the greater part in accordance with the Dutch Pharmacopoeia. Until the 1820s no patent medicines were shipped to Curaçao. However, one has to keep in mind that in the early eighteenth century patent medicines were scarce. In Great Britain the medicine 'Goddard's Drops' was patented in 1673. In the early 1700s the Halle Orphanage Foundations started the creation and lively export of a set of medications protected by local privileges and patents.[42] In 1711 the first American patent medicine appeared on the market. It was called 'Tuscaron Rice' and comprised a kind of consumption cure. A second patent was granted in 1712 to 'Stoughton's elixir'. Certainly the interest in and importance of some proprietary medicines drew the attention of the Curaçaoan physicians, as is shown in an attempt in 1707 to reproduce a Halle Orphanage proprietary medication by Dr. L.R. Horst.[43]

The WIC traffic included many medicinal preparations, which are still in use and originated during the seventeenth and eighteenth century. The formulas of these drugs are found in such works as the *Pharmacopoea Amstelredamensis* 1636 and the *Pharmacopoea Amstelaedamensis renovata* 1726. These works give a very good impression of what kinds of drugs were received in the colonies during the eighteenth century.

The non-official *Pharmacopaea Amstelredamensis*, translated into Dutch under the title *d'Amsterdammer Apotheek* (Ph.A.) (1686) with about 749 simples and 361 compounds, includes 108 roots, 20 barks, 15 woods, 152 herbs, 35 flowers, 96 seeds, 76 fruits, 9 poultice masses, 5 moulds and 70 inspissated juices. Also included are 78 animalia, 64 mineralia/chymica and 9 marina. Less than 4% of the simples are of North- and South-American origin such as cochineal, civet, bezoar occidentale and herbals such as Peruvian and winterani bark, jalap, sarsaparilla, contrayerva, mechoacana, sassafras, tobacco, piper braziliense (achi), copaiba and Peruvian balm. Cowen's study sheds light on the limited impact of the Indian materia medica.[44] A look at the bill of sale of the medicine chest of the slave ship *De Vergulde Vrijheyt* (1701) reveals that it contained 71 Old World materia medica with only four items of American origin: Peruvian and copaiba balsam, jalap and elemi.[45] Besides, each compound in the Dutch translation of the Ph.A. (1686) has a description in Dutch indicating the therapeutic use to which the compound could be put and an index of diseases to facilitate prescribing. These pharmacopoeias were forwarded to and used in the Dutch possessions overseas, where they were set up as standard works of reference.

In the Ph.A. West-Indian guaiac, gum anime, gum caranna, gum tacamahaca, pimento, brazilwood and aloe is mentioned. Simples such as ambra grisea, senna and grana paradisi (melegueta pepper) represent the materia medica of African origin. Drugs and spices played an important role in daily life and new Oriental and Occidental simples were included in current European pharmacopoeias. Sarsaparilla, for example, was brought to Europe by the Spaniards about the year 1536 as a specific for the cure of syphilis. Compound decoction of sarsaparilla and sublimate, called Lisbon Diet Drink, appeared in the 18th century as a remedy for syphilis. The preparation was introduced in the *Pharmacopoeia Londinensis* of 1788 under the title Sirop de cuisinière. The same indication on medical grounds was ascribed to guaiac wood. Taken internally they excited a sense of warmth in the stomach, increased the heat of the body and produced diaphoresis and diuresis. Tobacco, first used as a magical medicine, soon became a stimulant. Tobacco smoke was injected into the rectum by means of bellows, acting as a stimulant in reviving the vital powers in some kinds of asphyxia. Internally chewed it relieved toothache and as a powder it proved an excellent sternutatory when snuffed up the nostrils.

SHIPBOARD MEDICINES SENT BY AMSTERDAM AND OTHER WIC CHAMBERS

A few examples may illustrate the importance of slave trade in WIC medicine traffic. The various chambers of the WIC equipped slave-ships for the triangular voyage to Guinea → Curaçao → United Provinces. On the 1st March 1701 the Amsterdam bewindhebbers paid to pharmacist Justinus Versteegh *f* 209: 7: 8 (guldens: stuivers: duiten) for a chest of medicines to be used on board the slave-ship *Duynenburg* destined for Loango-Angola. The same apothecary delivered the medicine chest for the ship *Guntersteyn* on 2 May 1713 and received an amount of *f* 403: 6. Apothecary Lambertus Bidloo furnished a surgeon chest on board the slave-ship *St. Marcus* on 12th December 1712 for *f* 921: 9. Slave-ship *De Faam* destined for the coast of Guinea received a medicine chest from apothecary Wilhelmus de Penijn, valued at *f* 376: 8. Apothecary Lambertus Bidloo also furnished the chest on board of the slave-ship *Bosbeeck*, for the price of *f* 244.16. These were all ships equipped by the WIC Chamber Amsterdam.

On 19 March 1715 the Zeeland Chamber had to pay *f* 482: 6 for a chest delivered by apothecary Michiel Pille. The Stad en Lande Chamber at Groningen paid an amount of *f* 217: 4 for medicines on board the vessel *Africaansche Galey* with destination Elmina, Angola and Curaçao to the pharmacy of the Widow Dinckgreve-van der Kist, and an amount of *f* 311:14 for the ship *De Nieuwe Post* to Elmina and Curaçao to the same pharmacy. The Noorderkwartier Chamber at Enkhuizen paid *f* 526:8 for a surgeon chest on the ship *Margaretha Catharina*, destination Loango and Curaçao. [46] For comparison suffice it to say that the annual salary of a carpenter in those days amounted to about *f* 350.

VOLUME AND KIND OF WIC MEDICINES

It is not feasible to highlight medicines considered important from table 3.3 in this study. It is clear, however, that one of the most admired products shipped during the whole eighteenth century was Theriac. This confection contained nearly 60 ingredients: leaves, roots, aromatic barks, seeds, opium, resins, gum, minerals, vipers, honey and wine. It was an invention of the famous Mithridates VI Eupator, King of Pontus (132-63 B.C.), who was the first student of toxicology. Damocratis, a physician to Nero, later improved the confection. Due to its content of olibanum (frankincense), theriac has an anti-inflammatory activity. Boswellic acids in the resin act as non-redox inhibitors of 5-lipoxygenase, as we know today.[47] Theriac was believed by many physicians to be a specific against dysentery, colitis, arthritis and states of anxiety. In Curaçao there was an increasing demand for it by the slave doctors and surgeons.

The famous theriac maintained itself till the middle of the nineteenth century and in 1850 the Amsterdam pharmaceutical producer D'Ailly still had theriac prepared and dispatched to Japan. The Amsterdam Gasthuis pharmacy was not the only supplier of this favourite drug. In an emergency the government bought the missing remedies from local civilian surgeons or merchants of drugs. There were a number of such Spanish, English, French and German wholesalers of drugs. They needed no special medical or pharmaceutical background. In Curaçao the WIC surgeons often bought theriac and other drugs from these local dealers as well. Surgeons and captains of the slavery ships maintained a brisk trade in medicines. It is rumoured that the WIC surgeons derived profits from failure to report shortages of medicines, in order to be able to sell them to the Company from their own stockpile at exorbitant prices. In 1704, 1708 and 1709, for example, WIC surgeon Sigismund Druschke delivered medicines from his private stock to the Curaçaoan fort pharmacy. In 1703 the Government paid a certain Master

Christiaen for delivering 8 pounds of theriac; in 1705 a Mr. Tamme Degenaer supplied some emplastra (price 20 guilders) and 4,5 pounds of theriac at *f* 22 ; in 1709 the surgeon Isaac Nucella sold 8 boxes of theriac to the hospital pharmacy for about *f* 30 and a bottle of copaiba balsam for *f* 10. The WIC had to bear the costs. The increasing demand for theriac is shown in the following data: in 1701 13 pounds were ordered, in 1705 26 pounds, in 1707 32 pounds and in 1709 20 pounds. In 1710, a year that only two slaveships arrived at Curaçao, hardly any theriac was asked for. Medicines were annually ordered from Amsterdam and with few exceptions were always received in the colonies.[48]

The WIC entered into business relations with the Curaçaoan Jews or their representatives in Amsterdam from the earliest days of their settlement. The Jews supplied the Government of Curaçao with nearly everything necessary for the garrison and slaves.[49] Imports consisted of all kinds of products manufactured in Europe such as comestibles, drugs, wood and brick, arms and munitions. The major portion of the goods was re-exported to the Caribbean Isles and the Spanish Main. In exchange Curaçaoan merchants obtained cocoa, tobacco, sugar, indigo, lemon juice, vanilla, cochineal, cotton, gold powder and hides. One may suppose that parallel to the WIC supplies of materia medica to Curaçao, the Jews imported the necessary remedies for the medicine chests of their Jewish civilian physicians in Curaçao.[50] The Jews had not only representatives in Amsterdam but also in other European cities and elsewhere.

The assortment of drugs received by the Curaçao government in the eighteenth century was only intended to take care of the WIC servants. The free population of Willemstad, a small town that gave access to the St. Ann Bay, increased to 2760 whites and Jews in 1713. They had to apply to civilian physicians in case of sickness. According to the personnel rosters in the first decade of the century the WIC had to take care of an average of 240 WIC employees and 80 soldiers of the garrison, sailors and craftsmen. Besides there were nearly 2400 Company slaves in Curaçao to take care of.[51] Also the island Bonaire received drugs and a number of slave ships had to be supplied with drugs during their stay in the harbour of Curaçao. During the first decades of the eighteenth century Dr.med. Horst and the surgeons Pieter Scholtz, Jan Ribijn and Sigismund Druschky served the WIC. The remedies were supposed to assist nature in restoring the patient's physiological imbalance to its natural state. Table 3.3 deals with compounds ordered during the eighteenth century and facilitates comparison with the Ph.A register. Starting in 1700 with numerous compounds, doctor Horst discovered after a period of experimentation and patient observation the necessity to eliminate many obsolescent preparations and to minimize the application of antimonium and mercury compounds.

In addition to the shipped drugs, miscellaneous supplies, apparatus for chemical operations and pharmaceutical equipment were received, including scales and weights, distilling stills, refrigerators, retorts, crucibles, funnels, marble, brass and glass mortars and pestle, spatulas, bolus knife, plaster spatula, leather skins, linen, lint, vials and ink powder. Surgical instruments shipped to Curaçao included forceps, catheters, amputating and trepanning instruments, lancets, tourniquets and syringes. Table 3.3 further shows that anodyne preparations such as Philonium and Requies Nicolai, confections, syrups and aromatic waters were omitted in the second half of the period. Salts such as absinthe and centauri, which can be regarded as potassium carbonate, became obsolete as well. The volume of the traffic is shown in figure 3.1 Only in 1701 the weight of composites was greater than that of simples. The amount shipped yearly varied between 150 and 400 pounds. A sharp rise in drug consumption is noted in 1742, likely due to an outbreak of a severe smallpox epidemic causing the death of more than 1000 Negro slaves.[52]

As can be seen in table 3.3 several compounds described in the *Pharmacopaea Amstelredamensis* such as aceta, many aromatic waters, some electuaria (Benedictum laxativum, Confectio Hamech, Lenitivum, Diaphaenicum) are absent. Also cut out are plasters such as betonica, miniis, sparadrapum and griseum. The lists also failed to include essential oils such as those of orange, lime and fennel. Products such as Helleborus niger, Plumbi and pulveres chymici (Crystalli

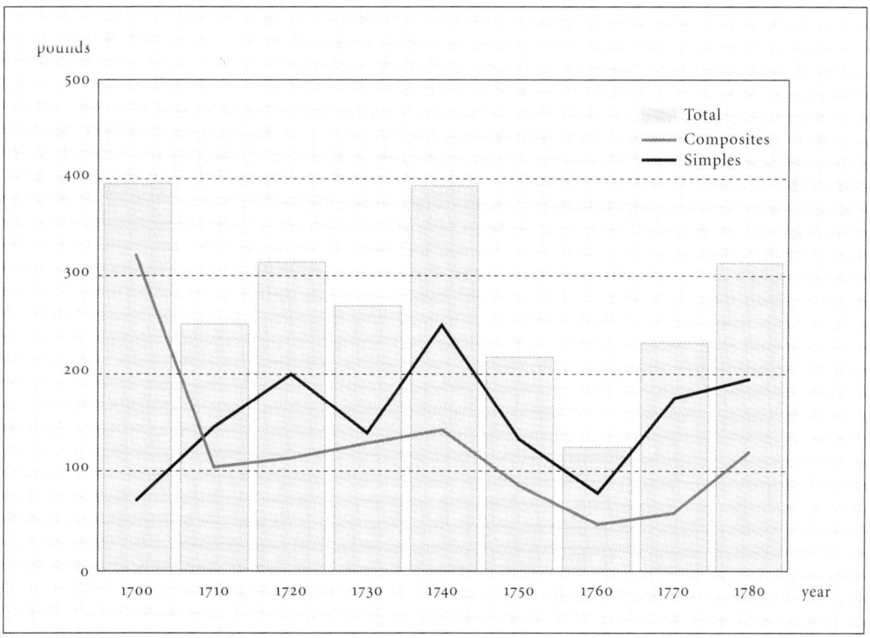

Figure 3.1 Volume of WIC medicines shipped to Curaçao 1700-1780

tartari and Magisterium corallorum) are absent. No purging powders were prescribed except the compound Hiera. The salts of absinthe and fabarum, the syrups of altheae and diacodium, trochisci such as alhandel or alkekengi and compounds such as Ruffi pills, turiae and vitrum antimonii obviously were considered of less importance by the profession. Scabies ointment was only needed in the year 1735 and 1744. Ointments such as basilicum, aureum, martiatum and oculare, appearing in the *Pharmacopaea Amstelredamensis* were also omitted.

SALE AND PURCHASE OF MEDICINES BY THE GOVERNMENT

The Curaçaoan Government often sold medicines received from Amsterdam at a profit to ships of their own WIC or to the VOC. An example of some prices is given in table 3.2. In 1706 Captain Jan de Roy of a VOC ship bought an assortment of medicines from the hospital pharmacy in Curaçao. The VOC ships entered the Pacific by the Cape Horn route. In 1743 shipper Andries Graan of the Company ship *De Catharina Galey* paid the exorbitant amount of 40 pesos to WIC surgeon Carel Doerffel for some medicines.[53] In 1714 the government bought 25 pounds of recently imported sassafras root.[54] A mixture of sassafras and opium was a popular anodyne and narcotic household remedy in Great Britain in 1722, named Godfrey's Cordial, chiefly used to prevent the crying of children. When the charter of the WIC was renewed and radical changes stripped the Company's trading activities of their monopolistic character, numerous commercial goods and drugs were shipped by private trading.[55] The port of Willemstad was opened to foreigners against a recognition fee. On the list of recognition fees in 1740 several medicinal products are mentioned such as sarsaparilla, ginger, guaiac, cochineal, indigo, wild cinnamon, campeche, carscarilla, anise and other liqueurs. The tax varied between 2 and 8 per cent of the value of their cargoes.[56] Often the origin of the medicines is obscure: the neighbouring Caribbean islands, North America or, most likely, the Spanish Main. In 1720 the barque *Satisfactie* arrived with two physic chests from the Danish St. Thomas. We suppose they contained patent medicines.[57] The chests were accompanied by popular medicine texts, assuming the user could read. Popular medical literature such as Buchan's manual for lay readers was also available and could inform the reader e.g. on the smallpox inoculation in the West Indian islands.[58] Inoculation or variolation, performed by rubbing the liquid of a pock into a scratch made on the arm, was well known in The Netherlands. A pupil of Boerhaave used the procedure in 1748 during his stay in Amsterdam. Surgeons were well aware of the fact that red colouring substances were believed to cure smallpox [59]. The red substance mercurius praecipitatus rubeus was recommended by d'Amsterdammer Apotheek (1686) to treat smallpox patients.[60] According to

Quincy (1736:178) carmin-red cochineal, made from females of a tropical American insect, was also used in the treatment of smallpox and measles. It is not surprising we come across Governors keeping medical books on their shelves, not only to be informed on diseases but also to learn about drugs.[61] Later on, in the nineteenth century, Curaçaoan merchants obtained a lot of drugs from New York.[62] A local pharmacist for example imported sarsaparilla in massive quantities.[63]

More often than generally assumed herbal simples and composites were re-exported by merchants from Curaçao to Amsterdam. Some examples will suffice. Manuel de Crasto sent orlean (annatto, roucou) to an Amsterdam enterprise in 1700.[64] In 1702 an amount of 7553 pounds of orlean were shipped to Jan Donker at Amsterdam.[65] Orlean was not only a valuable dyestuff, but it was used internally in diarrhea, lithiasis and haemorrhoidal affections as well.[66] In 1724 surgeon Willem Colomba dispatched one chest of elemi resin to Reynier van Weert in Amsterdam. [67] In 1735 Rudolph van den Clooster shipped 175 bags of sarsaparilla to Thomas Meijer/Aron Jesurun at Amsterdam.[68] In 1736 Willebord Horst also sent 14,977 pounds of sarsaparilla to the 'Societeit van Vredensburgh'.[69] Johannes Stuylingh dispatched in 1737 more than 2000 pounds of Peruvian bark (cinchona) to the business house Thomas Meijer, established in the Reguliers Breestraat in Amsterdam and to the Amsterdam firm Van Bunschoten & Boulder. Anthony Cadart shipped a box of 14 seroons of Peruvian bark to the widow of Fred. Bolmeyer in Amsterdam on 4 February 1737.[70] In 1738 Jan Veeris shipped a large amount of Peruvian balsam and lemon juice from Curaçao to Simon Leyen in Amsterdam.[71] Curaçaoan orange peels (laraha) proved an excellent stomachic and carminative and was used to make liqueur. In 1743 both the Widow Henriques and Dr. L.R. Horst shipped this product to the Amsterdam enterprises of Jan Westerburgh and Aron Jesurun.[72] Johannes Clemens shipped 6 packets of sarsaparilla to the merchant house of Elias van Laar at Amsterdam in 1743.[73] Return cargoes from Puerto Rico to Amsterdam contained a resin (gum anime?) to which a medicinal efficacy was ascribed. [74] A French ship seized on his voyage to Curaçao by a privateer carried 3000 pounds of cascarilla. With the barque *Subtile* Jean Michou of Martinique delivered in 1742 at Curaçao port 5089 lb. sarsaparilla and 29,003 lb. campechewood.[75] Campechewood, the dyewood of *Haematoxylon campechianum*, was also called 'Brazilwood', 'bluewood', 'peachwood, Provinciehout', 'stokvishout', heartwood or 'logwood'.[76] Commercially important dyewoods from South America and the Caribbean that were also exported via Curaçao were redwood or Fernambuco (*Caesalpinia echinata*); yellow wood (*Chlorophora tinctoria*)[77] and the West African (Angola) tacúla (*Pterocarpus tinctoria)*[78] Their most important use was found in dying textiles, but they were used in medicine as astringent, styptic and febrifuge as well.[79]

A small number of composites reached the United Provinces through Curaçao. In 1744 medical doctor Isaac Cardozo shipped 'een klyn vaatje met aptekers salve' (a small case of apothecary ointment) to the enterprise Elias Gomes Swaris in Amsterdam.[80] An attempt to smuggle medicines was made in February 1740 by the French shipper Du Ponhay. Under the false pretence of being hampered by leakage of his barque, he sailed into the small port of Piscadera where he sneakily discharged 8000 pounds of the medicine sarsaparilla root. His mission was to evade the Curaçaoan recognition fees but he was caught and had to pay. [81] In this way smugglers could also escape discomfort and delay by quarantine measures in case of communicable diseases. Illicit traffic, indeed, was the Dutch islands' fount of life.

Table 3.1 List of simples and compounds shipped to Curaçao in 1700 [82]

Aqua antiepileptica	Gummi tragacanthi	Sal centauri
Aqua cinnamomi	Lapis calaminaris	Sal prunellae
Aqua euphrasiae	Lapis haematitis	Sal succini
Aqua flores sambuci	Lithargyrium argenteum	Sal tartari
Aqua formicae	Lithargyrium aureum	Sal volatile cornu cervi
Aqua hyssopi	Manna electa	Sal volatile oleosum
Aqua melissae	Mater perlarum	Semen anisi
Aqua plantaginis	Mel rosatum	Semen cardamomi
Castoreum	Mercurius dulcis	Semen carvi
Conserva mellitum	Mercurius vitae	Semen papaveris albae
Corallium rubrum	Oculi cancri	Semen santonici
Cornu cervi ustum	Oleum hypericonis	Specifici cephalici Dr. Michael
Crocus optimus	Oleum lumbricorum	Spiritus carminativus
Diagridum	Oleum nardini	Spiritus cochleariae
Diamargaritum frigidum	Oleum dest. chamomelini	Spiritus cornu cervi
Diascordium Fracastorii	Oleum dest. foeniculi	Spiritus crani humani
Empl.ad fract Fernelli	Oleum dest. lavandulae	Spiritus formicae
Empl. defensivum Vigioni	Oleum dest. maioranae	Spiritus lumbricorum
Emplastrum diachylum	Oleum dest. rutae	Spirit salis armoniacum
Emplastrum diapalmae	Oleum dest. rorismarini	Spiritus salis communis
Emplastrum mucilaginum	Oleum dest. salviae	Spiritus vitrioli
Emplastrum oxicroceum	Radix angelicae	Spiritus nitri
Emplastrum stichticum	Radix calami	Succinum album
Extractum catholicum	Radix chynae	Succus liquiritiae
Flores absinthii	Radix cichorei	Syrupus adianthus
Flores chamaemeli	Radix consolidae	Syrupus artemisiae
Flores lavendulae	Radix iridis florentinae	Syrupus berberaceae

Flores meliloti	Radix jalappae	Syrupus papaveris
Flores rosarum	Radix pyrethri	Syrupus violarum
Flores sulphuris	Radix rharbarbari opt.	Tartarus crudum
Folia sennae	Radix rubiae tinctorum	Theriacum venetum
Gummi ammoniacum	Radix tormentillae	Trochisci myrobalani
Gummi anime	Radix zedoariae	Unguentum aegyptiacum
Gummi elemi	Sal absynthii	Unguentum diapompholygos
Gummi mastiche	Sal armoniacum	Unguentum populeum
Gummi olibanum	Sal cardui benedicti	Unicornu fossil. pp.
		Vitriolum cyprinum

This list reveals that the 109 drugs comprised 35 herbals, 13 mineral and 6 animal simples and that only 2 New World products were used. Jourdan (1828:II, 65) reported that 'Specific cephalicum' consisted of cinnabar, hartshorn, paeoniaroot, succinum, corallium rubrum and cranium hominis (dried human brain) and was used as an anti-epileptic. Diascordium Fracastorii was a powerfully astringent electuary containing opium, gum Arabic, cinnamon, styrax, cassia, and having a kaolin-like action through the presence in it of Bolus armenia, a Lemnian sealed earth (Ph.A.111)

Table 3.2 Prices of medicines delivered by the Curaçao Government to the slaveships 'De Coninck van Portugal' (6th February 1708) and to the 'Carolus secundus' (17th May 1708)[83]

Medicines	Quantity	Purchase	Sale
		Price in Dutch guilders	Price in Dutch guilders
Aloe hepatica	3 ounce	1,25	1,50
Antimon. diaphoreticum	2 ounce	0,75	3,00
Camphora	1 ounce	0,60	2,00
Cinnamon water	2 ounce	0,25	1,50
Mercur. praecipitatus	1 ounce	0,30	0,50
Oleum anisi	1 ounce	1,00	1,00
Oleum terebinthinae	4 ounce	0,45	3,00
Radix sarsaparillae	1 pound	0,75	2,75
Sal cornu cervi	1 ounce	0,75	1,25
Sal prunellae	2 ounce	0,35	1,50
Sanguis draconis	2 ounce	0,40	3,00
Spiritus cochleariae	6 ounce	2,25	6,00
Spirit. sal. armoniacum	2 ounce	1,00	2,00
Theriacum venetum	1 pound	4,00	5,00

Table 3.3 List of compounds dispatched to Curaçao 1701-1777

Legenda: amount in lb = pound, otherwise u = ounce

Medicinal products	1701	1709	1722	1735	1744	1751	1765	1775	1777
Source	84	85	86	87	88	89	90	91	92
Aqua alexipharmaca	4							2	
Aqua antiepileptica	4								
Aqua antinephritica	2								
Aqua antiparalytica.	3								2
Aqua chelidon. majus	2								
Aqua cinnamomi	2		3	2	3			2	3
Aqua cochlearium	4								
Aqua foeniculi	4								
Aqua hysopi	4								
Aqua hysterica	4		2	1		1			
Aqua lilior. convallar.	4								
Aqua melissae	4							2	
Aqua menthae	4	2			2				
Aqua rosarum	6	6	3		2				
Aqua sambuci	4								
Aqua styptica	2								
Aqua theriacalis	4	6			3	3			
Aqua tiliae	2								
Balsamum Locatelli	2		1	½		2			
Balsam.sulph.anisat.	2		½	½	2		1	1	
Butyrum antimonii					4u			½	
Cinnaber antimonii		½			3u		2	1	
Confectio alkermes	1	1	1	½	½	½			
Confectio hyacinthi	1	1	1	½		6u			
Conservum rosarum		2							
Corallorum	2		2						
Cornu cervi	2		1	2		5	4		
Cremor tartari	2	1	4	3	10	3	6	10	
Diascordium fracastorii	3	3	4	6		2	2	4	
Elect. diaphoenic.	3								
Elect. diaprunum	3								
Elect. hiera picra	2								
Elect. benedict. lax.	3								
Elect. diacatholic.	3								
Elixir proprietatis		½							

Medicinal products	1701	1709	1722	1735	1744	1751	1765	1775	1777
Empl. defensivum	8			7	8	3			6
Empl. diachyl.gum	3	2		6	6	3	3	6	6
Empl. diapalmae	6	8		6	8				12
Empl. ad fracturas	4		2	3					
Empl. gratia dei	2							4	4
Empl. labdanum	4		8	7	8	5	2		4
Empl. meliloti	6	3	4			2			4
Empl. mucilagin.	4	2	4						
Empl. opodeldoch									4
Empl. oxycroci	4	3	3	2			3	4	4
Empl. ranarum merc.	4	6	2	8	4	2	4	6	
Empl. ad rupturas	4								
Empl. stichticum	4			3					
Flores sulphuris	2		2	1	6				
Lapis prunelli	2						2		
Laudanum opiat	1		2u	1					
Margaritarum	2u		½						
Mel rosarum	4	3	4		1		1		
Mercurius dulcis			½	1	1	1	2		
Mercuri. pp. rubr.	6		½	2	½	2		½	
Mercurius sublim.	2				½			½	
Mithridatium	4				1				
Oculi cancri	3		4	3		2	1		
Oleum anisi	3	½		3	½u	3u		½	3
Oleum bacca junip.	4				2			1	1
Oleum caryophyllor.		1u		2u	1u		2u	½	1u
Oleum cinnamomi	½u	3u		½u		2u	2u	½	1u
Oleum hypericae	2								
Oleum laurinum	2	4			3	4			1u
Oleum ligni rhodii	½u	1u							
Oleum macidis	6u					½			
Oleum majoranae	6u			2	3u				
Oleum nardinum	2								
Oleum nux moschatae	1		2	½					
Oleum origani	2u	1u							
Oleum rorismarini	½u								
Oleum sabinae	3u					½			
Oleum spicae	1			2				½	1u

Medicinal products	1701	1709	1722	1735	1744	1751	1765	1775	1777
Oleum succini	6u			1					1
Oleum terebinthinae	4	6	3	6	10	5			
Oleum vitrioli	2	4							
Opium	0,5	3		1		1		2	
Oxymel scillae	3								
Philonium	1	2	1	4	1	1			
Pil. aloephanginae	½			4	1	1			
Pilulae cochiae	½								
Pil.extr.catholici								½	1
Pil. majernae	1								
Pil.pestilent. comp.	1								
Pulv. adstringens	3								
Pulv. diamargarith. frigid.	1				3u				
Requies Nicolai	1	1							
Sal absinthii	½	2u					2		
Sal armoniacum	6			2	6	2		2	
Sal centauri minor	½								
Sal prunellae	4		3	6	3			1	
Sal succinum	3u	2u	2u						
Sal volat.cornu cervi	1	6u	3	1	½	½			
Spir.carmin. Sylvii			2	2	3			½	2
Spir. cochleariae	4	2				6		½	2
Spir. cornu cervi	3		1	½		2		½	1
Spir. crani humani	½								
Spir. nitri dulcis	2		1	2	4	6		½	2
Spir. sal. armoniacum	4		3		3		2		
Spir. sal. commun.	1								
Spir. sal. dulcis			4	2	3	2			
Spir. sal. vol. oleos.	4		3	3			1	1	2
Spir. sulph. p.camp.	½								
Spir. vitrioli	1		½		½				1
Syrup. capilli veneri	2				2				
Syrup. diartemisiae	2								
Syrup. glycyrrhizae	2								
Syrup. papaver errat.			2	2	2	1			
Syrup. rosarum	4	2	3						
Syrup. rosarum solut.	2					1			
Syrup. violarum	4	1	2	1	2				

Medicinal products	1701	1709	1722	1735	1744	1751	1765	1775	1777
Tartras emeticus		2u	1u	1u					
Tartar. vitriolatum	2		1				2	6	8
Theriacum	13	10	4	12	12	5	4	4	
Tinctura bezoardi		½	4		2				1
Trochisci alhandel	½								
Trochisci de myrrhae	2u		2u						
Ungt. aegyptiacum	3	2		2				4	
Ungt. album camph.	4	3	4		4				
Ungt. altheae	4	3	4		4	3	2		2
Ungt .apostolorum	4					2	2	2	
Ungt. archanitae	3		2						
Ungt. diapompholigos	4								
Ungt. digestivum	6		2						
Ungt. lithargyri	4								
Ungt. nervinum	6	6			4			4	2
Ungt. nutritum	3								
Ungt. pectorale	2								
Ungt. populeum	6	3	2		4			2	2
Ungt. refrigerans	2								
Ungt. rosaceum	2		1½			2			
Ungt. ad scabiem				2	1				

Notes

1 Goslinga, *The Dutch in the Caribbean*, 95.
2 Harris, *Storm van 's Gravesande*, 284.
3 De Haan, *Nederlanders over de Zeeën*, 11.
4 Romieux, 'Les coffres de mer', 428-436.
5 Ratelband, *Vijf dagregisters*, 394.
6 Rutten, 'Slavenhandel', 389-406. See also Steele, *Atlantic Merchant-Apothecary*, xi-xxv.
7 Emmer, *The organization of Interoceanic Trade.*
8 Morton, *Atlas*, 324.
9 Postma, 'West African exports', 53-74.
10 Goslinga, *The Dutch in the Caribbean*, 95.
11 WIC 570 (1709) 212, 372.
12 WIC 200 (1700) 215.
13 Emboden, *Narcotic Plants*, 12.
14 Scagliola, *Apothecaires de Paris.*
15 Old Archive Curaçao (1818) 1579; See also *De Curaçaose Courant* 30 November 1816.
16 WIC 572/3 (1716) 745 mentions the exchange of 100 slaves for indigo from St. Domingo.
17 See for example WIC 586 (1739) 751.
18 Rutten, *Apothekers en Chirurgijns*, 220.
19 Coxe, *Dispensatory*, 320.
20 Pereira, *Beginselen der materia medica*, 854.
21 Rutten, 'Indigomaker', 39.
22 Benjamin, 'Medicine, mortality', 165
23 Meilink-Roelofsz, *Dutch authors*, 255-279.
24 Wilson, 'Halle Orphanage medications', 5-22.

25 Rutten, 'Geneesmiddelen leveranciers', 726-8.
26 Rotterdam. Raad ter Admiraliteit, *Lijst.*
27 Amsterdam. *Lijste der medicamenten en instrumenten.*
28 Vieyra, 'Lijst van geneesmiddelen', 1931-1935.
29 WIC, 590 (1742) 300-336. Monsterlijsten garnizoen.
30 WIC 137 (1766) nr. 4.
31 Hering, *Beschrijving*, 37.
32 Van Zanen, *David Ricardo Capriles*, 109.
33 Sesseler, 'Wilde salie', 49.
34 WIC 29/30 (1675) nr. 12.
35 Rutten, 'Drinkbaar goud', 126-30.
36 Hartog, *Bovenwindse Eilanden*, 250.
37 Klooster, *Illicit Riches*, 177
38 Rutten, *Apothekers en Chirurgijns*, 214.
39 WIC 566 (1700) 25.
40 WIC 570 (1709) 374.
41 WIC 1156 (1736) 5.
42 Wilson, 'Pietist universal reform', 133-54.
43 Rutten, 'Drinkbaar goud', 129.
44 Cowen, 'The impact of the materia medica', 51-63.
45 Rutten, 'Slavenhandel', 400.
46 Rutten, 'Geneesmiddelleveranciers', 727.
47 Sabieraj, 'Hemmstoffe', 278-9.
48 WIC 564 (1706) 14.
49 Emmanuel, *History of the Jews, I*, 69.
50 Rutten, 'Ziekten en geneesmiddelen', 246-50
51 See for example Emmanuel (1970) 102, 109; See also WIC 567 (1702) 25, 56; Hartog, *Geschiedenis Curaçao*, 343, 370.
52 WIC 589 (1742) 290.
53 WIC 590 (1743) 647.
54 WIC 205 (1714) 434.
55 WIC 582 (1735) 402.
56 WIC 587 (1739) 75.
57 WIC 570 (1720) 830.
58 Buchan, *Huislyke geneeskunde*, I, 302.
59 Neuburger, *Geschichte der Medizin* II, 369, 502.
60 *Pharmacopaea Amstelredamensis*, 136.
61 WIC 585 (1738) 930.
62 Anon, *De Curaçaose Courant* 23-12-1820; 16-2-1822 and 14-6-1828.
63 WIC 202 (1708) 410 and 576 (1720) 356.
64 WIC 566 (1700) 35.
65 WIC 200 (1702) 299.
66 Dragendorff, *Heilpflanzen*, 448.
67 WIC 578 (1724) 183.
68 WIC 582 (1735) 388.
69 WIC 1156 (1726) 5.
70 WIC 1156 (1737) 44, 57
71 WIC 1156 (1738) 77.
72 WIC 590 (1743) 30, 42, 295, 527.
73 WIC 590 (1743) 521.
74 Klooster, *Illicit Riches*, 77.
75 WIC 590 (1742) 245.
76 Wilson, 'Logwood trade', 1-15.
77 Tschirch, *Handbuch* 1, 745 and 3.2., 924, 934.
78 Dalziel, *The useful plants*, 256.
79 Githens, *Drug plants of Africa*, 59.
80 WIC 591 (1744) 231.
81 WIC 587 (1740) 470.
82 WIC 566 (1700) 25.
83 Rutten, 'Farmaceutische prijsgeschiedenis', 260-2.
84 WIC 566 (1701) 442.
85 WIC 570 (1709) 198.
86 WIC 576 (1722) 421.
87 WIC 1155 (1735) 165.
88 WIC 591 (1744) 287.
89 WIC 598 (1751) 298.
90 WIC 604 (1765) 1373.
91 WIC 610 (1775) 117.
92 WIC 211/12 (1777) 508.

Chapter IV
LETTERS FROM GUIANA

MAD ABOUT DRUGS

Between Brazil and Venezuela, the coast of Guiana extends along the Atlantic Ocean. The old authors and cartographers used to refer to this coast as the Wild Coast. Alonso de Ojeda, one of Columbus' fellow travellers, was supposedly the first to have visited this region in 1499. Subsequently, several expeditions were dispatched to the town of El Dorado in Guiana's interior, where according to legend gold and silver could be found.[1] The Spanish were soon followed by Zeelanders and Hollanders, who from the end of the 16th century maintained a regular trade with Guiana in order to explore salt from the lagoons on the Venezuelan coast and who bartered with the Indians. Due to the good relations with the Indians one was capable to exchange letterwood, cassava, tobacco, copaiba balsam, the vegetable oil pressed out of the nut of the Crab-wood tree (*Carapa procera)* and orlean (annatto) for European goods, such as copper, fishing gear, weapons, glass, ceramics and textile. Orlean or roucou is a dyestuff from the seeds of *Bixa orelllana*. There was an annatto dye-store on the Massaruni River. Timber was of importance to commerce but of equal, if not greater value were the trees and plants from which medicinal substances could be obtained. The rootstocks of cassava were cultivated throughout the tropics where it provides a staple food. Various species of *Dioscorea* or Yam of southern Asia origin but widespread in West Africa, had been brought in by slaves into Guiana in the course of the 16th and 17th centuries and had largely displaced the native cassava. Cassava however, travelled in opposite direction. Also akees and mango from Africa were introduced by the slave trade. The staples of cassava and plantain, however, have a protein content of less than 1 per cent; yams, rice and maize are better, but have only 2-3 per cent protein. As cattle could not be reared the intake of both animal and vegetable protein was low.

The oldest Dutch report of a reconnoitre expedition to the Wild Coast is by A. Cabeliau from Ghent, who was dispatched as 'Commies-Generaal' or supercargo of the two vessels that performed the journey to Guiana and Trinidad in 1599, and submitted this account to the States-General upon his return.[2] There was so much interest in the prospect of the coast that Zeeland merchants started to establish trading posts. The Zeelanders' stations on the Wild Coast were, however, weak and badly managed and were not sufficiently supported by the fatherland. Colonisation, if it took place at all, was primarily commercial and geared towards trading. Establishing settlements only came in the second place.

Already in 1616 trading posts were established along the Essequebo and Pomeroon Rivers and around 1625 a few forts were built, which were under the control of the Zeeland Chamber of the WIC. On the Surinam River an English colony was established in 1651, which was transferred to the Dutch in exchange for New Netherland. The States of Zeeland as of 1667 governed the colony of Surinam. In 1682 it was actually transferred to the WIC but already in 1683 it was incorporated in the Chartered Society (Geoctroyeerde Societeit) of Surinam, so that this colony is outside the scope of our subject. Berbice – originally a patron's colony of the Zeeland Van Pere family – was controlled from Amsterdam by the Society of Berbice after 1712. The WIC had a certain influence in it and the parties were mutually bound by contracts.[3] The aim of the settlements on the Wild Coast was the promotion of the cultivation of profitable staple products that might only be supplied to and transported by the WIC. That monopoly, however, formed a serious obstacle to the growth of powerful settlements. The settling of planters as well as the import of slaves was essential to the development of a healthy economy. But the WIC supplied the plantations with too few slaves to enable adequate exploration. Of the almost 345,000 slaves that were transported to Guiana, 185,000 went to Surinam and only 21,000 to Essequebo and Berbice together.[4] Why did the Bewindhebbers hesitate to meet these urgent requests? The answer is that planters were repeatedly delinquent in the payment of debts incurred by the slave purchases. The agrarian system upon which Essequebo's economy depended was characterised by small plantations with monoculture and compulsory labour. The staple products of the colony consisted of sugar, rum, coffee, cotton and cocoa. In 1747 the colony Essequebo produced 559 tierces or half-hogsheads of sugar which were carried to Amsterdam in two schooners. The exports in 1761 were only 878 hogsheads of sugar, 28 bales of cotton and 45 tierces of coffee. Some molasses was exported to Boston from which distillers made their rum for personal use. Rum and molasses were not only bought from the Dutch and the English but also from the French, who, since rum was unsaleable in France, sold it more cheaply than the English merchant.

HEALTH CARE

Though Guiana is situated in the Torrid Zone, it comparatively enjoys a more temperate climate than other countries at the same latitude. Nonetheless, Guiana was considered hot, unhealthy and detrimental to European immigrants and those who had the courage to move there suffered particularly from malaria. The fierce attacks of intermittent fever and the accompanying hallucinations that affected the mind sometimes resulted in the strangest decisions on the part of the commanders and were the cause of utter misery. Dysentery formed a second health hazard, immediately followed by smallpox, which especially could cause a massacre among black slaves and Indians.[5] Less lethal were cases of trachoma, typhoid, hydrops, scurvy, hookworm disease (ancylostomiasis), leprosy, filariasis and schistosomiasis. Filariasis was spread by many species of mosquitoes; vectors of *Wucheria bancrofti*, the microfilaria penetrate after the mosquito bite and cause severe sickness (pulmonary symptoms, elephantiasis, and blindness). Schistosomiasis (Bilharziasis) is a severe debilitating disease caused by infection with blood flukes of the genus *Schistosoma* (trematodes). It is endemic in Africa, certain West-Indian islands and Guiana and was a common cause of severe a-naemia. Both Schistosomiasis and Leishmaniasis (Dumdum fever, transmitted to man by sandfleas) were treated with antimony compounds. Today's treatment with antimonii potassium tartrate (tartras emeticus) is a classical example of old drugs (the antimonials) being used to combat old diseases. Yellow fever did not present a problem until the 19th century.[6] Moreover, alcoholism meant the ruin of many colonists and the Zeeland Chamber frequently had to discipline a drunken commander.[7] The body's innate ability to heal itself was impaired by the use of alcohol. Despite the threat of diseases, boredom and nuisance of swarms of mosquitoes, the land along the rivers the Berbice, Demerara, Essequebo and Pomeroon with their fertile soil, kept posing a challenge to young planters.[8]

The colonies in Guiana were of a cosmopolitan character and Spaniards, Dutchmen, Englishmen and Frenchmen lived together in more or less harmony. With the construction of the Fort Kijk-Overal, the raising of a hospital and surgeons shop and the laying out of sugar and coffee plantations, the seeds were sown for a gradually expanding health care system. Around 1750 the WIC still had authority over the African forts and lodges, the Netherlands Antilles and the colonies on the Wild Coast: Essequebo and Demarara. The latter colony developed favourably after its foundation in 1746 and soon numbered several sugar plantations. In 1769 the Dutch pharmacist Otto van Rens settled here, who set up a pharmacy annex Hortus Botanicus.[9]

The white medical profession came into touch with a variety of medical cultures overseas. Alongside – and sometimes opposite – the surgeon in the colonies was the traditional healer: the Curaçaoan curioso or curandero, the Indian shaman or hechicero and the African 'fiticheerder'. They considered the secret knowledge of herbs as their personal property that could not simply be transferred to others. Here the effect of their medicine was clearly based on a combination of social relations and magical significance. Health care for the WIC personnel and slaves was mainly the domain of WIC surgeons. With these 'fixers' as they were sometimes called, one was lucky one time and unfortunate the next. One gets the impression that the medical practitioners in Curaçao and in Guiana were of a better quality than those in Guinea, but in general they were honourable and quite competent, and some of them showed remarkable results. Most of them tried to heal according to Galenic principles; others made it their aim to publish on health problems and diseases in their area. In the 17th century surgeon Samuel Brun (1624) wrote about health care on Mori and Dr. Van Focquenbroch (1668) about the Gold Coast.[10, 11] On Curaçao the 18th century started with statements and letters by medical doctor Laurentius Rudolph Horst about health care and founding of a pharmaceutical laboratory. In the 1750s chief surgeon Carel Doerffel wrote about diseases, food and therapy in Curaçao. [12] In Berbice in 1727 surgeon Rutger Tenhoute wrote an accurate report on life at a sugar plantation: food, punishments, diseases and healing practices.[13] In 1796 Dr. Ernst Karl Rodschied closed the eighteenth century by a study on health care and state of health in Essequebo.[14] The two latter medical practitioners are of the opinion that the black slave in Guiana, compared to the Dutch Antilles, received little humane treatment.

The surgeons, who often acted as 'ziekentrooster' (a clergyman who tends the sick) treated sick and wounded Europeans as well as black slaves.[15] The sick could be admitted to the hospital of Carthabo situated close to Fort Kijk-Overal where the hothouse was also located. Carthabo was the centre of Dutch authority, which was moved to the new Fort Zeelandia on 'Vlaggeneiland' (Flag Island) in the estuary of the Essequebo River in 1733. The central repository for medicines was also located in Carthabo, from where the surgeon's chests at the various WIC plantations were provisioned. Around 1730 there were 25-30 private and 3-5 Company estates and the WIC payroll at that time contained 66 officials including 15 soldiers and 854 black slaves. The total population in 1735 comprised approximately 3000 persons.[16] For the surgeon such a labour force entailed a considerable amount of work. In 1750 plans were made for the construction of a spacious hospital of 40 feet long, 20 feet wide and 7 feet high, with departments for black and white patients who had to undergo the 'cure'.[17] That 'cure' consisted of a treatment with mercury ointment and decoctions of sarsaparilla, smilax china and guaiac (lignum vitae), both for treating yaws (Indian pox or framboesia) and Spanish pox (syphilis). The surgeons were not involved in the medical care for the Indians. Indians could never be enslaved, as they were 'under the Company's protective wings' and they did not appreciate absorbing European medicine. The Government not only protected the Indians but also at the same time monopolised the trade with them. They had their own medicine man, which disposed of an extensive knowledge of the rain forest herbs, and they lived mainly from gathering forest products, fishing and hunting. Part of the yield of turtles, jarou (fish), tobacco, orlean, indigo, wild vanilla, copaiba balsam (maraan oil), beeswax, crabs, lobsters and fowl, they sold or exchanged with the inhabitants of the fort or with private planters. Another part was occasionally sent with the shipments of sugar to Amsterdam or Middelburg, two cities of which the Bewindhebbers were always at odds with each other in matters concerning the management of the colony. Especially the 'kleine vaart', the short-haul shipping – particularly profitable for the colony – and the forbidden trade with Surinam or with the smugglers formed a source of irritation to the Zeelanders.

The colonial pharmacotherapy of the whites was restricted to European medicines. Whites only wanted Dutch fare and Amsterdam remedies that were brought in by transatlantic shipping. Native medicinal herbs and traditional healing practices were unknown to the white colonists, except for the bark of *Simaruba amara* and that of *Carapa procera* which were both used against fever and diarrhoea. With more or less success diarrhoea and flux were also treated with theriac and tragacanth; yaws with mercury salts or the leaves of *Jacaranda acutifolia*; trachoma and other eye disease with trochisci albi Rhazis or unguentum oculare. One treated hydrops with syrupus cichorei, oxymel scillae, colocynth and calomel; smallpox eruptions with mercurius praecipitatus rubeus; influenza, cough and pulmonary disorders with tartras emeticus; venereal disease and yaws with oleum guaiaci and mercury; pustules and swellings with unguentum basilicum or diachylon plaster; scurvy with tamarind pulp and lime juice; malaria with quassia wood; leprosy with unguentum nutritum; filariasis, bilharzia and leishmaniasis (dumdum fever) with an antimony preparation. Antimony was strongly recommended as an emetic and expectorant by Basilius Valentinus (Johan Thoelde 1565-1624) in his book *The Triumphal Chariot of Antimony*.[18] In small quantities it operates as a diaphoretic, heavier doses acted as a purgative and emetic, which expelled intestinal worms.

Many diseases could be traced back to alcohol abuse, poorly balanced diet, poor state of sanitation, vitamin deficiency or to food poisoning. Throughout the entire Torrid Zone *Ipomoea batatas* is growing, originally native in Central America and an important food crop, known by the name 'batata'. Often Fusarium fungi that produced toxic phytoalexins like ipomeamaron infected the tubers. [19] Manioc (*Manihot utillissima*), another staple food, contains cyanides and rhodanides.[20]

In horse beans (*Vicia faba*) pyrimidine derivatives such as vicine and convicine occur, of which the aglycon may cause acute hemolytic anaemia in persons with a lack of glucose-6-phosphatedehydrogenase.[21] Yams from *Dioscorea alata* and other species, native to subtropical countries, contain the toxic dioscorine.[22] Akee, the fruit of *Blighia sapida* may contain poisonous hypoglycine, The unripe fruits of *Mangifera indica* or Mango are the possible source of contact dermatitis, caused by alkylphenoles.[23] Rye received from Holland could contain toxic indole alkaloids of the ergoline type, produced by a fungus (ergot) that grows on cereal grains. Many vegetable medicines could be contaminated by aflatoxins due to fungal infection, and food poisoning could put a heavy pressure on the medicine supply.[24]

THE SURGEON'S MEDICINE SHOP

Table 4.1 gives an insight into the medicine assortment that was ordered for the hospital pharmacy in Essequebo at the end of the 17th century.[25] At the Fort Kijk-Overal an estimated 25 servants and 78 slaves were present at the time. The colony as a whole numbered 88 whites and 77 black slaves at the WIC plantations, whereas approximately 50 Europeans and 440 slaves and a total of about 760 persons lived at the private plantations.[26] The list of medicines was drawn up with the utmost care and knowledge by surgeon Jan de Bruyn and signed by Commander Abraham Beekman. A total of more than 170 pounds of medicines was shipped to the Fort Kijk-Overal, a large and expensive shipment. Also later shipments, when the governor's seat was transferred to Fort Zeelandia at Flag Island, were quite substantial. This was also the case with the shipments destined for Berbice. In 1731 the Zeeland Chamber had already asked the pressing question of what happened to those excessively large quantities of drugs.[27] Did they really come into the possession of those responsible for health care, the surgeons, or did they disappear into other channels? For a long time the surgeon's medicine shop had been allowed to supply the drugs to private persons as well, but the WIC put an end to this in 1749. One distrusted the surgeons and suspected them of putting the proceeds into their own pockets. The scorn the surgeons in Guiana encountered is remarkable when compared with the recognition they received in other colonies. Especially Berbice has a bad reputation in this respect.

It is clear that at least part of the medicines Holland or Zeeland dispatched did not find its way to the WIC employees and plantations, but vanished into private objectives. The director of the Hoogelande sugar plantation in Berbice, who confiscated the medicine chest in 1727 so that the responsible surgeon Tenhoute could not dispose of the necessary drugs, set a particularly bad example. Also

Table 4.1 List of medicines for Essequebo 1 May 1687. Weights given: lb = pounds, u = ounces 31

Emplastra		**Aquae**		**Unguenta**	
Diapalmae	1 lb	Cinnamomi	1 lb	Aegyptiacum	1 lb
Diachylon cum gummi	¼ lb	Foeniculi	2 lb	Agrippae	½lb
Mucilaginibus	1 lb	Antiparalytica	½ lb	Album caphuratum	1 lb
Meliloti	1 lb	Vitae Matthioli	½ lb	Altheae simplex	2 lb
Ranis quadrupel	1 lb	Spiritus cochleariae	1 lb	Basilicum	4 lb
Diapompolygos	½ lb	Antinephriticum	½ lb	Digestivum	4 lb
Opodeldoch	½ lb	**Farinae**		Martiatum	1 lb
Oxicroci	3 u	Altheae radix	1 lb	Nervinum	1 lb
Defensivum	½ lb	Foenugraeci	1 lb		
Ad Rupturas	4 u				
Herbae		**Radices**		**Flores**	
Absinthi	2 lb	Aristolochiae longae	½ lb	Croci occidentalis	2 u
Altheae	2 lb	Chinae	12 lb	Centauri	½ lb
Scordii	1 lb	Glycyrrhizae	6 lb	Chamaemeli	1 lb
Sabinae	¼ lb	Polypodii quercini	3 lb	Meliloti	1 lb
Olea		Sarsaparillae	12 lb	**Opiata**	
Juniperi bacci	3 u	Hermodactylorum	2 lb	Laudanum opiatum	1 u
Laurinum	1 lb	Lignum guaiaci	12 lb	Theriaca veneta	7 lb
Palmae	1 lb	Angelicae	½ lb	Philonium Romanum	½ lb
Amygdalarum amarum	1 lb	Graminae	1 lb	Diascordium fracastorii	1 lb
Hypericae	1 lb	Bardanae seu Lappa minor	2 lb		
Mandrini	½ lb	Asari	2 u	**Laxativa**	
Origani	1 u	Contrayervae	2 u	Scammonium	2 u
Anisi	2 u	Hellebori albi	2 u	Pilulae foetidae maioris	2 u
Succini	3 u	Pyrethri	1 u	Confectio Hamech	1½ lb
Petrae	1 lb	Rubiae tinctorum	1 u	Diacarthamum	2 lb
Terebinthinae	3 lb	Consolidae maioris	2 u	Diaphoenicum	1 lb
Guaiaci	1 u	**Mellita**		Extractum catholicum	6 u
Trochisci		Rosarum	1 lb	Pilulae Ruffi	3 u
Albi Rhazi	2 u	Diamorum	½ lb	Radix Jalappa	1 lb
De myrrhae	1 u	Sirupus papaveris	½ lb	Radix rhabarberae	½ lb
Alkekengi	4 u	Altheae Fernellii	1 lb	Folia sennae	1 lb
Pulveres		Cichorei cum rheo	½ lb	Resina jalappae	1 u
Pluritis	1½ u	**Conserva et Rob**		**Cortices-Fructi-Ligni-Semina**	
Ad dysenteriam	2 u	Conservum rosarum	1 lb	Cortex guaiaci	2 lb
Cremor tartari	1 lb	Rob acaciae	½ lb	Cortex granatorum	1 lb
Aloe	½ lb	Confectio alhandel	2 lb	Semen anisi	1 lb

Ammoniacum	2 lb	Rob sambuci	1 lb	Semen foeniculi	2 lb
Camphora	2 u	**Mineralia et marina**		Semen zedoariae	2 lb
Elemi	1 lb	Aerugo	½ lb	Fructus cardamomi minoris	3 u
Mastiche	1/2 lb	Argentum vivum	1/2 lb	Nigellae	4 u
Myrrha	1/2 lb	Alumen crudum	3 lb	Auricula judae (Fungi sambuci)	6u
Glycyrrhizae succus	1 lb	Cerussa	6 lb	Jemu indorum (Gutta gamba)	4 lb
Terebinthina veneta	2 lb	Tutia praeparata	4 u	**Chimica**	
Asa foetida	1 u	Coralli rubri	4 u	Extractum absinthii	1 pint
Tragacanthum	1 u	Vitriolum cyprium	¼ lb	Vitrum antimonii	½ u
Animalia		Lapis hematites	1 u	Antimonium diaphoreticum	2 u
Axungia porci	2 lb	Antimonium crudum	2 lb	Aqua fortis	½ lb
Oculi cancri	½ lb	Sal absinthi calcinatus	2 u	Crocus martis	3 u
Cantharides	1 u	Spermaceti	1 u	Saccharum saturni	1 u
Cera flava	3 lb	**Utensilia**		Sal prunellae	½ lb
Cera alba	1 lb	Mortars and pestles, glass jars		Mercurius praecipitatus rubeus	½ lb
Cornu cervi raspatum	1 lb	Scales, weights and measures		Elixir proprietatis Paracelsi	2 u
Sapo venetus	6 lb	Canules, tubes, syringes			
Castoreum	1 u	Lint, sheets, lancets			

from Essequebo complaints are heard that medicines disappeared into thin air via the many plantations. In 1733 the directors of the Zeeland Chamber once more expressed their anxiety about the substantial shipments of medicines Essequebo needed and demanded that the surgeon's shops would be inspected three times a year.[28] Whether this made a lot of difference is not known.

Later, during the administration of Laurens Storm van 's Gravesande (1743-1772), the voluminous shipments of medicines were minimised, as well as those of food and tools. The Surgeon Major Jacob Dijkman does complain in 1753 about receiving so few medicines for the three Company plantations Duynenburg, Pelgrim and Agtekerke (Poelwijk) that even the bare necessities were lacking. In the same year Storm van 's Gravesande points out to the Zeeland Chamber that 'a number of whites and 712 slaves need quite a lot of drugs, especially when the seasons are bad and also the dose for the Negroes is much higher than for the whites'.[29]

Not only medicines, but also other products were embezzled. According to the Zeeland Chamber in Middelburg too much kiltum (rum) and molasses disappeared from the production of the sugar plantations without any justification, so that the Essequebo colony became increasingly costly and more burdensome to the Company.[30]

During the administration of commander Laurens Storm van 's Gravesande an attempt was made to bring more order into the management of the colony and to strengthen Essequebo economically by attracting English and Zeeland planters, who were expected to lay out sugar and coffee plantations along the rivers.[32] The abuses in the health care system were also tackled and improved.[33] At the Fort more than 200 servants and militia and twenty Company blacks are present at the time. Probably with a view to the substantial and costly 'long distance movers' of medicines, Laurens already in his first letters to the bewindhebbers at Middelburg argues in favour of a scientific study and a better appraisal of the native medicinal herbs he supposes to find in his district, such as sarsaparilla, gutta gamba, aloe and other medicinal products.[34] Laurens had a fair – even if theoretical – knowledge of medicinal plants. Besides, knowledge of European plant species and recognition of the same or similar species presumed to have analogous properties to those already known helped new arrivals in Guiana. Laurens also described in great detail the processing of the fleshy rootstocks of cassava or yucca (*Manihot utillissima*), an indispensable foodstuff for the slaves and grown in the bread plantations The starch made of this root, called manioc or tapioca, was popular in the Netherlands for curing gastrointestinal disorders. The white officials received rations of flour and rye meal sent from Europe, but in case of shortage they consumed cassava as well. In his letters from 1750 he emphasises once more the commercial perspective the pharmacobotany of Essequebo offered. According to Laurens, an abundance of cardamom, copaiba balsam, elemi, mastic, tacamahac, caranja gum, copal, guaiac wood, bezoar stones, cassia varieties, simarouba bark, jalap root, orlean, honey, yellow wax, quassia and ipecac was available for export. Ipecacuanha is a perennial growing in shadowy moist situations in the forests of the interior and was used by the Indians as an emetic before their connection with Europeans. Piso described its use fully in his *Natural History of Brazil* as early as 1618 and brought the root to Europe, yet it was scarcely used before the year 1700. In 1726 it was listed in the Dutch *Pharmacopoea Amstelaedamensis renovata.* It is prescribed in amoebic dysentery and in small doses as a diaphoretic and expectorant. Quassia (*Quassia amara*) and other febrifuge vegetable drugs such as *Simaruba* and *Malpighia* species were found on the border of the River Berbice. The locust tree (*Hymenaea spp.*) furnished the gum animé. Many trees, Storm mentioned were famed for their fragrant resinous juice and healing properties and slaves knew how to exploit the natural environment for medicinal purposes. Natural remedies are still used worldwide in traditional systems of medicine and were central to healing in pre-modern times.

'It is unnecessary – wrote Storm on June 19, 1750 – to dilate upon the advantages which would accrue from the above-mentioned project both in dues and taxes to the Honourable Co. and in the consumption of merchandise and the increase in navigation, since anyone will, upon consideration, easily grasp this. Just as our neighbours, the Portuguese and Spaniards, ship many products besides the mentioned sugar, coffee, cocoa, we should be able to do the same, for we enjoy the same climate and like them have high and low, dry and humid regions...'[35] Oddly enough the Zeeland directors hardly react to his proposal to trade in these medicines. As export articles mainly guaiacum, simarouba and copaiba were known. The latter remedy had been introduced in Europe in 1625 by Samuel Purchas and was recorded in the Amsterdam pharmacopoeia of 1636 and in the London pharmacopoeia of 1677 as Balsamum Capivi. The balsam was used externally as a wound ointment and as a liniment against rheumatic joint pains, internally against diarrhoea, urinary tract complications and venereal disease. A less known but popular export product was orlean, which was marketed as a dye and as a medicine in the Republic. The indifferent attitude of the Zeeland directors is the more noticeable because in 1684 and 1737 they had ordered the surgeons to pay more attention to the herbs of their resident countries.[36] Essequebo, however, was treated as the Cinderella under Laurens' administration. Zeeland was much more interested in Surinam than in Essequebo, as the colony brought in larger revenues and could count on a regular import of slaves from West-Africa as labourers for the sugar and coffee plantations, whereas blacks for the plantations in Essequebo and Demarara were in short supply.[37] The bewindhebbers' unwilling and uninterested attitude is also expressed in the supply of tools and medicines from the Netherlands in the second half of the century. Around 1750 surgeons complain about the poor quality of the medicines and surgical instruments shipped and commander Laurens writes an angry letter about barrels of adulterated flour and tainted meat received. [38, 39] On February 1745 Laurens wrote to the directors: 'There is a general dearth of everything – no victuals, no ammunition, the warehouses already long empty, the smithies at a standstill for want of coal and iron.... If we had no supplies from the English we should all very long since have been brought to making shift with a crust of dry bread'.[40] Thus, the colony fell from one complaint into the other until General Whyte in 1796 with three British regiments took possession of Essequebo and Demerara, and under the protection of Great Britain agriculture and commerce made rapid progress.

EXPEDITION TO POMEROON

Pomeroon, together with Essequebo, was one of the first settlements of Zeelanders on the coast of South-America. By the end of the 18th century Pomeroon was virtually deserted and Essequebo was entirely surpassed economically by the colony of Demerara, established around 1750. The commander of Essequebo, Abraham Beekman (1686) considered the colony of Pomeroon, situated west of the river Essequebo, as part of his territory and he did not appreciate the attempts to make Pomeroon into an independent colony. Those attempts frequently failed anyway due to diseases among the colonists, lack of black labourers and English raids. In the middle of the 17th century the towns of Middelburg, Flushing and Veere jointly tried to inject new life into the colony of Pomeroon by accommodating Jewish fugitives from Brazil there.[41] The settlement that then developed, Nova Zeelandia, was lost after occupation and looting by the English. Yet the idea of a settlement in the fertile Pomeroon region kept haunting the colonists on the Wild Coast. In 1685 a certain Jacob Pietersz de Jongh, former plantation owner in Essequebo, succeeded in interesting the Heren X (Assembly of Ten) in a new expedition to Pomeroon. After consultation with the Amsterdam Chamber, the Zeeland directors decided to appoint De Jongh as prospective commander of the Pomeroon colony. This was completely against commander Beekman's wishes, who did not want to separate Pomeroon from Essequebo, but could not do much against a decision imposed by his superiors. Accompanied by the Rotterdam surgeon David van Cassel and a few relatives, De Jongh departed from Flushing in 1686.[42] His expedition is a striking example of laborious transatlantic medicine traffic in the late 17th century. Besides tools and foodstuffs, a big wooden chest with medicines was taken along. Pharmacist Gilles Heyndricksen, the city pharmacist of Middelburg, supplied its contents. The medicines shipped are shown in table 4.2.

As this table indicates, 103 drugs were shipped, divided into 20 classes. The classification is mixed: sometimes galenical, sometimes botanical, chemical or pharmacological. Noticeable in this list is the large amount of antimonium crudum and vitrum antimonii, of which a total of about 15 ounces was shipped, although when compared to the medicine list of the Amsterdam Admiralty from 1692, it appears that a mere 1½ ounces would be sufficient for 100 heads.[44] These medicines must have been intended for the cure of malaria, schistosomiasis and visceral leishmaniasis; for antimony was deemed the proper remedy in cases of lengthy, persistent and intermittent fevers and infestation with parasites.[45] The quantity of 10 pounds of guaiac wood is also much larger than the 4 pounds advised on the Amsterdam list. With a total of 16 pounds of guaiac, sassafras, sarsaparilla and smilax china, one apparently wanted to be on the safe side for any future syphilis or framboesia (yaws) treatment. The 3½ ounces of mercury and a half pound of mercury-containing emplastrum de ranis we may consider to be adjuvant to that therapy. Of theriac twice as much is present as was thought necessary on the Amsterdam Admiralty list. The pharmacological classification of the shipment of medicines for Pomeroon is shown in table 4.3.

Table 4.2. Drugs shipped to the Dutch colony of Pomeroon in 1686. Weights given: lb = pounds, u = ounces[43]

Antidota et opiata		**Olea per destillationem**		**Flores**	
Theriaca Andromachi	12 u	Anisi	½ u	Meliloti	½ lb
Diascordium fracastorii	8 u	Juniperi	1 u	Balaustiorum	1 u
Philonium romanum	4 u	Therebinthinae	1 lb	Chamaemeli	1 lb
Electuaria		Caryophylli	2 u	Crocus	1 u
Diacarthamum	½ lb	**Olea per inf/expr/descensum**		Rosarum	1 u
Diacatholicum	½ lb	Laurinum	1 lb	Hypericae	2 u
Condita		Amygdalarum	¼ lb	**Aquae**	
Rosarum	1 lb	**Pilulae**		Cinnamomi	8 u
Cydoniarum	1 lb	Ruffi	½ u	Fortis	2 u
Mel rosarum	1 lb	Extracti catholici	½ u	Rosarum	16 u
Emplastra		Laudani opiati	½ u	**Gummi et succi**	
Diapalmae	2 lb	**Mineralia et Chymica**		Tragacantha	1 u
Meliloti	½ lb	Balsamum sulphuris	2 u	Balsamum peruvianum	1 u
Mucilaginum	¼ lb	Mercurius pp rubrum	½ u	Camphora	2 u
De ranis c. mercurio	½ lb	Mercurius dulcis	1 u	Gutta gamba	2 u
Defensivum	¼ lb	Sal absinthi	2 u	Gummi caranna	2 u
Griseum	½ lb	Turbith minerale*	1 lb	Succus liquiritiae	2 u
Unguenta		Crocus metallorum	2 u	Mastiche	2 u
Arthanitae	2 u	Spiritus salis armoniaci	1 u	Myrrha	2 u
Basilicum	½ lb	Elixir propriet. Paracelsii	4 u	Opium	½ u
Digestivum	¼ lb	Ruptorium	2 lb	Therebinthina veneta	2 lb
Ad scabiem	¼ lb	Spiritus cochleariae	8 u	Sanguis draconis	½ u
Desiccativum	¼ lb	**Radices**		Scammonium	1 u
Album camphoratum	¼ lb	Aristolochiae	2 u	Aloe hepatica	2 u.
Ligna		Contrayervae	1 u	Ammoniacum	2 u
Guaiacum	10 lb	Glycyrrhizae	4 lb	Spanish soap	6 lb
Sassafras	3 lb	Jalappae	¼ lb	**Farinae**	
Folia et Herbae		Lappa minor	¼ lb	Foenugraeci	1 lb
Centauri	½ lb	Polypodii	1 lb	Radicem altheae	1 lb
Absinthii	1 lb	Rhabarbari	2 u	Lupinorum	½ lb
Altheae	1 lb	Sarsaparillae	2 lb	**Animalia**	
Scordii	½ lb	Chinae	3 lb	Oculi cancrorum	½ lb
Sennae	½ lb	Bistortae	2 u	Spermaceti	½ lb
Fructus		Hermodactylorum	1 lb	**Mineralia et chymica**	
Alkekengi	2 u	Rubiae tinctorum	1 u	Alumen ustum	2 u
Myrobalani	2 u	**Semina**		Antimonium crudum	4 lb
Piper album	2 u	Anisi	½ lb	Vitrum antimonii	1 u
Tamarindorum	6 u	Foeniculi	1 lb	Lapis haematitis	½ u
Colocynthis	½ u	Jujubae indae	2 u	Lithargyrum aureum	1 lb
		Zedoariae	1 lb	Vitriolum cyprinum	1 u
				Argentum vivum	2 u

*Mercuric sulfate

Table 4.3. Pharmacological classification of medicines shipped to Pomeroon in 1686

Dermatologicals	28%
Purgatives	13%
Analgesics and narcotics	9%
Syphilis therapy	8%
Expectorants	8%
Diuretics	6%
Astringents	4%
Mouth and throat preparations	4%
Anthelmintics	4%
Bitters and gastric sedatives	3%
Antipyretics	3%
Carminatives	2%
Stimulating agents	2%
Diaphoretics (Sudorifics or Hidrotics)	2%
Alexipharmaca (antidotes)	2%
Antiscorbutic agents	1%
Arthritis and related disorders	1%

No more than a global significance may be ascribed to this classification. Theriac, for example, is classified as an antidote, but was mostly applied in cases of diarrhoea and dysentery. Although theriac contains opium, little is left of the narcotic and analgesic effect a few weeks after preparation.[46] This is understandable, for the fermentation following the preparation and the influence of oxidases and peroxidases from the gum Arabic incorporated in it, will not have left the unstable morphine molecule undisturbed. Theriac, however, did possess quite different valuable properties, such as an anti-inflammatory activity. Contamination of theriac by Saccharomyces species during fermentation contributed to the effect of the end product as anti-diarrhoicum due to possible bonding of bacterial endotoxins, recovery of the intestinal flora and inflammation-inhibiting effect.[47]

The travel report of De Jongh's expedition shows how the medicine traffic took place.[48] After a successful crossing aboard the ship *De Vrijheyt* to Essequebo, De Jongh was assigned 10 black male slaves and 9 female slaves, a number of soldiers, ammunition and provisions by commander Beekman. The expedition then sets sail on board *'t Casteel Rammekens*, a barque with Gerrit Schonck as captain, and for the prospective colonists trouble now is really just beginning. The water level in the river is not high enough everywhere and impedes sailing. Sandbanks, waterfalls and rapids require constant attention and swarms of mosquitoes, stinging flies, frogs and chirping crickets prevent the travellers from sleeping, particularly the children.

When arrived at his destination, the surgeon can unload the more than 70 pounds of medicines and begin setting up a temporary hospital. Initially, letters from the new colony are cheerful: the soil is excellent, it must be possible to collect a lot of copaiba balsam, orlean, dyewood and letterwood, and one starts cultivating cassava, cotton, sugar and tobacco. The colonists' state of health gives much less reason for cheerfulness. A few planters soon die and the surgeon has a burdensome job with diseases such as malaria, dysentery and infestations with worms. It soon becomes clear that a colony like the former Nova Zeelandia can no longer be realised. Lack of work force and negligence on the part of De Jongh accelerate failure. Three years after settlement, French privateers with the aid of some Indians attack the colonists. De Jongh is able to escape, but the plantations in Pomeroon are looted and set on fire. The hospital and surgeon's shop are also burnt down. In the meeting of Heren X in November 1689 it is then decided to give up the colony definitively.[49]

DRUGS IN A VICIOUS SOCIETY

Berbice developed from a small trading station in 1624 into a rather flourishing plantation colony under the Van Pere family but the colony's growth never came up to expectations.[50] Trade with the Indians in the interior such as in Essequebo and Surinam, was almost non existent here. The conditions for colonisation – set down in the minutes of the 'Vergadering ter Camer' (Meeting at the Chamber) on 12 June 1627 – included that each settlement should consist of at least 20 families, accompanied by a blacksmith and a surgeon. [51] The latter condition was difficult to fulfil, for surgeons were not very fond of working in the unhealthy river region. So, Amsterdam had a lot of trouble to keep the half dozen of surgeons up to strength. In Berbice the WIC constantly kept a finger in the pie and initially demanded a recognition fee of *f* 300 from the Society of Berbice for each ship trading with Berbice. Later the Society, founded in 1720, was able to circumvent the WIC monopoly by means of a patent, obtained from the States-General in 1732, allowing all residents of the Republic to export sugar, coffee, cocoa, dyes and drugs from the colony and import them duty-free into the Netherlands. The modest growth of the colony appears from the fact that under commander Anthony Tierens (1714-1733) there were 9 plantations with sugar, 3 with cocoa, cotton and coffee and many cassava plantations in that year. In addition private persons owned a number of quite profitable plantations. Entanglement of private interests and those of the Society could not always be avoided. The rule that WIC employees were not allowed to start their own plantations was frequently violated. Sometimes those in charge turned a blind eye to it, as in the case of governor S.H. de la Sablonière (1768-1773).[52] Through the years more and more sugar plantations were established along the banks of the Berbice River and later the Canje River. To safeguard the river against a hostile invasion the Fort Nassau was built at the Berbice River estuary. Besides the 'bottelierskamer' (commissary's room), it was equipped in 1757 with a surgeon's room and a hospital.[53] Apart from the surgeon-in-chief in the fort, there were another six surgeons divided among the Society's plantations.

The profession of surgeon on Berbice was exhausting and the many deaths among them caused a constant lack of medical aid. From 1751-1762 no less than 38 surgeons were sent to Berbice at different times to keep the number up to strength. In 1763 the colony had grown to 95 plantations with 4200 slaves. The heavy work at the sugar plantations and the brutal treatment of the slaves brought many sick and injured blacks to the hospital, where especially lung disorders caused numerous victims. Medical treatment for slaves was only extended to working slaves and children who had the potential to grow into productive labourers. It was orientated toward preserving the fitness of the labour force and its economic productivity. Slaves experienced incapacitation ranging from fevers, dysentery and other gastrointestinal disorders, aches and pains in body joints and skin disorders, so considerable quantities of drugs were required. The list of medicines (table 4.4) that were shipped to Berbice by Amsterdam, however, gives rise to the suspicion that the remedies were not only used for the Society's sick employees and slaves, but were also exchanged or sold.

The medicine assortment is excessively large for the Society's personnel. Syrups do not occur on the list, because the bewindhebbers refused to send those and there was enough sugar in the colony for the surgeons to prepare their own syrups and electuaria. [55] The large quantities of liquiritia, althaea (Marsh Mallow) and anise must have been intended for the treatment of colds and 'breast diseases'. [56] Consumption or phthisis was unknown on the coast.[57]

What difficulties the surgeons had to overcome before they could dispose of the arrived medicines emerges from the report by Rutger Tenhoute, who was appointed as a surgeon at the Hoogelande sugar plantation in 1726, as successor of Dr. Benjamin Pousset. The sugar estate Hoogelande was both factory and farm. Plantation director and council member A. van Heesel apparently was someone who was constantly at odds with the commander Tierens because of the brutal treatment of slaves. On 12 March 1727 the commander reprimanded him because he had got a slave pregnant and administered an abortifacient (probably eup-

Table 4.4. Medicines sent to Berbice, March 1727[54]

Emplastra		**Radices**		**Gummi et resinae**	
Diapalmae	4 lb	Sarsaparillae	12 lb	Succus liquiritiae	8 lb
De ranis cum mercurio	1 lb	Radix jalappae	1 lb	Aloe	½ lb
Defensivum	2 lb	Rhabarberi	1 lb	Camphora	3 u
Diachylon	1 lb	**Herbae**		Tragacanth	3 u
Unguenta		Absinthi	2 lb	Spermaceti	1 lb
Aegyptiacum	1 lb	Sabinae	½ lb	Cera flava	4 lb
Album camphoratum	1 lb	**Opiata**		Cantharides	3 u
Altheae	2 lb	Theriacum	7 lb	**Mineralia**	
Basilicum	4 lb	Philonium	2 lb	Argentum vivum	1 lb
Digestivum	4 lb	Diascordium	1 lb	Vitriolum album	½ lb
Olea		**Purgantes**		Lapis haematites	1 lb
Oleum cinnamomi	½ lb	Confectio Hamech	2 lb	Vitrum antimonii	2 u
Oleum lauri	1 lb	Extractum catholicum	2 lb	Antimonium diaphoreticum	1 lb
Oleum hypericae	1 lb	Folia sennae	1 lb	Saccharum saturni	½ lb
Oleum anisi	¼ lb	Euphorbium	½ lb	Mercurius praecip.albus	½ lb
Oleum juniperi	1 lb	Scammonium	½ lb	Mecurius praecip. ruber	½ lb
Oleum rosae	¼ lb	**Farinae**		Mercurius corrosivus	½ lb
Oleum terebinthinae	2 lb	Altheae	1 lb	**Aquae**	
Flores		Foenugraeci	1 lb	Cinnamomi	1 lb
Chamomillae	5 lb	Lignum guaiaci	12 lb	Antiepileptica	1 lb
Majoranae	1 lb	**Semina**		Spiritus cochleariae	½ lb
Radices		Cardamomi	½ lb	**Cortices**	
Aristolochiae	1 lb	Nigellae	½ lb	Cinnamomi	3 u
Liquiritiae	8 lb	Anisi	2 lb	Granatorum	1 lb
Chinae	6 lb	Lini	1 lb	Ebuli	3 u
Contrayervae	½ lb	Phellandri	¼ lb	Macis	3 u

horbium) that resulted in death.[58] Most planters appeared to have been well informed about the effects of drugs, poisons and the treatment of sick slaves, and Van Heesel was no exception. The planters not only treated the sick with the remedies imported from Europe, but sometimes resorted to local folk medicines. This soon led to differences in opinion between surgeons and plantation director. In a letter of complaint to commander Tierens, surgeon Tenhoute is critical about the 'quacking' by planter Van Heesel, who confiscated the supply of medicines so that the surgeon could not dispose of it. According to Tenhoute, slaves who suffered from diarrhoea or dysentery were wrongly treated by Van Heesel with toasted bread, bananas and with 'little balls looking like musk that were boiled to a slime', in the words of the surgeon. Apparently Tenhoute was not familiar with this Indian remedy of toasted arrowroot (the nutritive starch obtained from the rootstock of *Maranta arundinacea*), a therapy for diarrhoea that has maintained itself until well into the twentieth century. That sugar planters liked to meddle in medical affairs is not only reported from Guiana, but also from Jamaica.[59]

It is fascinating to see how surgeons had to struggle to overcome daily problems, heavily burdened, tormented, ill and provided with insufficient resources. Numerous surgeons have contributed to the advancement of health care on the Wild Coast. Some appear to have preserved their distance from the patients persistently; others got involved, built a relationship and tried to look at the patients not only as medical problems, but also as human beings. The psychosocial role of a number of those surgeons is certainly worth mentioning. In Berbice, it was surgeon Rutger Tenhoute who struggled relentlessly against the molesting of slaves on the Hoogelande plantation, where 57 male slaves and 36 female slaves worked. On 29 July 1727 Tenhoute writes to the commander about the problems a surgeon encounters who wants to dedicate himself dutifully and conscientiously to the health and wellbeing of the slave community, but is boycotted by the planter in this and robbed of his medicines. Tenhoute's letter cannot be given in full, but a few salient details may be extracted. The original text extracts have been provided with modern punctuation and capital letters.

The Noble and Right Honourable Sir, The Commander Anthony Tierens
Berbice, 29 July 1727

I cannot tell you how painful it is to me to be continually exposed to the slander and abuse by this planter. He knows I fear him. He kicks, bites, and scratches like a stallion. If there were a Collegium Medicum here he would sing a different tune. But here I have to let myself be ruled in an intolerable way by a fellow I would not even entrust with my pigs, let alone my Negroes. I have been involved in the art from my youth and many an ordination of decent doctors have passed through my hands. A large number of patients I have treated both internally and externally. If I were in the mother country, I would know how to stop him. There are two fellows in the rasp house[60] who also had surgeons under their command, but I do not believe that they were half as vicious as Van Heesel was to me... As an example I mention to you the care of a Negro from the sugar manufacture who had dysentery. Thanks to the medicines I gave him the patient's life was no longer in danger, which I reported to the plantation director.... Immediately he (Van Heesel) ordered to beat the slave from the hospital and put him to work, despite my protest. But Your Honour, if I have no say in such a matter, I am

> unnecessary here. The planter has taken the medicine chest sent from Amsterdam into his own home, and I have to give an explanation about everything I need. I am worried about the fact that Van Heesel is able to dispose of strong poisons and appears to have extensive knowledge about their effects. I pretend to have a reasonable knowledge of harmful medicines and poisons, but he knows far more than I do... A recently arrived young Negro accidentally cut his leg. Van Heesel subsequently had the man whipped into the hothouse. That was empty at that moment, for the Negroes were in great fear of it because so many died there... I begged him to get the young man out of there, but instead of showing compassion, he had him drowned... This concerned the husband of the Negress I wrote you about. Van Heesel had the Negress pass between two whips during mustering and he bit her in the shoulder – as the previous surgeon Pousset can testify – because she was not sufficiently compliant to him. As a result of that whipping the Negress for a long time walked around with two holes in her leg that would not heal... There is yet another Negro of whom I am afraid he will die. He has dysentery and loses mucus and blood. The day before yesterday I had some hope that I had overcome it by means of medicines and reported to Van Heesel that the Negro was out of danger. Immediately he sends a slave to the hospital who has to tell the patient that he should go to work straight away, or else he would be whipped outside. Since then the Negro has decided to die, he can no longer urinate and refuses to ingest anything at all. And that, then, is the best Negro he had on the plantation. Sometimes the beating and the cursing turn into intimacies. His treatment of Negroes changed in such a way that he began taking them into his house, yes, even into his bedroom and you, Sir, can easily imagine that such goings on brings me little esteem with the Negroes. When the sugar cane stands, he allows the Negroes to take it home as food, so that they fall ill frequently, the one gets diarrhoea, the other abdominal cramps...

The behaviour of this planter is not an isolated case. Loneliness and boredom, lack of diversion and the continuous threat of diseases, delirium caused by malaria or syphilis, all this contributed to the slow but sure moral degradation of many whites. The boundaries and norms between man and woman, good and bad, virtue and vice, order and chaos had become blurred. What is noticeable here, is that the colonial relation often was pre-eminently characterised by macho behaviour.[61] Traders and colonisers saturate old colonial historiography with continuous admiration for tough male display. With regard to the slaves that meant brute force. The opinion of some authors that the treatment of the slave by the West-Indian planters was humane is contestable.[62] Craton already stipulated this, at least as far as British West-India is concerned.[63]

Macho behaviour also formed an obstacle for an adequate health care system of the slaves, as the case of Van Heesel illustrates. According to commander Storm van 's Gravesande, at the Company plantations in Essequebo slaves were never beaten or their rations withheld and they were treated well.[64] At any rate Berbice and Surinam had a much worse reputation in this respect than Curaçao or Essequebo and Demerara.

Thirty years later the harassed Berbice slaves revolted and in a panic the governors of St.Eustatius and Surinam were called on for help. Once more a surgeon stood up for the rights of his black fellow man. After arriving in Berbice, surgeon J.C. Mangemeister of the Surinam detachment joins the rebels, takes care of them as well as possible and prepares medicines for the blacks. After the suppression of the revolt in 1764 he does not escape execution in Surinam: his hand is chopped off, his head severed from his body and he then is buried in the gallows-field....[65]

Notes

1 Bankroft, *Beschrijving van Guiana.*
2 De Jonge, *Nederlands gezag in Oost-Indië.*
3 Netscher, *Geschiedenis*, 166.
4 Van Goor, *Nederlandse koloniën*, 148.
5 WIC 1027 (1745) 144.
6 Benjamins, *Encyclopaedie*, 282.
7 WIC 812 (1715), 25 March.
8 Hartsinck, *Beschrijving van Guiana.*
9 Pop, *De geneeskunde bij het Nederlandse Zeewezen*, 400.
10 Brun, *Schiffarten.*
11 Godschalck van Focquenbroch, *Alle de Werken*, II, 425.
12 Doerffel, 'Aanmerkingen', 331, 408.
13 Archive Societeit van Berbice 61 (1727) 29 July.
14 Kesler, 'Duitsch medicus in Essequebo', 241.
15 Netscher, *Geschiedenis*, 82, 343.
16 Goslinga, *The Dutch in the Caribbean*, 440.
17 WIC 1027 (1750) 307-387.
18 Basilius Valentinus, *Triumphal Chariot*, 158-166.
19 Kolodziej, 'Phytoalexine', 1385-89.
20 Essers, *Removal of cyanogens.*
21 Teuscher, 'Biogene Gifte' (1992) 230, 236.
22 Lötschert, *Elseviers Gids van Tropische Planten*, 183.
23 Teuscher, *Biogene Gifte* (1994) 44.
24 Roy, 'Aflatoxin contamination', 842-43.
25 WIC 1025 (1687) 317.
26 WIC 1026 (1691) 430.
27 WIC 814 (1731) 14.
28 WIC 814 (1733) 5 and 26 February 1733.
29 WIC 1027 (1753) 516.
30 WIC 814 (1731). Letter 14 March.
31 WIC 1025 (1687) 317.
32 De Villiers, *Storm van 's Gravesande.*
33 Rutten, 'Storm van 's Gravesande', 72-79; see also WIC 1027 (1756) 690.
34 Harris, *Storm van 's Gravesande*, 195, 506.
35 Harris, *Storm van 's Gravesande*, 263-265.
36 WIC 770 (1684) 57, art. 7 and 814 (1737) Letter of 4 November.
37 WIC 1027 (1758) 731.
38 WIC 1026 (1732) 421.
39 WIC 1027 (1751) 516, 707, 730.
40 Harris, *Storm van 's Gravesande*, 160.
41 Netscher, *Geschiedenis*, 73.
42 WIC 1025 (1686) 208-239.
43 WIC 1025 (1686) 252.
44 Amsterdam, *Lijst der Medicamenten 1692.*
45 Sieur de Saint Hilaire, *Les rémèdes*, 684.
46 De Farvacques, *Medicina pharmaceutica*, 181; see also Lemery, *Pharmacopée universelle*, 487.
47 Caspary, 'Saccharomyces', 1280.
48 WIC 1025 (1686) 208-259.
49 Rutten, 'Medicijnkist voor Pomeroon', 6-14.
50 Van Berkel, *Amerikaansche voyagien.*
51 Netscher, *Geschiedenis*, 351.
52 Bosman, *Nieuw Amsterdam in Berbice*, 17.

53 Hartsinck, *Beschrijving van Guiana,* 365.

54 Archive Societeit van Berbice 61 (1727) 3 March.

55 WIC 814 (1735) letter of 20 January.

56 WIC 1027 (1751) 410, 419.

57 Schomburgk, *Description of British Guiana,* 27.

58 Archive Societeit van Berbice 61 (1727-46) 6 April.

59 Sheridan, *Doctors and Slaves,* 294.

60 A House of Detention and Correction whose prisoners rasped guaiac and dye wood to powder.

61 Van Goor, *Nederlandse koloniën,* 152.

62 See for example: Oostindie, *Het paradijs overzee.*

63 Craton, *Testing the chains.* Idem 'Reshiffling the pack', 23-75.

64 Harris, *Storm van 's Gravesande,* 72-79.

65 Hartsinck, *Beschrijving van Guiana,* 510.

Chapter V

MEDICINE TRAFFIC TO DUTCH WEST AFRICAN FORTS

THE WHITE MAN'S GRAVE

On June 7, 1494, the Treaty of Tordesillas between Spain and Portugal had settled conflicts over lands explored by Columbus and other early voyagers. Spain was given the rights to the region west of the line of demarcation from pole to pole 370 leagues west of the Cape Verde Islands; the Portuguese were to keep the east. The treaty (1494-1750) enabled Portugal to claim the coasts of Brazil and Africa. After it had emerged that black slaves were better able to cope with the climate and the harsh labour conditions on the plantations in Spanish America than the Indians were, Spain wanted to import slaves itself. According to the Treaty however, Spain was not allowed to possess any trading stations on the African coast, so it was not able to provide its colonies with African slaves. There was a continuing division of the political and mercantile spheres of influence according to the line drawn of Tordesillas. Africa was Portuguese territory and both the settlements on the West Coast and in Arguin were utilised as slave stations. Thus, Spain was forced to make contracts – so called asiento de negros –, an agreement between the Spanish crown and private merchants or another sovereign power by which the latter was granted a monopoly in supplying African slaves. The first such contractor was a Genoese company that in 1517 agreed to supply 1,000 slaves over an eight-year period. In 1528 an agreement was reached with the German Hendrik Eynger that concerned the supply of 4,000 Africans.

The West Coast of Africa comprised two regions that were important for the slave trade, usually indicated as the Guinea and Angola coasts.[1] The area between the Cameroon and Congo rivers was known to the Dutch as Angola, sometimes also called Loango. It was an important supplier of slaves and redwood. The most interesting area to the Dutch trade was the Gold Coast, which approximately corresponds to what is now Ghana. The western coastal area of the Gulf of Guinea, the Grain Coast and the Ivory Coast was less suitable for loading and unloading of goods, due to the lack of proper landing sites. To the east of the Gold Coast, the Slave Coast was situated, where Ouidah (Juda or Fida) developed into important slave stations in the second half of the 17th century. In the vicinity of Ardra one had a lodge at Benin.[2] After 1612 the WIC took possession of the fort Mori on the Gold Coast and in 1637 it drove the Portuguese from Elmina, which became the WIC headquarter on the African coast.

Between 1637 and 1871 the Dutch possessed approximately 15 forts and castles on the West African coast. The Elmina castle was established in 1482 by a Portuguese expedition under Don Diogo d'Azambuja. The castle was equipped with a hospital and a medicine shop. Four years later King John assigned Elmina the full rights and privileges of a town. Until 1637 health care and drug supply were in the hands of the surgeons, who lived in the castle with almost sixty Portuguese servants. Subsequently, the organisation was taken over by the Dutch Company personnel. These consisted for half to three quarters of military men, who were entrusted to the health care of the WIC surgeons. The highest authority in Elmina was the director-general, who enjoyed wide powers. He was followed in rank by the minister and next by the superintendent (fiscal), who had to guard against illicit trade. Surgeons belonged to the rank of lower servants, which was also manifest in their salaries. The director-general received *f* 300 a month, the chief merchant *f* 100, while the chief surgeon's monthly salary of *f* 40 was considerably lower than that paid at the Dutch East India Company (VOC). So, in various ways one tried to make some extra money by means of private trade, which was forbidden until 1742. The authority that had to supervise this, and in particular the superintendent, who was at the same time criminal investigator and public prosecutor, failed or proved corrupt. The determining factor for appointing officials was health rather than service history. Management in Elmina had to be entirely based on control and regulation. That was only necessary, of course, if servants moved too fast and not if they contributed too little.

Elmina was the main port of export for the trade in gold, ivory, slaves, grain, African sandalwood, palm oil, civet, cola nuts (*Cola acuminata*), redwood, salt, gum arabic and limejuice. Medicinal resins and gum resins obtained from African plants and part of the return goods were African kino (obtained from *Pterocarpus erinaceus*), African bdellium (from *Commiphora Africana*) and African myrrh (bisabol), which are exudates from the bark of species of *Commiphora* and are used as wound dressings or plaster bases and internally in dysentery. Kino was first described by Fothergill in 1757 (gummi rubrum adstringens Gambiense) and was incorporated as an astringent in the London Pharmacopoeia of 1787 and the Amsterdam Pharmacopoeia of 1792. Sugar, tobacco and hides, brought in by Portuguese slave carriers, were also part of the return goods.[3] Around 1720 gold represented a value of approximately 74% of the total WIC trade, the slave trade amounted to 14% and ivory 8%.[4] The remaining 4% mainly consisted of the pharmaceutical products mentioned, which also included beeswax that was used for the preparation of candles and ointments. In 1715 the medicinal products kaolin (clay) and sandalwood are also mentioned. These were shipped together with a return cargo of crevelles (small elephant tusks) and limejuice.[5] Even today clays are still included in a number of pharmacopoeias and used to control diarrhea. Recent scientific research has proved that the bactericidal effect is based on an agglutinating effect on the adsorbed bacteria. The initially lucrative trade of the WIC was clearly declining by 1720, not only because insufficient marketable barter goods were sent from the Netherlands, such as coloured textiles, napkin cloths, burned beads, bracelets, iron, copper bars and Dutch linen, but also because competition by the English and the French was growing.[6] Spirits, cowries (shell money) and firearms were popular as barter goods as well.[7] On board the merchant ships a supercargo was present, a trader who was responsible for the sale of the cargo and the purchase of return goods. In consultation with the English a 'Marktbrief' (Price guide) was drawn up giving prices, as shown in table 5.1. The list reveals that the drug sarsaparilla root was one of the barter goods.

The WIC tried to maintain a strict monopoly in its territory. At its founding in 1621 an early exception was made for the salt trade of the West Frisian towns, who were involved in the important salt shipping to Punta d'Araya. In its possessions in the Caribbean and Guiana, the WIC presented itself as a tame, peaceful organization. On the African coast, however, it turned out to be an aggressive, intolerant enterprise, prepared to use every available means to maintain its position. Victims of this attitude were, for example, the ships of the Ostend Company (Compagnie impériale et Royale des Indes Orientales établie dans les Pays-Bas autrichiens), established in 1723. In 1719 the WIC ship *Amsterdam* immediately seized the ship *Le Marquis De Prié*, sent to West Africa by the Ostend Company to collect gold, ivory and medicines. It had a cargo of 69,000 lbs. of melegueta grain, 11,000 lbs. of redwood, 12,000 lbs. of rice, 144 lbs. of cardamom and 20,000 lbs. of gum on board. On 12 January 1719 it was taken to Elmina, where Director-general William Butler confiscated ship and cargo and sent everything to the Netherlands.[8] The same fate befell the ship *La Marquise de Prié*, sent the following May. After that, the Southern Netherlands did not undertake any other attempts to penetrate WIC territory. The Ostend Company was able to carry on a profitable trade with India and China.

The false cardamom, mentioned here, probably concerns the fruits of *Amomum stipulatum* or *A, angustifolium*, which was applied in the same way as grain.[9] Axim was the major cardamom supplier.[10]

Table 5.1. Part of a Marktbrief (Price guide) 1689. Prices in Engels. One Engels is two guilders[11]

Product	Engels	Product	Engels
Vinegar	1/7	French brandy	12
Sarsaparilla 5 lb	1	Black mirrors 5 st.	64
Powder	30	Sheepskin	4
Pintado	4	Platillos	2
Linen	7	Iron bar	2
Knives	4	Brandy 10 stoop	21
Coral	48	Carpet	8

Note: Example of the Marktbrief issued 21 January 1689 by Director-General Nicholaas Sweerts at Elmina, listing the current purchase and sales prices of all merchandise bought and sold on the Coast. Important list at the beginning of the WIC trading voyages carrying their European commodities to Guinea or Angola in exchange for slave cargoes, which continued until the Charter's change in the 1730s. Interlopers had always blatantly ignored charters and monopolies.

The exclusion of private trade eventually proved disadvantageous to the Company. The directors of the Gold Coast Headquarter frequently complained to the Amsterdam Chamber that they did not receive sufficient barter goods, whereas private traders could dispose of them in abundance. By the time the goods arrived from the United Provinces, demand often had already decreased or had ceased altogether. So, both high- and low-ranking Company servants resorted to illegal trade. The Chief Factor Pieter Nuyts, for example, was sued because he traded with interlopers in Axim and the trading station at Mori via black women.[12] That the interlopers were not concerned with small shipments is shown by the cargo of a ship confiscated in Apam, which carried 8,678 lbs. tusks, 56,700 lbs. of melegueta, 34,500 lbs. of rice and 600 Marks of gold (one Mark = 320 Guilder or £ 32 in contemporary sterling value). Interlopers were hardly interested in the slave trade and their activities were often organised from Zealand. Bosman estimates that 50% of the Dutch share in the gold trade was in the hands of interlopers.[13]

Apart from melegueta pepper, used in the spice trade as well as in breweries and medicine, other local products found a technical or medical application. Ivory was applied in jewellery, but was also used as a medicine called Ebur ustum. Tamarind was exported as a laxative and served to make spoiled drinking water on ships usable again. Tamarind, obtained from *Tamarindus indica*, which despite its name may be of African origin, is common in the savannas. West African elemi from *Canarium Schweinfurthii* was used in wound ointments. Coloquinte apples were used as a purgative across all of Africa.[14] In 18th century Europe coloquinte played an important role and remedies such as pilulae cochiae and unguentum arthanitae were very popular, but the trade preferred Syrian and Cypriot items to African ones. Gum Arabic was obtained from the trunks and twigs of various *Acacia* species. Blacks carried the gum – sometimes referred to as 'barnsteen' or 'amber' because of its colour – in shiny lumps of as much as 18 kg on their heads during a 10 to 12 days' walk from the West African interior to Elmina.[15] The gum also arrived in the port of Portendick, situated below Arguin, via caravan routes across the Sahara.[16] The French had founded a trading station at Portendick in 1717 and from this port it was shipped to Europe as well. Between 1675 and 1731 an amount of 357,981 pounds of gum was exported via Elmina.

A randomly selected example illustrates the share of pharmaceutical ingredients in the total weight of goods sent by the ship *Sonnensteyn* to the Netherlands on 3 July 1721 (figure 5.1). This diagram does not include the simultaneous despatch of 350 Marks of gold.

In 1730 the WIC monopoly ended. By the edict of 4 January 1731 the 20th article letter was adapted in such a way that interlopers with a proper passport were free to anchor in all WIC ports in Africa, without having to pay the WIC.[18] After 1740 civil servants were allowed to engage in so-called 'kleine negotie' (private trade) up to certain limits, varying from £ 33½ down to £ 10 per member. In many cases one tried to bribe the captain or supercargo, in order to get the goods out of the country. When discovered, cargo and ship were confiscated. WIC employees begrudged the free traders their trade in colonial goods and slaves and tried to obstruct it in every possible way.

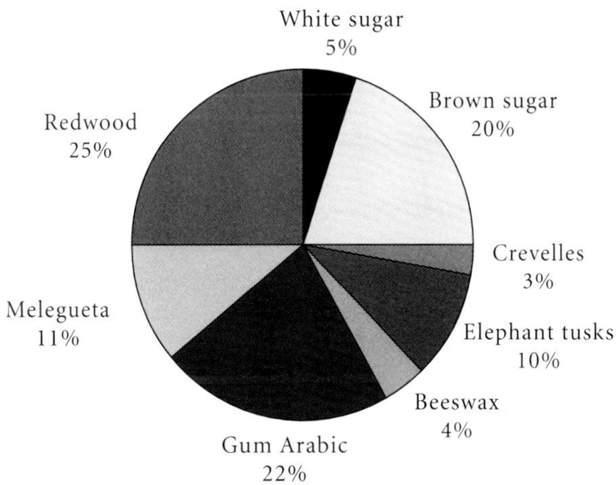

Figure 5.1. Percentage of goods carried in 1721 by the ship *Sonnensteyn*[17]

MEDICAL CARE

After the capture of Elmina by the Dutch in 1637, medical and pharmaceutical care of Company personnel became a task of WIC surgeons.[19] Elmina castle boasted a beautiful park and a vegetable and herb garden, where lettuce, beets, carrots, endive, parsley, sorrel, radish, melon, turnips, red and white cabbage, cucumbers, celery, chervil, rosemary and bay were growing.[20] The fresh vegetables and herbs were delivered to passing ships and to the sick in the hospital. The surgeon could obtain a number of fresh medicinal herbs from this 'hortus botanicus'. Initially he probably used the supply of drugs left by the Portuguese in their storerooms, while he could get remedies that were lacking from the chests of the ship's surgeons. Soon the need for a regular supply of medicines became so urgent that each year an order list was sent to Amsterdam.[21] These lists reveal that the assortment of medicines of the Dutch had already significantly expanded by 1645, compared to that of the Portuguese list. At the forts and lodges on the Gold Coast, 215 whites and 407 slaves were staying at the time. These numbers hardly changed during the first decades of the 18th century. Despite the fact that the number of servants remained about the same, the use of some drugs strongly increased in the course of the years (table 5.3). This cannot simply be explained by a shift from the gold trade to the slave trade, as the Gold Coast initially had a modest share in the slave trade. From 1675 to 1699 this only concerned 136 slaves, but from 1702 to 1709 about 3000 slaves were transported to Curaçao and Guiana and the English shipped more than 30,000 slaves to Barbados and Jamaica.[22] The slaves, brought in from the interior and kept in stock in the castle dungeon and old warehouses, not only imported diseases, but also required medication. Besides their pathogenic share, also poor public hygiene, lower resistance, an increased number of sick among the Europeans on the coast and embezzlement, must have been responsible for the growing use of medicines.

The assortment of medicines destined for Africa (table 5.2) is considerably different from that destined for Curaçao and Guiana. The not very flattering, but cutting adage 'Guinea not only absorbed men, they destroyed them by disease', makes one suspect a growing use of medicines. Antimony compounds – no longer used because of their toxicity and around 1710 hardly any longer prescribed in Curaçao either – were increasingly needed on the Gold Coast for the treatment of the greatest plague: threadworm disease (strongyloidiasis).[23] Also the use of the well-known syphilis remedies, such as guaiac, sassafras, sarsaparilla, smilax china and the use of drugs against flux and dysentery, such as kaolin (bolus) and theriac, had grown considerably in half a century (table 5.3).

The number of abdominal complaints probably also increased, in view of the quantity of Philonium romanum needed. The components of hyoscyamus seed, opium, saffron and white pepper made Philonium into an effective carminative and spasmolytic remedy, with abdominal pain, flatulence and meteorism as indications. A disadvantage of Philonium was its hallucinogenic effect. The Dutch on the Gold Coast were apparently known for their excessive flatulence. The quaintest remark in the context of Negro manners was made by Samuel Purchas (1577-1626) who recorded that 'it is holden a shame with them to let out a fart, which they wondered at in Hollanders, esteeming it a contempt'.[24] The question whether this was due to the consumption of the so-called 'potspeyse' (pot fare) with a lot of beans, peas and bacon, remains unanswered.[25] The supply of frankincense (olibanum), mentioned in table 5.3, has been used partly for fumigating hospital wards, but the internal application to inflammations such as in the case of rheumatic joint pains, was more important.

In 1713 the assortment of medicines was considerably extended. The surgeons started to use Peruvian bark[26] – lacking on the Curaçaoan list because malaria does not exist on that island – on the Gold Coast and in Guiana to treat malaria and the reddish-brown contrayerva or the red stuff mercurius praecipitatus rubeus to treat smallpox.[27] The association of magic with medicine is well illustrated by the doctrine of 'signature'. This taught that nature had provided signs how each simple was to be used. A red herbal or mineral could cure flow of blood, scarlatine or smallpox; a yellow flower inflammation of the liver. That year for the first time 1 pound of ipecac was shipped to the WIC drugstore on the Gold Coast, it was initially used as an emetic, but later prescribed for amoebic dysentery.[28] Contrayerva, the roots of *Dorstenia contrajerva*, a perennial growing in South America and some of the Caribbean islands, was known as a stimulant, diaphoretic and febrifuge. It is also given in exanthematous diseases. The Spanish Indians on account of its alexipharmic qualities gave its name of Contrayerva.[29] The medicines ordered arrived in the hospital pharmacy of Elmina via Amsterdam, but not always trouble-free. In 1700 director-general J. van Sevenhuyzen wrote that he was impatiently waiting for medicines and that he had taken over a chest from the ship *Carolus Secundus* for *f* 200.[30] Quality and packaging were continually criticised. In 1702 the frugal director of the Amsterdam Chamber first had pharmacist Justus Versteegh in Amsterdam calculate the cost of the order, before they decided to ship the goods required. Chief merchant for the Dutch at the Elmina fort, William Bosman, describes how one was vexed by 'corrupted medicines and unskilled physicians, who bring several into the utmost danger of their lives', but that may have been exaggerated.[31] Bosman's misrepresentations have been pointed out before.[32] On the other hand there were also expressions of appreciation e.g. for surgeon Frederick Spancker, who received an ample reward for his 'extra-ordinary services' after Director-general Pieter Nuyt's death. So, Bosman's complaint may be caused by the use of simples that were

Table 5.2 Medicines shipped to Elmina to provide hospital, lodges and ships – 16 January 1726
Legends: amount in lb. = pound; otherwise u = ounce; p = pint[34]

Emplastra		**Semina**		**Herbae**		**Electuaria**	
Diapalmae	12 lb	Lauri	1 lb	Cardui benedicti	1 lb	Theriacum venetum	4 lb
Diachylon c. gum.	6 lb	Zedoari	½ lb	Phellandri	1 lb	Diascordium	6 lb
Oxycroceum	3 lb	Foenugraeci	2 lb	Salviae	2 lb	Confectio alkermes	1 lb
Meliloti	3 lb	Lini	2 lb	Scordium	4 lb	Conf rosarum rubr.	3 lb
De ranis c.mercurio	4 lb	**Aquae**		Menthae crispae	4 lb	Mel rosarum	2 lb
Griseum	2 lb	Foeniculi	1 p	Agrimonium	2 lb	Syrupus papaveris	3 lb
Unguenta		Menthae	6 p	Malvae	2 lb	**Miscellaneous**	
Altheae comp.	2 lb	Theriacalis	8 p	**Chimicalia**		Terebinthina veneta	8 u
Basilicum	8 lb	Cinnamomi	6 p	Tutia preparata	2 u	Extractum catholicum	8 u
Digestivum	4 lb	Rosarum	8 p	Bezoardi minerale	2 u	Alumen crudum	2 lb
Aegyptiacum	3 lb	Alexipharmaca	6 p	Mercur. praec. rubrum	2 lb	Laudanum opiatum	2 u
Populeum	2 lb	**Spiritus**		Mecurius dulcium	1 lb	Succus liquiritiae	3 lb
Defensivum rubrum	2 lb	Carminativum filis	1 lb	Mecurius sublimatum	2 u	Minium	2 lb
Olea		Matricalis	2 u	Argentum vivum	8 u	Elixir proprietatis	10 u
Anisi	1 lb	Nitri dulcis	8 u	Saccharum saturni	1 lb	Sal prunellae	8 u
Juniperi	1 lb	Sal armoniacum	8 u	Vitriolum album	3 lb	Cantharides	10 u
Spicae	1 lb	Sal volat.oleos.	6 u	Vitriolum cyprinum	4 u	Diagrydum	8 u
Terrae	½ lb	Vitrioli	2 u	Antimonium diaphoret.	1 lb	Sal absinthi	8 u
Succini	½ lb	Cochleariae	1 lb	Oculi cancri	2 lb	Sal armoniacum	2 lb
Terebinthinae	4 lb	**Radices**		Cornu cervi ustum	8 u	Antimonium crudum	2 lb
Caryophylli	2 u	Angelicae	1 lb	Balsam. sulphur. anis.	1 lb	**Tincturae**	
Cinnamomi	1 u	Chinae	2 lb	Resina jalappae	8 u	Bezoardica	1 lb
Macis express.	1 u	Galangae	1 lb	Tartras emeticus	4 u	Castoreum	3 u
Menthae	2 u	Liquiritiae	6 lb	Pilulae ruffi	4 u	Succini	4 u
Lauri	3 u	Jalappae	4 lb	Laudanum crudum	4 u	Croci	5 u
Flores		Rhabarberi	3 lb	Extractum absinthi	1 lb	**Gummi**	
Rosarum	1 lb	Iris florentinae	8 u	Corallium rubrum	1 lb	Camphora	4 lb
Sambuci	2 lb	Sarsaparillae	10 lb	Cremor tartari	1 lb	Olibanum	2 lb
Crocus orientalis	½ lb	**Ligna**		Cerussa	4 lb	Myrrha	3 lb
Meliloti	1 lb	Sassafras	6 lb	Crocus martis	6 u	Mastix	4 u
Chamomillae	2 lb	Guajacum rasur.	6 lb	Sal cardui benedicti	8 u	Asa foetida	4 u
Semina		**Folia**		Sal cornu cervi	4 u	Terebinthina	3 lb
Anisi	1 lb	Sennae	4 lb	Nitrum	2 lb	Balsam. peruvianum	6 u
Cumini	1 lb	Absinthi	4 lb	Viridis aeris	10 lb	Balsam. copaivae	2 lb

Instruments				
10 Lancets	12	Razor knives	4 Syringe clyster	2 Syringe mouth
6 Basins	2	Funnels tin	20 lb Spanish soap	Red leather
4 Mortars glass		Scale and weights	200 Vials glass	100 Jars

adulterated, contaminated or had become ineffective or toxic because of fungal growth.[33] What can be derived from the order lists up to 1720 is that the surgeons' level of expertise was clearly lower than that of their Curaçaoan colleagues.

Table 5.2. gives insight in the order list for medicines drawn up in 1726 by chief surgeon Balthazar Charles.

SEASONAL DRUGS

'Helsch (Hellish) Del Mina' doctor Focquenbroch (1640-1670) called his station on the Gold Coast. Life was hard there and the climate was considered unhealthy.[35] But people die of diseases, not because of climate. The question as to why the WIC servants on the Gold Coast were more afflicted by disease in the months of July and August than in the other months remains unanswered (figure 5.2). The months of May and October are characterised by the occurrence of travados, i.e. line squalls, prevalent on the coast when the inter-tropical front is in the vicinity. They seemingly did not cause any deterioration in the state of health. Africa's most effective defence against colonisers, however, was a wide range of tropical diseases. Whereas in Curaçao one was mainly up against dysentery and yellow fever, in Guinea a far greater number of health hazards were looming. This shows up in the orders for medicines. There was a continuous shortage of drugs, for, as Director-general De La Palma wrote in 1703, 'one decays here in a cruel manner as to body and soul... experience teaches that two hundred whites on the coast here in this unhealthy climate need more medicines in one year's time than three thousand in Europe'. He does not mention the black's consumption of drugs. The complaints about shortages of medicines especially emerged in the bad seasonal months. By means of those medicines one had to fight intestinal disorders, elephantiasis, venereal disease, leprosy, malaria, filariasis, eye disorders, rheumatism, intestinal worms and scabies, to mention just a few. Clear cases of falciparum-malaria are indicated in Director-general Butler's letters.[36] Pox occurred in 1713, 1724 and 1729, but already around 1700 Bosman reported that the disease had caused thousands of victims among the natives during the preceding fifteen years. Prior to vaccination smallpox was one of the most feared scourges of mankind. It always concerns variola major (smallpox) here; the mild variola minor only emerged late in the 19th century. Most deaths or blindness caused by smallpox occurred in June and July. According to surgeon Samuel Brun (1580-1668), the sand flea (*Tunga penetrans*) formed a threat to the settler's foot soles and the skin between the toes. Paludanus (1550-1633) considered the major disease encountered the Guineaworm-infection or dracontiasis (dracunculiasis).[37] The infection follows ingestion of water containing infected crustacean (cyclops), which acts as an intermediary host for the worm embryos. The treatment consists of slow extraction of the adult worm (*Dracunculus medinensis*).

Besides the diseases mentioned, wound infections, dysentery, malnutrition, avitaminosis and alcohol abuse constituted a menace to the white newcomers, so that 25-30% of them died within four months after arrival. The new environment made different demands on immunity. The effect of nutritional status on drug action is a factor, which must not be underestimated. The coast did not carry the meaningful qualification of 'White Man's Grave' without reason. In 1701 director-general Van Sevenhuyzen wrote that some of the servants were in very poor health due to the lack of medicines.[39] The 'bewindhebbers' in Amsterdam were constantly trying to economise on the costs of the medicines to be shipped. The problems of cost control in health care seemed to last forever. As a rule the medicines dispatched were handed out to the WIC personnel free of charge, but in 1704 Amsterdam ordained that patients from then on had to pay for the remedies.[40] Director-general De la Palma ignored the command and replied that he would continue to provide the sick and injured with medicines pro Deo, but that in case of venereal disease the patient's account would be charged doubly, so that enough money would be available to cover expenses.[41] Amsterdam put up with this. Apparently many high-ranking civil servants had a private medicine chest

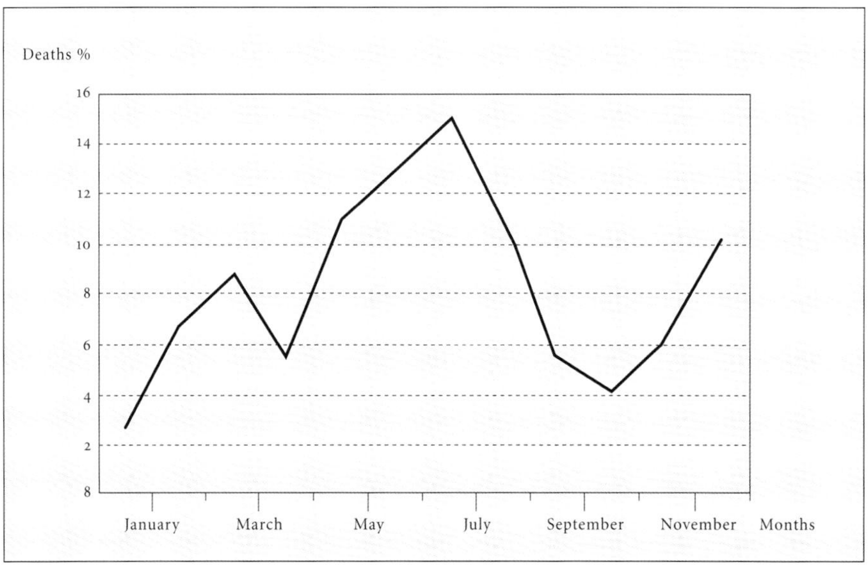

Figure 5.2 Monthly mortality of WIC servants on the Gold Coast 1721[38]

to provide first aid when necessary. Director-general Abraham Houtman left a well-fitted medicine chest behind when he died and chief merchant Cornelis van Eerkens's small chest fetched nine guilders after his death in 1723.[42]

Sometimes the need of medicines was so dire that the surgeon had himself rowed along the coast by canoe to the English Cape Coast Castle, to buy the necessary provisions there.[43] The surgeons were just as rare as the required drugs. In 1712 Holland had to report that the surgeons requested were not available because it was impossible to hire them and for that reason the salary of the chief surgeon in Elmina would be raised as a compensation for the extra work.[44] There was little interest in employment in Elmina, where living conditions were considered extremely unhealthy and payment was unattractive.

A°. 1715.
WEST-INDISCHE
COMPAGNIE.

DE Bewindhebberen van de Geoctroyeerde West-Indische Compagnie, ter Kamere Amsterdam, zullen by openbare opveylinge aan de meestbiedende Verkoopen, een partye van

220000 ℔ Guinees Gryn, en
20000 ℔ West-Indische Gom.

De Verkoopinge zal geschieden, op Woensdag, den 7 Augusty, 1715. 's Morgens ten 9 uuren, op 't Nieuwe West-Indische Huys, op de Cingel.

De voornoemde Goederen zyn leggende op het Oude West-Indische Huys, op Rapenburg; alwaar deselve op Maandag en Dingsdag, voor de Verkoopinge van een yder zullen konnen gesien worden.

Seg 't voort.

Figure 5.3 Announcement of Public Sale of melegueta pepper and West Indian gum[45]

When receiving the annual requests for medicines, which had to be shipped across the Atlantic at high costs and with a fair chance of contamination or decay, the directors in Amsterdam undoubtedly must occasionally have wondered whether these could not be replaced by native drug plants. Records do not show any real concern for this, except for a hint from 1644 and an instruction to shippers from 1684 about the gathering of herbs.[46]

The WIC was first and foremost a commercial enterprise and was in general not interested in studies on the medicinal use of native plants. If the practice of colonial pharmacobotany could lead to an increased self-sufficiency and the saving of medicines, the Company did show some interest, but it did not lend a helping hand. In the beginning of the 18th century, Bosman had already pointed out that a number of ill compatriots could be cured by means of local herbs, whereas the surgeons with their European medicines were powerless.[47] He had a higher opinion of the native herbs than of those from Europe. Later attempts to get the *bewindhebbers* (directors) interested in plant drugs and aromatic herbs from Guinea came to nothing. In 1719 Director-general Butler shipped a small chest of 'aromatic beans in pods' to Amsterdam as a possible economic asset.[48] A few years later he thought he had found coloquinte apples, 'which in Holland would cost at least thirty to forty stivers a pound' and of which he dispatched a few specimens.[49] In the archives no indication can be found of a substantial export of these products. Forty years later director-general J.P.T. Huydecoper raised the matter anew in a letter to Amsterdam. He points at 'the infinitely large number of curative herbs, unknown to Europeans, which Negroes use to cure internal and external diseases... and that would certainly yield a good branch of commerce if only a botanist were present'.[50] As far as we know Amsterdam did not respond to this. Political patronage, resulting in the appointment of incompetent persons to important positions, played a major part here. Decision-making in health care was often based on political rather than medical considerations. On the other hand the bewindhebbers did devote themselves to the introduction of the cultivation of sugar cane, cotton, indigo, peanuts, cubeb pepper, cardamom and cinnamon on the Gold Coast. Their attempts failed, however, due to an uncooperative administration in Elmina, which was not keen on novelties imposed by the motherland. Some of Bosman's contemporaries characterised that attitude as 'one wined, one dined, but that was all'. [51] The export of pepper species formed an exception. There were also a considerable number of species of indigo plants, both wild and cultivated in West Africa, from which blue indigo dye may be obtained. A number of spices indicated as 'pepper' was shipped from the Gold Coast and an important export product was melegueta pepper or grain, the seed of *Aframomum melegueta.* In the middle of the 13th century it was transported as 'grana paradisi' or 'Guinees gryn' along caravan routes from the Grain or

Pepper Coast, situated on the west of the Gold Coast, to the European markets. It was in great demand as a spice, commonly used for seasoning stews etc., and as a medicine.[52] It is an interesting early example of a commodity, which had been a luxury and had become an article of general consumption. The seed contains the alkaloid piperine and essential oil with cineole, alpha and beta pinene, sabinene and limonene. The resin of the seed skin contains pungent-tasting hydroxyphenyl alkanones, including gingerol, also found in ginger, and paradol.[53] Gingerol was supposed to have an anti-emetic, cardiotonic and anti-serotonin effect and to curb the prostaglandin biosynthesis.[54] This might explain its favourable effect on rheumatism and gastrointestinal disorders. Around 1700 a lively grain trade existed in Elmina. Despite its characteristic flavour this product was later completely pushed from the world market by real pepper. Melegueta belonged to the 'sacred plants' of the Africans. They were so attached to it that the slaves carried its seed from Africa to Guiana.[55]

More than a 1000 species of pepper are known to grow in the Torrid Zone. They contain essential oil in leaves, berries and seeds, and also resins and alkaloids such as piperine, chavicine etc. Many pepper species were used to treat gonorrhoea. Real pepper species among the African export products were *Piper Clusii* (Ashanti pepper) and *Piper guineense* (Guinea pepper), that was collected from Benin, situated to the east of the Gold Coast, and was traded in Elmina.[56] Attempts to introduce the cultivation of *Piper cubeba* or cubeb – with the aid of the king of Benin – to the African West Coast succeeded. [57] João Afonso d'Aveiro who visited Benin in 1485 brought cubeb or 'Benyn pepper' to Europe for the first time. Furthermore, one was familiar with the fruits of *Xylopia ethiopica* (Negro pepper), a native of the Anonaceae family from the Ivory Coast, which appeared via Elmina on the European market as a spice and drug as early as the 17th century. Besides as a spice, both Ashanti and Guinea pepper were used in traditional medicine as a carminative, vermifuge and diuretic and externally in ointments against rheumatism and headache. As a specific remedy against headache the slaves also used tacúla wood or 'redwood', which was obtained from a tall African tree, *Pterocarpus tinctoria*. The Loango-Angola coast was the major supplier of this wood. According to the 'Instruction for the Skippers in the Slave Trade' of 1675, each slave ship had to have a supply of tacúla on board for distribution among the slaves.[58] Another type of medicinal wood among the shipments from Elmina was the African sandalwood (Santal d'Afrique), the core wood of *Pterocarpus santalinoides*.[59] Much confusion exists as to the botanical identification of various specimens of redwoods known as Barwood (*Pterocarpus*) and Camwood (*Baphia*). Besides being the supplier of melegueta pepper, the Grain Coast or Rio Cestro was also the major source of rice. This not only served as food for the soldiers in the Elmina castle, but it was also exported. The presence of all these commercially attractive products enticed many greedy merchants to the coast. Figure 5.4 shows the percentage of foreign ships that visited the Grain Coast from 4 June 1716 to 30 January 1717. It is clear that mainly the English merchants are in control of the trade. The British Navy had become so powerful that it decided all by itself in what part of the Atlantic it would display its activities. Should it want to do so, it was capable of conquering all Dutch and French Atlantic possessions.[60] In 1701 the director-general in Elmina already complained that the trade on the Gold Coast gradually declined and that there was an increasing number of English ships on the coast. Trade dropped because insufficient barter goods were available and wars among the Negro tribes impeded purchasing. The English certainly knew how to make use of this impotence.[61]

HOSPITAL AND PHARMACY

The St. George d'Elmina Castle was equipped with a hospital and barbershop or 'meesterwinkel'.[63] The shop also provided the lodges and yachts along the coast with supplementary drugs for their surgeon chests. Of all the settlements in the WIC territory, Elmina was the only place with stringent regulations for the daily practice in the hospital and for the care of the sick. The hospital, later also called 'garrison infirmary', was an oblong two-storey building. In 1702 the director-general spoke of 'a clean hospital for injured sailors, soldiers and Company servants'.[64] Castle slaves or Company blacks, employed as manual workers, were

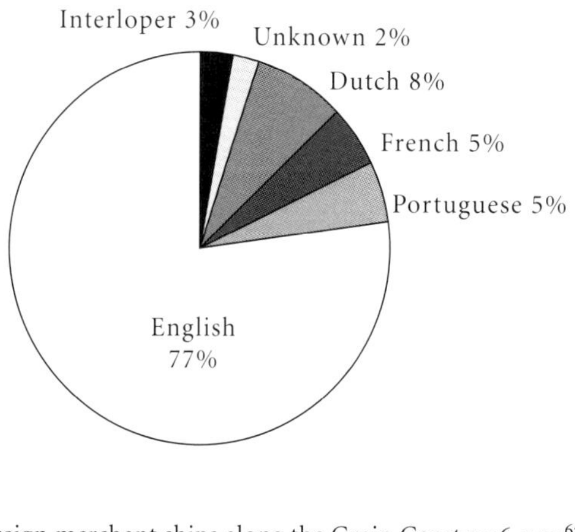

Figure 5.4 Percentage of foreign merchant ships along the Grain Coast 1716-1717[62]

also admitted. In 1722 there were 621 Company blacks, including those on the WIC ships, on the Gold Coast. Sick domestic slaves were supposed to be looked after in their houses or huts, but could also rely on the surgeon's aid. Their main task was to plant maize (Sorghum) and look after it.[65] Later, problems arose about the management of the hospital, so that the director-general and the Council decided to issue an 'Instructie voor de Binnenvader van het Edele Compagnies Hospitaal aan het Hoofd Casteel St. George d'Elmina, waaraan hij zich met alle stiptheid zal hebben te houden' (Instruction for the Warden of the Noble Company Hospital at the Main Castle St.George d'Elmina, to which he has to adhere with the greatest accuracy).[66] The instruction contains 21 articles and includes a regular visitation of the hospital and inspection of the distribution of medicines. As the trade on the Gold Coast declined, less attention was paid to the hospital. Around 1813 G. Ruhle described the hospital as neglected and dirty.

From 1612, when the Dutch settled in the Nassau fort at Mori, health care on the Gold Coast was entirely in the hand of surgeons. Medical doctors were not found on the payroll. A medical doctor hired in 1668 was not employed in health care, but got a job as a superintendent (fiscal). The surgeon's task was treating the sick and injured, preparing and delivering medicines, examining slaves, detecting possible poisonings, performing autopsies and – incidentally – giving chemical advice to the workers in the mining operations, who were looking for minerals in the vicinity of the St. Jago mountain.[67] The white personnel was distrustful of native medicines from the very beginning, but later the Europeans learned from the Negroes about the use of palm wine, the fermented sap of the oil or raffia palm, against kidney stones, jequirity seed for ophthalmic purposes and about cola nut, coloquinte and strophanthus as effective products.[68] The blacks did not apply phlebotomy, a routine operation for the European surgeons in Elmina. The Africans were accustomed to inoculation against smallpox in the beginning of the 18th century.[69] Mather learned from his Cormantin slave in 1706 that variolation was probably known and practised in West Africa by the late seventeenth century and rarely any person died of it. As early as 1770 H. Meredith recorded that the practice was known on slave ships at Whydah[70] and P. Isert noted in 1784 that the practice of variolation was quite common on the coast.

The black population on the Gold Coast, on the other hand, had a sympathetic attitude towards the European medical practitioners and their remedies. European medicine was incorporated quickly into the Ashantic medical practice; this in contrast with the aversion Javanese and Chinese had against the use of European medicines in the East Indies.[71] European directors and officials on the coast sometimes supplied the Ashanti with medicines, such as tincture of rhubarb (a laxative) and tincture of cinnamon (relieves flatulence).[72] The young king of Akwamu (near Accra) had been suffering for years from a venereal disease that could not be cured by his own medicine men. He went to the surgeon in Elmina castle for treatment in the 1700s and could return home as 'almost cured'.[73] When in 1645 a large number of deaths occurred in the castle, the captains and caboceros of the natives offered the help of a 'fiticheerder', a black medicine man and fetish priest (from the Portuguese feitiço = magic). According to them, this man would be able to put an end to mortality among the Europeans. Director-general Jacob van der Wel rejected the offer as 'godless', however, and even wanted to have those who proposed it punished. When Van der Wel himself fell ill, he had his brother send a quantity of extractum catholicum, a senna-containing laxative, from Holland.[74] The Fetishman is not content merely with the sacrifices and other ceremonial observances, which he enjoins, he makes particular inquiry respecting the nature of the disease and is able, from his medical experience, to prescribe such medicines as very frequently effect a cure.[75]

Table 5.3 shows that medicine use per capita increased significantly in Elmina in the period 1645-1708. The exact reason for this cannot be retrieved. The number of WIC employees on the forts, lodges and yachts along the Gold Coast fluctuated between 200 and 500 men, depending on the one hand on the variable number of servants and on the other hand on the number of deaths. An explanation may be that in the period concerned the number of malaria infections increased

Table 5.3 Some important drugs sent 1645-1708 by Amsterdam to the hospital pharmacy at Elmina (Dutch Gold Coast)

Year	1645	1699	1704	1708
Source	76	77	78	79
Number of Employees	200	251	203	188
Number of Slaves	408	401	398	400
Amount of drugs (pounds)				
Philonium romanum	0,5	6	4	20
Theriaca	0,8	6	6	15
Antimon. diaphoret.	0,2	0,6	2	3
Bolus armena	0,5	–	2	15
Lignum guaiaci	4	8	10	40
Lignum sassafras	1	4	6	25
Radix chinae	0,5	12	2	30
Radix jalappae	0,3	–	6	4
Radix sarsaparillae	4	6	10	30
Olibanum	0,5	–	1	6

strongly. After a journey to Apam and Mori, director Willem de la Palma behaved very aggressively and soon died of malaria in delirium and paralysis.[80] In letters to Amsterdam the director-general wrote that 'the servants in the fort were a spectacle of misery and that many a disease prevailed for which so few medicines were in stock that a chest had to be taken over from a ship's surgeon'.[81] Occasionally no bearers were available for the transportation of coffins.

The medicine lists show that mineral remedies – still hardly used in Columbus's time – were being applied here. The medicines destined for the Gold Coast in 1645 included antimony, copper, lead and zinc compounds, in addition to mercury preparations. Antimony compounds were used as an emetic, to suppress fever and to treat threadworm infections.[82] Copper, lead and zinc compounds were used in skin ointments and eye preparations. The increased use of guaiac wood, sassafras and sarsaparilla in table 5.3 may indicate a growth of syphilitic patients in the colony. In addition to the growing number of deliverable slaves kept in depot, bringing an increased risk of infection, a further explanation may be found in the weakening state of health of the white Company personnel and the pattern of treatment. Moreover, due to the decline of the WIC, the provisions in the area of health care were breaking down. In the 4th Anglo-Dutch War (1780-1784) the WIC lost almost all forts, except Elmina, to the English. The lost possessions were returned later on, but in 1791 the WIC ceased to exist. In 1871, after more than two hundred years, the Dutch presence in West Africa came to an end by transferring all possessions to England.

ARGUIN'S MEDICAL INGREDIENTS

Although the supply of medicines to Arguin presented here took place in the 17th century, we like to include the list for comparison in our discussion of Africa. On the island of Arguin or Argyn, situated off the coast of West Africa and south of Cabo Blanco (now Mauritania), the Portuguese had already built a strong castle as a depot for the slave trade in 1481. The Zealand Chamber of the WIC appropriated the castle in 1634 and Daniel van Pere was appointed commander. The island served as a base and refurbishing centre for the trade on the West Coast of Africa.[83] The Zealanders built warehouses and equipped offices and a small hospital. In 1677 Cornelis de Lincourt was appointed as commander and a total of 25 officers, sailors and soldiers and about 40 Moorish labourers lived in the castle. One traded in gum Arabic, in salt extracted from saltpans at about a 6-mile distance from the castle, and also in elephant tusks, ostrich feathers, beeswax, bezoar stones and ambergris. Gum Arabic could also be shipped, moreover, from Portendick that was situated to the south and functioned as a terminal of an important caravan route.[84]

Gum Arabic or gum acacia has been used as an article of commerce and medicine for more than 5000 years. The gum is an exudation of several *Acacia* trees that occur in a wide belt of semi-arid land. Because the gum reached Europe through various Arabian ports it acquired the name gum Arabic. Blacks carried the gum from the West African hinterland to Elmina.[85]

The gum also arrived in the port of Portendick, situated below Arguin, via caravan routes across the Sahara.[86] From this port the gum was shipped to Europe. Between 1675 and 1731 an amount of 357,981 pounds of gum was exported via Elmina. Gum Arabic was used in glues, inks, as an emulsifier and in medicines to combat diarrhoea and cough.

In 1677 Arguin was overpowered by the French Africa Company, but later it again came into the possession of the Dutch and in 1720 trade under the WIC was described to be flourishing. Eventually, the island was recaptured by the French and was definitively lost to the Dutch.

Fort Arguin was an important port of export for gum Arabic. Packed in leather bags, the gum was brought in from the Sahel by caravans of 10 to 20 camels. The gum trade was the cause of continuous conflicts between the Dutch, who tried to maintain trading posts on the African West Coast, and the French, who already possessed a key position in the port of St. Louis (Map 5.1). The good relationship the Dutch entertained with the emir of Trarza, Ali Shandora, the Moorish ruler of the Arguin fort and the Portendick harbour, was a thorn in the flesh of the French. They tried to frustrate the Dutch activities in every possible way and to extend their influence on the gum trade. In 1717 the Compagnie du Sénégal managed to establish a trade centre in Portendick and to obtain concessions from

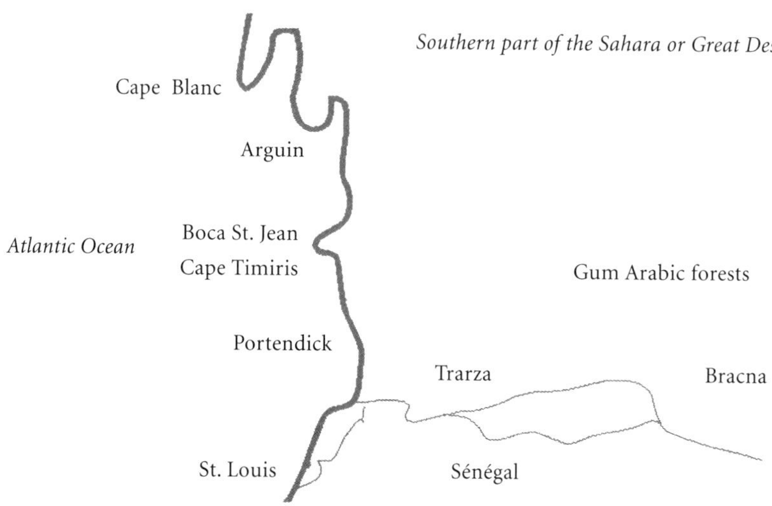

Map 5.1 Coastal regions of West Africa

Ali Shandora. Initially he promised the French to exclude all other nations from the gum export, but at the instigation of the Dutch he broke his promise in 1722.[87]

Table 5.4 shows the medicines shipped by the WIC to Arguin in 1676.[88]

Table 5.4 Medicines stored in the hospital of Arguin 1676

Aqua cinnamomi	Mel	Semen foenugraeci
Aqua plantaginis	Mel rosarum	Semen myristicae
Aqua rosarum	Myrrha	Syrupus diamorum
Camphora	Oleum chamaemeli	Theriacum vulgaris
Conservum rosarum	Oleum rosaceum	Unguentum apostolicum
Extractum catholicum	Olibanum	Unguentum defensivum
Farina lini	Philonium mesue	Unguentum digestivum
Flores meliloti	Radix altheae	Unguentum populeum
Mastix	Radix consolidae	

The medicine chest for Arguin contains only radix altheae as a bronchitis and cough remedy, but for injuries and surgical operations various ointments and oils are available, such as unguentum defensivum, unguentum digestivum and fatty rose oil. These are remedies we find repeatedly in all medicine shipments. The presence of Philonium in the Arguin stock gives rise to the assumption that the castle residents, just as those on the Gold Coast, suffered from disorders of the abdomen and the gastrointestinal tract.

THE BENEFIT OF YESTERDAY'S DRUGS

As disease played such an important role in the history of the Dutch expansion overseas, it is remarkable that hardly any attention is paid to the medicines that had to make such a long transatlantic voyage to benefit the sick. The question is sometimes raised why all those medicines were necessary and whether they were effective.[89] Some authors are of the opinion that the patients would have been better off if all medicines had been dumped in the ocean.[90] Criticism also focuses on the physicians of those days, who are portrayed as incompetent and even as a direct threat to their patients.[91] Their medicines would be ineffective or harmful and even if they did have some result, this was ascribed to a placebo effect. Then there are those authors who wonder how it is possible to cure people by means of remedies from polypharmacy, such as theriac with 60 or more ingredients. For centuries these medicines have helped suffering humanity, however, and here the old motto seems fitting 'Non ridere, non lugere neque detestari sed intelligere' (Spinoza, Tract. Pol. I, 4): let us try to understand before we condemn.

According to Handler, medicated care slaves received was singularly deficient when judged by modern standards.[92] From letters and reports to the various WIC chambers, however, it becomes clear that the surgeons did their therapeutic work well. Ward concluded that also in the British Caribbean the plantation doctors and surgeons actually managed to obtain positive results.[93] If they were unable to cure patients completely, at least they succeeded in improving their health to such an extent that they could resume work. This gets rid of the picture of practitioners causing harm rather than providing cure. Any historian writing about any society at any time is faced with the problem of interpreting the past in its own terms rather than through today's eyes. The tendency to condemn the past if it does not confirms up to the ideals of the present has since 1931 often been known as 'whiggishness'.[94]

It is clear that a structural approach of medical aid was out of question. What could be offered was a pragmatic effort, treatment of symptoms and short-time solutions. It is true that patients died because of excessive bloodletting and purging, which were fashionable at the time, or by poisoning due to toxic metal salts. But the medicinal arsenal certainly contained usable and therapeutically effective remedies, which undoubtedly saved many people's lives and a number of these drugs are still being applied nowadays. Some protozoal and parasitic infections are treated today in the same way as two hundred years ago: with antimonials.[95] Already in the 1750s many surgeons no longer were in favour of bloodletting which often resulted in death, and instead they administered vegetable sudorifics and diuretics.[96] Increasing the patient's life span, slowing down the progress of a disease and getting physical symptoms under control belonged to the possibilities of a capable surgeon in the period under discussion. And we should consider the WIC practitioners in the overseas possessions capable and conscientious. If they were not, they would certainly be corrected roughly.[97] As statistical material is lacking, we have to be satisfied with data from rare colonial medical reports. One was familiar with opium, which could prevent death by dehydration in cases of diarrhoea and flux. Besides hyoscyamine-containing preparations such as Philonium, opium was also used as a soporific and an analgesic. One also knew effective laxatives, drastics and abortifacients; iron salts as a styptic; Peruvian bark as a febrifuge and tonic; quassia wood, simarouba and ipecac against dysentery; absinth oil against dracontiasis; anise-ammonia solution to treat common cold; carminatives – still in use today – against stomach disorders; effective wound ointments such as aegyptiacum and epispastic plasters such as diachylon. The use of zinc oxide and zinc salts, such as tutia praeparata and vitriolum album, externally as a skin remedy and internally as an emetic and a nervine, is still known at present. From experience one had learned that scurvy could be prevented or cured by eating fresh vegetables and fruits, and that hygiene, both on board and on shore, was important for the prevention of diseases. In the Netherlands Indies fleet which sailed in 1598, lemon juice was issued as a preventive against scurvy and the value of fresh fruit as anti scorbutics was fully recognized. The Dutch East India and West India Companies developed orchards and vegetable gardens at such ports and forts as St. Helena, the Cape, Mauritius and the Gold Coast, where their ships might call. One did not know anything about microbial infections and pathogenics, but had learned from experience that one could fight 'miasma's' or noxious vapours by means of what we now consider disinfectants: sulphur dioxide from burning gunpowder and phenols from burning pitch or juniper berries.

Undoubtedly overdosing of opium, mercury or antimony has had destructive effects. The administering of mercury and mercury salts has caused many poisonings, but also slowed down some sickness processes considerably.[98] What we have managed to unearth about pharmacotherapy is that the surgeon of those days could dispose of effective weapons. This is not only emphasised in the reports of some practitioners,[99] but also, for example, in a publication of 1990 about old-fashioned drugs.[100] When criticising the harmful treatments or the use of multi-compounds, one should keep in mind that there are present-day cancer therapies causing considerable damage because of toxicity and that even today medicinal cocktails play an important role in the treatment of, for example, leprosy and aids. One should also be careful to ascribe a therapeutic effect to the imagination. Disorders with strong psychological components such as pain, depression and fear, accounting for a not negligible part of the WIC servants' complaints, could be remedied by their medicines. That may have been a placebo effect but also a natural process or regression to the mean. Placebo effects are much more substantial and ubiquitous than is usually thought.[101]

The fact that the colonial surgeon often had better results in the treatment of diseases than is generally assumed, may be explained from a present-day viewpoint. For the spreading of malaria in Guinea, for instance, it is favourable when the patient is seriously ill, so that he is an easy prey for other mosquitoes that after stinging may function as a vector for the parasite. Even though one did not dispose of Peruvian bark (cinchona), one could intervene in this process by administering herbals like quassia wood, which lowered the fever and thus mobilised the patients. If the human being himself was vector, as with dysentery, the ill-making effect was low, so that he was capable of transferring pathogenic bacteria or amoebas to another host by means of his excrements. In such a case, the treatment consisted of administering drastics and emetics such as aloe, scammony, euphorbium, coloquinta or antimony, which confined the patient to his sickbed.

GALEN IN THE TROPICS

The medicines for the colonies in the territory of the New WIC were adjusted to the contents and prescriptions of the Dutch pharmacopoeias. They were the weapons against disease and disorders related to physical, social and disease environments of the area and to interactions with other disease environments. The assortment of drugs varied according to the disease pattern of the colony, but what is remarkable are the excessively large quantities of medicines that made the transatlantic voyage and the massive doses that were often prescribed. To leave the point aside that those drugs were embezzled, a number of explanations may be given for this fact. First, the Europeans were of the opinion that tropical diseases had to be treated quickly, by means of high doses and strong remedies. Second, over-medication was stimulated by the racist myth that blacks were less sensitive to strong medicines than whites. This is a direct consequence of the humours doctrine of the Roman practitioner Galen (130-200 AD) and his racist views. In Galen's doctrine the mental characteristics are explained by the physical quality. Even after Christianity had made the principal distinction between body and soul, his typology persisted. Without Galen's humours doctrine it is virtually impossible to understand Shakespeare's dramas. [102] The Negro and the donkey are dumb due to blood; a lion or an Indian is choleric due to yellow bile.[103] Galen does not want to prescribe goat's dung and human brain as medicines for prominent town's people, but thinks one should be familiar with them to be able to apply them, should the occasion arise, to sick peasants and farm hands who 'are no better than donkeys'. This was against the Hippocratic oath, which did not allow any social distinction.

Galen performs a kind of therapeutic anthropology based on town and country, on rich and poor, and that deems whites different – and better – than blacks. In the colonies Galen's doctrine was used to consolidate a racist theory, assuming a Eurocentric view of the World history.[104] Blacks belonged to the 'lower animal species', and were, for example less sensitive to strong medicines than whites.[105] Therefore, one had to administer those immediately and for a long time. The skin of a Negro 'was so thick that germs or insects could not penetrate it', which explained why not a single lower animal or black ever got malaria or yellow fever.[106] Moreover, 'was it not the black people's passion for dancing and their amoral way of life that accounted for the weakness of the race and which resulted in "cachexia" or gastro-enteritis'? Or was the black's pathology perhaps controlled by 'la complexion chaude qui rend les hommes fort adonnez aux femmes', as Père Labat, the prosperous sugar-plantation owner, observed with hardly disguised envy?[107] Anyway, the myth that according to Galen's doctrine the sanguine blacks could better cope with hard work and exhaustion than the phlegmatic whites and choleric Indians was used for a long time to extenuate slavery.[108] The vehement socially oriented discussions about race-related diseases clearly demonstrate the tendency of colonial society to rigidify in categories.[109]

Galen's racial doctrine still lives on. Present-day psychologists such as Rushton still support the age-old theory that robust differences exist between Asian, European and African due to both genes and environment. They try to substantiate this by means of data on brain size, intelligence, sexuality, personality, growth rate, life span, crime and family stability.[110]

A third explanation may be found in alcohol abuse, which was a serious problem for the health of the inhabitants of the castle.[111] Large amounts of alcohol usually cause significant clinical toxicity and tissue damage, nutritional deficiencies (vitamin B), susceptibility to infections, the development of characteristic deviant behaviour and the danger of withdrawal syndrome. As far as diseases are concerned, it is clear that the Europeans on the Gold Coast and in Guiana especially suffered from two of the world's major killers: malaria and dysentery that raised drug consumption. Malaria did not occur in Curaçao, but in this island smallpox, flux and yellow fever afflicted people. One did not possess a remedy against yellow fever (febris flava), one of the most notorious endemic diseases from the Atlantic region, caused by an arbovirus (Arthropod-borne virus) and carried by mosquitoes (*Aedes aegypti*). Antimony preparations were administered against the notorious blood vomiting but one rarely succeeded in keeping the patient alive by these means and 40% of the sick died. Yellow fever barely occurred on the Gold Coast and did not form a health hazard until the 19th century.[112] Malaria (ague), made a lot of victims both in Guinea and Guiana. The eighteenth century associated malaria (lit. bad airs) with mist or miasma. In Essequebo the pools and marshes along the big rivers formed ideal breeding grounds for malaria mosquitoes. The infection was stimulated because many sugar plantations and cassava gardens were established precisely in that region. So, we see the expansion of the sugar plantations in the rain forest run parallel to the outbreak of 'virulent fevers and pains in head and body' and the urgent request for European drugs. On the Gold Coast especially rain basins and water holes, necessary for the drinking-water supply, were the major culprits.[113] Four main types of malaria are recognised, caused by parasites that all belong to the *Plasmodium* genus: *P. falciparum. P. malariae, P. vivax* and *P. ovale*. The most lethal form is malaria tropica (malignant tertian fever), caused by *Plasmodium falciparum*. Without treatment and in case no immunity had been built up in advance, it caused death in ⅓ of the cases within a week. Less lethal was malaria tertiana, caused by *P. vivax* and *P. ovale* (benign fever). Plasmodium parasites are carried by mosquitoes of an *Anopheles* species, the female of which sucks blood and may transfer parasites to humans by means of her saliva. These parasites end up in the liver and multiply there. They then enter the blood where they nestle in the red blood cells. There they divide again and again. Frequent attacks of fever, preceded by chills, swelling of the spleen, anaemia, neuralgia's and a general malaise are the results of the infection. There often are accompanying symptoms, such as brain aberrations, resulting in death. Only after several years partial immunity is reached. Due to an innate physiological defect, sickle-cell anaemia, West and Central Africans are largely protected against the lethal consequences of malaria tropica infection. The therapy in the period discussed here was symptomatic. Until 1713, the African colonists did not have Peruvian bark at their disposal, but they may have learned the effect of the bark of *Crossopteryx febrifuga,* which contains the glycoside B-quinovin (found in other Cinchoneae) and served as a Peruvian bark substitute.[114] Around 1750 the bitter wood of *Quassia amara* was used to alleviate fever and to mobilise the patient. Later, in 1763, this wood was sent to Linnaeus by one of his pupils who was travelling in South America, with the information that it was a secret remedy in fevers used by the Negro slave Quassi in Surinam.

The major breakthroughs in medicine only came by the end of the 18th century with the discovery of vaccination against smallpox by Jenner in 1798, followed in the 19th century by Carlos Findley's discovery (1881) that mosquitoes are the carriers of yellow fever, and that of Amico Bignami (1896) that malaria was transferred by mosquitoes, but especially with improved hygiene in the 1850s and following years. Louis Pasteur (1822-1897) focussed the attention upon microscopic forms of life and the words 'microbe' and 'bacteria' first came into common use. Pasteur's demonstration and the work of the German physician Robert Koch (1843-1910) that microbes could cause diseases was followed by the experiments of Joseph Lister (1827-1912) to introduce antisepsis through the use of disinfectants in the treatment of wounds. Meanwhile Paul Ehrlich (1854-1915) tried to overcome infectious diseases by adminstering chemicals, toxic to the pathogenic bacteria, but with little affinity for human tissues.

Every trade, traffic or profession has a history. The influence of the past upon the present is in direct proportion to the wealth of tradition and history. Europeans found that their former imperial stance had become unprofitable or untenable. Physicians found that they should not look with disdain upon the ignorance of the old-fashioned surgeons in the tropics. Those who have preceded us in the trade and traffic of medicines have left clear landmarks to guide our way.

Notes

1 Goslinga, *The Dutch in the Caribbean*, 44.
2 Müller, *Die Afrikanische Landschafft Fetu.*
3 WIC 103 (1718) 481.
4 Den Heijer, *Geschiedenis van de WIC*, 131.
5 WIC 124/125 (1715). Register 25 March 1715.
6 WIC 104 (1720) 474; 105 (1720) 27
7 Den Heijer, *Goud, ivoor en slaven*, 116-125.
8 WIC 124/5 (1719), Resolution 18 March 1719.
9 Tschirch, *Handbuch*, 2.2., 1087.
10 WIC 104 (1719) 239.
11 WIC 124 (1689). Register 21 January, number 3.
12 WIC 98 (1705) 387.
13 Bosman, *Description of the Coast of Guinea*, 90.
14 Tschirch, *Handbuch*, 2.2, 1610.
15 WIC 104 (1718) 236.
16 Hair, *Barbot on Guinea.*
17 WIC 124/5 (1721). Letter of 3 July 1721.
18 WIC 127 (1731) 730.
19 Rutten, 'Geneesmiddel voorziening Goudkust', 385-96.
20 WIC 97 (1699) 26; 100 (1707) 62, 251.
21 Rutten, 'Geneesmiddelen leveranciers', 726-729.
22 WIC 105 (1722) 357; see also Postma, *The Dutch in the Atlantic slave trade*, 308.
23 Stirrett, *Medical book*, 56; see also WIC 104 (1719) 230.
24 Ransford, *The Slave Trade*, 57.
25 Rutten, 'Geneesmiddelvoorziening', 390.
26 WIC 102/3 (1713) 52.
27 Dalziel, *Useful plants of West Tropical Africa*, 314.
28 WIC 102 (1713) 53.
29 Coxe, *Dispensatory*, 226.
30 WIC 97 (1700) 280, 322.
31 Bosman, *A new and accurate description*, 106.
32 Lawrence, 'Some source books', 229-34.
33 Rutten, 'Slavenhandel', 396.
34 WIC 106 (1725) 726.
35 Feinberg, 'New data on European mortality', 357-371.
36 WIC 104 (1719) 311.
37 Rutten, 'Geneesmiddelvoorziening Goudkust', 385-96.
38 WIC 105 (1721) 265.
39 WIC 97/8 (1702) 500.
40 WIC 98 (1704) 212.
41 Rutten, 'Geneesmiddelvoorziening Goudkust', 389.
42 WIC 106 (1723) 114, 119.
43 WIC 100 (1708) 158.
44 WIC 813 (1722) 5 December.
45 WIC 1296 (1715). Announcement 7 August
46 WIC 770 (1684) 57.
47 Bosman, *A new and accurate description*, 225.
48 WIC 104 (1719) 239.
49 WIC 105 (1721) 102.
50 WIC 132 (1765) 3 April 1765.
51 Gramberg, *Schetsen van Afrika's Westkust*, 277, 307.
52 Van Harten, 'Melegueta Pepper', 208-16.
53 Githens, *Drug plants of Africa*, 42.
54 Wichtl, *Teedrogen*, 251. See also Jaspersen-Schib, 'Phytotherapie', 621.
55 Dalziel, *Useful plants*, 471.
56 WIC 104 (1719) 238. See also De Marees, *Beschryvinghe*, 238 and Griebel, 'Erzatzpfefferarten', 426.
57 WIC 104 (1718) 236.
58 Unger, 'Bijdragen slavenhandel', 154. See also: Instructie voor de schippers 1675 (*Instruction for the Skippers.*).
59 Tschirch, *Handbuch* 2.2, 963.
60 Steele, *The English Atlantic.*
61 WIC 97 (1701) 352 and 105 (1721) 167.
62 WIC 103 (1717) 207.
63 De Marees, *Beschrijvinghe*, 226.
64 WIC 98 (1702) 2.
65 WIC 101 (1709) 232.
66 WIC 131 (1741) 6 February.
67 WIC 104 (1718) 145.
68 De Marees, *Beschryvinghe*, 171, 180.
69 Maier, 'Nineteenth Century Asante Medical Practices', 70.
70 Meredith, *Gold Coast of Africa*, 235-43. See also Isert, *Voyages en Guinée*, 219.
71 De Knecht van Eekelen, 'Tropische geneeskunde', 407-13.
72 Maier, 'Asante Medical Practices', 76.
73 Bosman, *A New and Accurate Description*, 66.

74 Ratelband, *Vijf dagregisters*, 174.
75 Cruickshank, *Eighteen Years on the Gold Coast*, 146.
76 Ratelband, *Vijf dagregisters*, 394.
77 WIC 97 (1699) 30.
78 WIC 98 (1704) 292.
79 WIC 100 (1708) 267-69.
80 WIC 98 (1701) 605.
81 WIC 97 (1700) 280.
82 Stirrett, *Medical book*, 56.
83 Swaluwe, *De daden der Zeeuwen*, 316.
84 Den Heijer, *Goud ivoor en slaven*, 189.
85 WIC 104 (1718) 236.
86 Hair, *Barbot on Guinea*.
87 Catalan, 'Cent cinquantenaire'.
88 WIC 1025 (1676) 32.
89 Wright, *Economic History*, 1031.
90 Sheridan, *Doctors and Slaves*, 320.
91 Craton, *Searching for the invisible Man*, 129.
92 Handler, 'Slave medicine', 75.
93 Ward, *British West Indian Slavery*.
94 Butterfield, *Whig Interpretation*.
95 D'Arcy, *Tropical diseases*, 39, 67.
96 Doerffel, *Aanmerkingen*, 331, 408.
97 WIC 137 (1766) 4.
98 Leuftink, *De geneeskunde bij 's Lands oorlogsvloot*, 113. See also Bajon, 'Mémoires sur le pian (framboesia)'.
99 WIC 569 (1707) 295.
100 Stoll, 'Alte Rezepte modern betrachtet', 33, 40.
101 Enserink, 'Can Placebo be the cure', 238.
102 Haeser, *Leerboek geschiedenis der geneeskunde*, 65.
103 Hünerfeldt, *Korte geschiedenis van de geneeskunde*, 84.
104 Taffin, 'Calamités, catastrophes naturelles et maladies', 243.
105 Sheridan, *Doctors and Slaves*, 331.
106 Kiple, *The Caribbean Slave*, 178.
107 Labat, *Nouveau voyage*, 401.
108 Williams, *Capitalism and Slavery*.
109 Taffin, *Maladies et médécine à la Guadeloupe*, 140.
110 Rushton, *Race, Evolution and Behaviour*.
111 See for example the abuse of director general A. Engelgraaf-Robbertszoon, WIC 104 (1718) 111.
112 Gramberg, *Schetsen*, 101. The presence of yellow fever on the West Coast of Africa could easily be overlooked as there were not usually enough whites in one place to provide material for a real epidemic and the blacks were relatively immune to the disease.
113 WIC 103 (1717) 10.
114 Dalziel, *Useful Plants*, 396. The presence of B-quinovine claimed by Dalziel is unconfirmed by Irvine, *Woody Plants of Ghana*, 668.

Chapter VI
THE ORIGIN AND QUALITY CONTROL OF TRAVELLING SIMPLES

Soon after the discovery of American and African territory chroniclers wrote extensive accounts on their experiences that included information about exotic plants possessing healing properties. The virtues of the newly found materia medica supported the efforts of Spain and Portugal to break the Venetian monopoly on the import of drugs and spices. An obstacle in the employment of the new found drugs was the fact that in the Western medical system each drug action needed to be placed within a Galenic faculty and ascribed a temperament or quality as hot, cold, wet or dry. The number of plants that finally made a really significant impact on European professional medical practice was rather small. An early example of the economic importance given by the Spanish crown to American medical plants was guaiacum, a tree found in most Caribbean islands. Calumba root and gum Arabic are examples of African profits. From Ayuba's *Return to Africa* we learn that '... the next day he was going with Mr.Hull up to Yanimarew, from whence he would accompany him to the gum forest, and make so good an understanding between the Company and his country people, that the English nation should reap the benefit of the gum trade...'[1]

Throughout the 17th and 18th centuries an incessant coming and going of ships across the South Atlantic was kept in motion by Europe's insaturable appetite for sugar and need for the New World's drugs. Tropical crops such as sugar, tobacco, cocoa and vegetable drugs like sarsaparilla, guaiacum, sassafras, since they were packed in leather satchels, helped to encourage the raising of cattle. The Dutch practitioner was European trained and accustomed to Amsterdam medicines and semi-pharmaceutical goods. Surgeons in Curaçao asked for European purging plants, although there were a good number of local substitutes such as aloe and ricinus. The records of Doctor Laurentius Horst (1700) reveals that in the 109 medications listed, there were 33 vegetable simples and only 2 products of

American origin. Gall nuts of *Quercus lusitanica* travelled from Holland to the Dutch Antilles in order to make ink, although divi-divi beans could be used as a possible substitute.[2] The powdered nuts were shipped to the clerical staff of the Dutch Caribbean and African bases and were used to prepare ink powder by mixing 1 lb. of green vitriol (ferro sulfate), 2 lbs. gallnuts and 8 ounces of Arabic gum. Two ounces of this mixture in water made a pint of ink.[3]

The control on the quality and authenticity of the supplied drugs was a subject of constant concern to the critics. One of the most important areas of health care is that pertaining to adulteration of drugs. Both Athens and Romans had laws to prevent the adulteration of wine and spices and England in the 13th century prohibited the adulteration of certain foods and beverages. Fraud in the 18th and the first half of the 19th century was scandalously common and hardly any article of food and drugs appeared to have been exempt. People were cheated with adulterated medicines, which often turned to be worthless drugs. Calumba root (*Jateorhiza calumba*) was adulterated with *Bryonia* weed, coloured yellow and made bitter with *Quassia species*. It was said that one of the best friends of the medical doctor would prove to be the adulterator. In the year 1820 F.C. Accum wrote a book on adulteration with the scriptural text 'There is death in the pot' (the words of the biblical quotation 2 Kings iv.40). In 1850 the ambitious works of A. Chevalier appeared in which many chemical methods were described for the discovery of adulterations.[4] It was the great and original merit of A.H. Hassal to have applied the microscope to important uses in the examination of adulteration. He made known to the public the health destroying and fraudulent adulterations of drugs and paved the way for English legislation against fraud[5]. In 1875 England had enacted the adulteration of foods and drugs. In the USA an act prohibiting the adulteration of drugs was passed by Congress in 1848, but it did not prohibit the distribution of poisons or dangerous drugs till the 1906 Food, Drug and Cosmetic Act was finally passed.

In the 17th and 18th century adulteration was not easily detected and often was unintentional. Locally available substitutes or facsimiles with similar sensory properties to the main plant were often encountered in trade goods. The confusion and inconsistencies in botanical nomenclature and plant identification often formed a difficult problem. There were no chemical or physical analysing methods available as we have today. Experience was needed and olfactory characteristics were used based on smell, taste, colour, texture and physical tests on specific gravity and maturity were performed to detect good quality or adulterations. A pharmacotherapeutic test or investigation of the offered drugs was impossible as well. The practitioner's indications were entirely of empirical nature and not until the end of the 19th century pharmacological studies were to find a scientific basis. Often the probing surgeon was confronted with abnormalities arising either from ignorance or from a fraudulent desire of more quickly completing the merchant's contracts. The censors repeatedly met with adulterated vegetable and animal drugs. The role of the investigator was not particularly enviable. The tasting of cinnamon bark to ascertain their quality, for example, was a very disagreeable duty imposed on the surgeons, as it caused such intolerable pain of the tongue that it rendered it impossible for them to continue the preparations two or three days successively. They attempted to mitigate the pain by occasionally eating a piece of bread and butter. The high price of some drugs and spices gave rise to many modes of adulterating it. To increase the weight of some drugs sand and even lead particles were introduced into the satchels. Cascarilla bark, for example, was adulterated with worthless plant roots, coloured black with iron salts. Cinnamon was a trade product from the territory of the Dutch East India Company and the Dutch were accused of deteriorating their cinnamon by mixing it with a proportion of real cinnamon, but which had been deprived of its essential oil by distillation. Cinnamon oil was a valuable and expensive product used in medicine. The weaker smell and taste of the spice detected the fraud.[6]

A serious problem in the storage and transport of drugs was the hidden danger of occupational diseases. Contact with the dust of dried herbals, especially during cultivation, travelling, drying, handling, transport, storage or control of drugs could induce an inflammation of the mucous membranes of the upper respiratory passages or mouth by a specific allergen, toxic plant constituents or microbial contamination.[7] Workers exposed to wood dusts have experienced a variety of adverse health effects such as eye and skin irritation, allergy, and reduced lung function, asthma and nasal cancer.[8] Examination of tobacco snuff, shipped from St. Domingue to Amsterdam via Curaçao, over a period of years could give rise to injury of the nasal cavity.[9] Particular notorious were the plant families of Euphorbiaceae and Asclepiadaceae, inhalation of sapogenin containing dust (Smilaceae), natural gums such as gum Arabic and tragacanth, and goods like red cedarwood, indigo, barley and rye. Leather bags could be contaminated with spores of *Bacillus anthracis*.[10] Anthrax is a highly infectious disease of animals, especially ruminants, that is transmitted to man by contact with animal products such as hides. Human infection with anthrax is usually through the skin but inhaling spores under adverse conditions could result in pulmonary anthrax (woolsorter's disease) which was often fatal.

CONTRIBUTION OF THE NEW WORLD DRUGS

ARROWROOT starch is obtained from the roots of plants of *Maranta arundinacea* (Marantaceae). It is a cash crop in Guiana, which originated in tropical South

America and was transported to the West Indies by pre-Colombian Amerindians, who used the arrowroot in poultices for sores and wounds, including those caused by poison arrows. Over time, other uses for arrowroot were found. The sediment of the juice dried and powdered was a most forcible diaphoretic. The crushed root was applied externally in treating yaws, inflammations caused by scorpion and spider bites and internally for dysentery. Later, in the 18th century it was exploited as a food and substitute for other starches. The extensive use of this product in the diseases of the bowel etc. rendered it of great commercial importance and several Dutch colonies exported it in bales of 200 pounds to this market.

CASCARILLA. The shrub *Croton eluteria* (Euphorbiaceae) grows in the Bahaman Islands and Jamaica. Its dried bark is chiefly imported from Eleuthera on the Bahamas, packed in chests and bales and exported to Europe and the United States. It is said to be a valuable carminative and tonic and was used in bitter wine to alleviate dyspepsia, flatulence, dysentery and measles. Cascarilla was introduced in 1690 by Professor Johann Andreas Stisser (1657-1700) and was afterwards much used in Germany by Friedrich Hoffmann, the famous inventor of many remedies (1660-1742) and Ernst Stahl (1660-1734) at Halle University as a substitute for cinchona in the cure of intermittent fever. Often it was adulterated with roots of other *Croton* species or weed.

CASSAVA is the nutritious starch from several plants of the genus *Manihot* (Euphorbiaceae) Its fleshy tubers yielding a nutrition starch are cultivated throughout the tropics where it provides a staple food. The starchy material tapioca or manioc is prepared from the pulp of the roots of cassava by elution with water. It is used to treat gastrointestinal disorders.

CASSIA FISTULA (Leguminosae) was indigenous in India and Egypt, but the tree is cultivated in the West Indies. The fruit is a cylindrical pod. The inside is covered with a soft black pulp of a sweet taste. It is a gentle laxative medicine.

CINCHONA or Peruvian bark (Rubiaceae). According to Coxe (1827) more than twenty-four species of the important genus Cinchona were known. The branches of the Cinchona tree were decorticated in the dry season and collected. *Cinchona succirubra* or Red Bark was found in the Andes, growing in the woods on the banks of the mountain streams at Riobamba, Cuchero and Chacahnassi. Its bark is the Quina roxa of commerce The trees frequently died after the operation. The bark arrived in Amsterdam in chests made of slips of wood and covered with hides, of about 200 lbs. The Dutch pharmacopoeia of 1726 lists both Cortex Peruviana vel Chinae and Radix ipecacuanhae as American drugs. Hybrid barks, usually a hybrid between *C. succirubra* and *C. ledgeriana*, formed a large proportion of the bark of commerce. The bark of *Cinchona calisaya* (Quina amarilla) was preferred in South America to all the other cinchonas. It was also called cortex chinae fuscus and was found in the mountains of Loxa in the kingdom of Quito and those of Santa Fé. The bark yielded by this tree was shipped in chests containing about 90-100 pounds each. Prior to 1772 all the cinchona bark brought to Europe was shipped at the ports of the Pacific. Later it came by the way of Carthagena de Indias to Cadiz. The stories, which are related to the discovery of its febrifuge activity, appear to be unworthy of notice. Cinchona bark was entirely unknown as a febrifuge to the Indians in Loxa, Guaneabambo and far around as Alexander von Humboldt (fl. c. 1820) states. They even regarded it as poisonous. The countess of Cinchon introduced the bark in Europe on her return to Spain in 1640. Its fame soon spread as it was taken to Italy in 1649 and through the means of the Jesuits distributed over the continent. The Jesuits sold it for its weight in silver, yet Condamine relates that in 1690 several thousand pounds of it lay at Piura and Payta for want of a purchaser.[11] The bark sometimes was adulterated with the bark from Martinique, resembling the *Cinchona floribunda* or with black cherry bark made bitter by tincture of aloes. Cinchona is a bitter stomachic and has astringent properties, It was chiefly used to prevent or control overt attacks of malaria.

COCHINEAL. The dried body of the female of a hemipterous insect *Coccus cacti*. It is found chiefly in the Mexican provinces of Oaxaca on the leaves of *Nopalea* species. South Carolina, New Granada, Quito, Peru, Mexico and the Caribbean and Canarian islands were the suppliers. In the 1750s about 800,000 pounds were brought annually to Europe. The peculiar colouring principle of cochineal has been called carmine. Cochineal was used as a scarlet dye and in medicine as an antispasmodic and anodyne in whooping cough.

COPAIBA BALSAM. Both the thicker Brazil and Maracaibo balsam and the oily Pará or Maran balsam (Maraan oil) were shipped. Several *Copaifera* species (Leguminosae), native of Venezuela (*C. Jacquini*) Brazil (*C. Langsdorffii*) and Guiana, (*C. guianensis*) produce the oleoresin. A substitute was the West-African Illurin balsam. The resinous juice flows in considerable quantities from incisions made in the trunk. The balsam was often adulterated with turpentine, colophony and castor oil. Copaiba balsam promotes urine and was said to cure inflammations of the genitourinary tract.

ELEMI. The resin of several resinous Burseraceae, grown in Manila (*Canarium luzonicum*), Africa (*Boswellia spp.*), America (*Protium spp.*) and the West Indies (*Bursera spp.*) was known as elemi. The Curaçaoan 'elemi' of *Bursera tomentosa* was called tacamahac or West Indian gum. Incisions are made in the bark of the trees from which a resinous juice flows. *Bursera simaruba* (Curaçao) yields a sweet aromatic balsam, which is used as a medicine for internal (spasmolytic) and external application; it is known in the trade as Chiboue or Gomart resin.[12] Elemi acts as a local stimulant and was used to prepare wound ointments.

GUAIAC. The trees *Guaiacum officinale* (common Lignum vitae) and *Guaiacum sanctum* (Holywood) are natives of the West Indies. The wood of these Zygophyllaceae is heavier than water, very hard and resinous. The resin exudes in tears but was principally obtained by heating the wood receiving the melted resin into a calabash. Both the resin and the wood were used in medicine as a diaphoretic, diuretic and were slightly laxative. It was used in gout and acute and chronic rheumatism and in inflammatory conditions of the pharynx and tonsils as well. Oviedo gives us a description of how to combat syphilis with splinters or filings of the guaiacán, which were boiled with water. He had observed the trees in the West Indian islands but not in Tierra Firme and confirms that the Indians regarded the guaiacum as a holy tree, of whose wood they used to make their idols and sacred chairs.[13] Syphilis was considered by European physicians to be a cold poison, lodged in the blood. Guaiac was introduced as a hot antidote to replace the mercurial induction hitherto employed. Nicholas Pohl wrote in 1517 that 3000 Spaniards were cured with guaiacum and Uhlrich Von Hutten further spread its reputation. Boerhaave (1668-1738) was an advocate of guaiac and thought that the drug could reach spots in the body where mercury could not penetrate.[14] When the wood was discovered not to be an antisyphilitic as supposed, but simply a stimulant and diaphoretic, interest in it waned as rapidly as it had risen.

GUM ANIME is the resin of *Hymenaea courbaril* (Locust or Algarobe resin) and is synonymous with South American copal. The tree (Leguminosae) grows in West India and South America. In Mexico it is called Ambar del Pais. Externally is is incorporated in ointments to treat wounds and ulcers. It was also used to relieve asthma and in fumigating compounds on account of its aromatic odour while burning.

IPECAC is a perennial of the Rubiaceae, growing in shadowy moist situations in the forests of the interior of West-Brazil and was used by the Indians as an emetic before their connection with Europeans. Piso described its use fully in his *Natural History of Brazil* as early as 1618.[15] He brought the root to Europe, yet it was scarcely used before the year 1700. After collecting the dried root or rhizome of *Cephaelis ipecacuanha* it was packed in bales and shipped from Rio de Janeiro. In 1726 is was incorporated into the Dutch 'Renovata' pharmacopoeia. Powdered ipecac was employed as an emetic, in the treatment of amoebic dysentery and in small doses as a diaphoretic and expectorant.

JALAP consists of the dried tubercles of *Ipomoea purga* (Convolvulaceae). It is a climbing perennial and an inhabitant of Mexico and Vera Cruz. It grows also wild near Pensacola in West Florida and near the seashore in Georgia. It was often adulterated with dried potatoes. Jalap is a powerful purgative and is also used to alleviate inflammatory ailments

LOGWOOD, Palo Azul or Brazilwood is the unfermented heartwood from *Hae-*

matoxylon campechianum (Leguminosae). The tree was introduced from Honduras into Jamaica, St. Thomas, St. Domingue and other Caribbean islands where it is now common. In ancient and medieval times the brazilwoods imported to Europe from the Near East were *Caesalpinia braziliensis* and other C. species. When Portuguese explorers in the New World found a similar tree they named the country where brazilwood grew Brasil or Brazil. It was principally used as a peach coloured dyewood but also with considerable advantage in medicine as a mild astringent, usually in the form of a decoction, to treat hemorrhage, chronic diarrhoea and dysentery. Other dyewoods were Fernambucco or Red Brazilwood, obtained from *Caesalpinia echinata*, a native of Brazil and Mexico and *Caesalpinia crista* from Jamaica. 'Redwoods' came from *Baphia nitida* (Camwood) and *Pterocarpus* species in West Africa as well.

PERUVIAN BALSAM or balsamum Indicum nigrum is obtained by incision of the tree *Myroxylon Pereira* (Leguminosae) that grows in the warmest provinces of South America. Each tree delivers about 2 pounds balsam which, when insippated to the heat of the sun, turns redbrown and viscous. Often the product was adulterated with castor oil, colophony, tacamahac or alcohol. It was used internally to treat dysentery, externally for cleansing and healing wounds and ulcers, sometimes to alleviate rheumatic pains.

PIMENTO. *Pimenta officinalis* (Myrtaceae) is a tree native in Central America and is cultivated in Jamaica and East India. The full-grown unripe fruits are dried during which time they gradually lose their green colour and become of a reddish brown. It is used as a stimulant and tonic and as a condiment in dressing food. It was known as 'allspice' because it combined the flavour of cinnamon, pepper and cloves.[16] It was introduced to Europe from the West Indies about 1600.

QUASSIA. The bitter wood of *Quassia amara* and *Picraena excelsa*, two trees of the family of the Simaroubaceae. The first grows in Surinam and Brazil; the second is native to Jamaica. Quassia appeared on the market in the second half of the 18th century and is used in bitter tonics, in obstinate diarrhoea, dysentery, anorexia, and intermittent fever and to expel threadworms

RATANHY consists of the dried roots of *Krameria triandra* (Krameriaceae), a native to Bolivia and Peru, which grows in the mountains of the provinces of Huanuco, Tarna and Xauca. Several commercial substitutes existed such as Payta ratanhy and Savanilla of other *Krameria* shrubs, such as the Ratanhia das Antillas (*Krameria ixina*) found in Puerto Rico, Hispaniola, Brazil, Guiana, Venezuela and Curaçao. The name ratanhy signifies trailing plant. It is used medicinally as a wound styptic, astringent and tonic, to treat haemorrhoids, chronic rheumatism, headache and dysentery. Ratanhy root was long known to those who manufactured port wine and large quantities of its redbrown extract were prepared solely for this purpose in South America.

SARSAPARILLA. The dried root of several tropical climbing or trailing vines belonging to the *Smilax* genus of the lily family (Liliaceae). According to Monardes the name originates from the Spanish *çarça*, 'bremble' and *parrilla*, 'little vine'. The plants are native to the southern and western coasts of Mexico to Peru. The commercial species providing sarsaparilla are principally *Smilax officinalis* and *S. medica*, known as Mexican, Honduras and Ecuadorian items. The Mexican items were called 'macapatli'.[17] Other *Smilax* species include the 'red bearded sarsaparilla', cultivated in Jamaica. After washing and drying in the sun the roots were bound tightly into cylinders, packed in seroons of 80-100 pounds and then exported. The drug was first brought into Europe by the Spaniards about the year 1536 with the character of being a tonic, blood purifier and a specific for the cure of syphilitic diseases and chronic rheumatism. At the end of the 17th century Peru shipped huge quantities to England and Veracruz yearly delivered about 500,000 pounds. Today the saponin containing herbal is used to flavour and mask the task of medicines and in combination with wintergreen and other flavours in root beer and other carbonated beverages to create foam. Sometimes the strongly aromatic roots of the wild sarsaparilla (*Aralia nudicaulis*) and false or bristle sarsaparilla (*Aralia hispida*) were substituted for the true herbal. Other adulterants were roots of *Pteris* and *Philodendron* species.

SASSAFRAS ROOT. The dried bark of the root of *Sassafras officinale* (Lauraceae), a tree native of North America and Cochin China, was used as a gentle stimulating, carminative and diuretic remedy. It was prescribed in addition to a decoction of guaiac wood in the treatment of syphilis as well.

SIMAROUBA consists of the dried root of *Simaruba amara* (Simaroubaceae), native to Guiana, North Brazil and St. Vincent It has been used as a bitter, as an astringent and in the treatment of diarrhoea

TAMARIND is the sweet pulp collected from the tree *Tamarindus indica* ((Leguminosae), which grows both in tropical Africa and in the East and West Indies (Barbados, Martinique, Grenada, Curaçao). Its fruit is a broad ash coloured pod which contains a soft brown pulp. The pulp proved to be a mild laxative and purgative. It was taken aboard of slavers to prevent scurvy on the triangular trade. It was often adulterated with molasses and sometimes it is confused with dates in the literature. In Curaçao it was taken with cinnamon into a laxative soup.

VANILLA consists of the fruit of the wild *Vanilla pompona* (Orchidaceae), found in Mexico and Guiana, a species of tropical American orchids and an important article of commerce. Vanilla is one of the leading flavours for foods and pharmaceuticals. It is used in medicine to treat fevers, rheumatism and nervous disorders.

WILD CINNAMON. The tree *Canella alba* (Canellaceae), the white or wild cinnamon, is very common in Jamaica and some of the West Indian islands. It is native of Brazil and cultivated in Venezuela and Guiana. The interior bark was gathered and dried in the shadow and brought to us rolled up in long quills thicker than cinnamon. Its odour is slightly different from real cinnamon and it is used as a spice and in medicine in flatulence, as a carminative and to make aromatic wines. A mixture of the powdered bark with aloes is known as Hiera picra and is used as cathartic and emmenagogic.

REMEDIES OF AFRICAN ORIGIN

CLAYS are widely distributed in West- and Central Africa. An example of medical importance consisted of kaolin, which occurs most notably on Nigeria's Jos Plateau, on the Gold Coast and in Southern Africa. Clays are still official in a number of today's pharmacopoeias and are used to treat enteritis, colitis and diarrhoea. Recent scientific research has demonstrated its bactericidal activity.

COLOQUINTE consists of the dried pulp of the fruit of *Citrullus colocynthis* (Cucurbitaceae), an annual plant of the gourd type and a native of Turkey and tropical Africa. It is a most powerful and violent cathartic.

CUBEB is the unripe fruit of *Piper cubeba* (Piperaceae), native to the East Indies and Guinea. It was used as a spice and medicinally as a urinary antiseptic similar to that of copaiba and to alleviate colds, flatulence and shortness of breath.

GUM ARABIC or Acacia. This gum was originally brought from Arabia by the way of Egypt to Marseilles and it was not until the beginning of the 17th century that the Dutch made the gum of Senegal known in Europe. Gum was not 'rubber' and tamarind no 'dates' as some authors supposed.[18] The gum was packed in very large sacks of tanned leather and brought on camels and bullocks to certain ports of Senegal, of Elmina or Benin where it was sold to the Dutch, French and English merchants. In 1787 the annual quantity purchased by these merchants was about 1.200.000 pounds. Making an incision in the stem and branches of *Acacia Senegal* and other A. species and collecting the exudate repeatedly throughout the dry season produced gum Arabic. The sicklier the tree appears, the more gum it yields The dried exudation so obtained consisted of pale yellow lumps. For this reason they were sometimes called 'barnsteen' (succinum).[19] Examples of the true gum Arabic are gum Kordofan (shipped via Chartum to Alexandria) and gum Senegal (African West Coast to Bordeaux). It is also collected in North Nigeria, Tripoli, Egypt and a substitute called gum gatti is collected in Sudan. Is is used as a glue and in medicine as a mucilaginous demulcent in irritable states of the respiratory passages such as catarrh, cough, phthisis and gastrointestinal disturbances. Externally it was applied in powder as a styptic.

MELEGUETA, also called Guinea grains or Grains of paradise, is the pungent seed of *Aframomum melegueta*, a reedlike plant of the family of Zingiberacae. The seeds are contained in the acid pulp of the fruit and have a glossy dark-brown husk. They contain an essential oil and a viscid brown resin. Grain was obtained from the Grain- or Pepper coast and shipped via Elmina in bales of 40 pounds. It has long been used as a spice and as a drug. The wine known as Hippocras was flavoured with it and with cloves and cinnamon. Melegueta was used in intermittent fever, enteritis, exantheme and nausea.[20]

Notes

1 Curtin, *Africa Remembered,* 59.
2 WIC 1146 (1704) 134.
3 WIC 1156 (1736) 19.
4 Chevalier, *Dictionnaire des altérations.*
5 Clayton, *A memoir of the late Hassal,* 11-44.
6 Coxe, *Dispensatory,*377. Coxe was largely based on the Edinburgh New Dispensatory.
7 Weatherall, *Oxford Textbook of Medicine,* 6, 143.
8 National Institute for Occupational Safety and Health. *Hazard Control,* Publication no. 96-127.
9 WIC 574 (1719) 490; see also Amberger-Lahrmann, *Gifte,* 173-176.
10 Publicatieblad Curaçao Nr. 11; 10 July 1849.
11 Coxe, *Dispensatory,* 94.
12 Broeders, *Handleiding inheemse en ingevoerde planten,* 67-69.
13 De Oviedo, *Natural History,* 88-9.
14 Rutten, *Apothekers en Chirurgijns,* 220.
15 Piso, *Historia natural,* 433.
16 Tschirch, *Handbuch,* 2.2.1239.
17 Tschirch, *Handbuch,* 2.2.1506.
18 Postma, *The Dutch in the Atlantic Slave Trade,* 60, 234.
19 WIC 104 (1717) 25.
20 Githens, *Drug Plants of Africa,* 62.

EPILOGUE

In the eighteenth century the Dutch West India Company (WIC) bought relatively large quantities of medicines in Amsterdam and shipped them to the Atlantic region on behalf of the Company's surgeons working there. As return cargoes medicinal herbs and other goods were shipped back to the metropolis from the overseas possessions. Facts about the type of products involved here, the volume of shipments and the eventual life span of the shipped drugs are scarce and have so far been reported on only fragmentarily. Books on the Dutch overseas expansion or on the medico-pharmaceutical history hardly pay attention to the trade and shipment of medicines that form the subject of the present study.

The Dutch Atlantic activity had been coordinated by the WIC, founded in 1621, but in 1674 this uncontrollable and top-heavy organization was transferred into a New or Second Company; a semi-official body for the management of American and African settlements, with far more restricted monopoly rights than its predecessor. The basis of the relative prosperity which enabled this Company to prolong its existence in the eighteenth century was formed by the trade in black slaves, gold, gum and melegueta pepper from Africa; the trade in sugar, tobacco, hides, cocoa and cotton from Guiana or from the colonies of other New World powers; the collection of recognition fees from the private trade for sailing its monopolized domain; and – for a smaller but not insignificant part – the return cargoes of spices, medicinal herbs, dyes and woods from its overseas territories. In the WIC's trade network Curaçao was a vital link. This Dutch possession in the Caribbean was the storehouse of European and North American goods and a market for slaves and colonial products. Tropical agriculture on the Spanish-American continent was provided with slaves from Curaçao, while crops and plant medicines were shipped home as return freight. Between 1760 and 1790 the island St. Eustatius was a succesful Dutch entrepót in the Caribbean as well.

In this book the Dutch settlements and colonies in the Caribbean, Guiana and West Africa form the target of the shipments of drugs destined for the health and comfort of the swelling staff of the Company's servants and employees, soldiers and black slaves. As far as we know, this is the first attempt to present an overview of the Dutch transatlantic medicine trade and traffic in the eighteenth century in a book. Spices and herbs formed the foundation of the apothecary's recipe book. Europeans were pre-occupied with the search for wonderful drugs which travelled from distant and unknown places. The adventurer who could return with a shipload of these exotics was assured of riches and honours. The thousands upon thousands of travelling herbs were to be utilized in countless ways to make most of medicines of man. The trade in plants remained the cornerstone of pharmacy.

APPENDICES

APPENDIX I

CONTENT PHARMACOPAEA AMSTELREDAMENSIS 1686

SIMPLES KEPT IN APOTHECARY SHOPS

RADICES
acetosae
acori
alkannae
alii
altheae
angelicae
apii
ari
aristolochiae
asari
asparagi
bardanae
bistortae
brusci
bryoniae
calami
capparis
cardui benedicti
carlinae
caryophylatae
caevae
cepae
chelidon major
chelidon minor
cherefolii
chinae
cichorei
consolidae
contrayervae
costi utriusque
cucumeris
curcumae
cyclaminis
cynaglossae
ciper longi
dentis leonis
dictamni alb
doronici
ebuli
enulae
eringii
esulae
filicis
foeniculi
fraxinellae
galangae
gentianae
glycyrrhizae
graminis
helenii
hellebori albi
hermodactylor
hirudinariae
hyoscyami
jalappae
ibisci
imperatoriae
iridis florentinae
lapati
lappa minor
levistici
liliorum alborum
liquiritiae
malvae
mandragorae
mechoacannae
narcisci
nympheae
ononidis
osmundae
ostrutti
oxalidis
oxylapathi
pastinacae
paeoniae maris
pentaphylli
petasidis
petroselini
peucedani
phu
pimpinellae
plantaginis
polypodii
porri capitati
pyrethri
raparum
raphani hispanici
raphani horrensis
raphani rusticana
restae bovis
rhabarberi
rhapontici

rubiae tinctorum
rusci
sambuci
satyrii
saxifragiae
scorzonerae
scillae
scrophulariae
sigilli salomon
spicae nardi
taraxaci
tormentillae
turbith
tussilaginis
vincetoxici
zarzaeparillae
zedoariae
zingiberis

FUNGI
agaricus
auriculae
fungus vulgar
moxa
orbicularis

CORTICES
aurantiorum
cassiae lignae
cinnamomum
citriorum
castanearum
ebuli
fraxini
glandium calices
granatorum
juglandium
kina kina
ligni guaiaci
limonum
macis
mali chinensis
malicorij
quercus
radicis capparum
sambuci
tamarisci
xylocassiae
winterani

LIGNA
aloes
aspalatum
brasilianum
buxinum
colubrinum
guajacum
juniperinum
moluccense
nephriticum
rhodium
santalum album
santalum citrinum
santalum rubrum
sassafras
visci quercini

FOLIA & HERBAE
abrotoni
absinthii romani
absinthii marini
absinthii vulgaris
acetosae
acetosellae
adianti
agrimoniae
alchimillae
alsines
altheae
anagallis (becabunge)
anethi summitatis
apii
argentinae
artemisiae
asari
asplenii
atiplieis
basilici
bellidis
betae
betonicae
bismalvae
boraginis
botryos
brancae ursinae
brassica
buglossae
bursae pastoris
calaminthae
capilli veneris
caprofolii
cardui benedict
cardui mariae
caulaequinae
caulium
centauri minor
ceterach minor
chamaedryos
chamaepytios
chelidoni major
cherefolii
cichorei
cicutae
cochleariae
cuscutae
dentis iconis taraxaci
dictamni creticae
ebuli
endiviae
epithymi
equiseti
erysimi
eupatorii aquatici
eupatorii cannabini
euphragiae
farfarae
foeniculi
fragariae
fumariae
gallitrichi
herderae arborescentis
herderae terrestris
hellecebrae
hepaticae
hyoscyami
hyperici summitatis
hyssopi
ibisci
lactucae
lapathi
lavendulae
lauri
lentis palustris
lichenis
lingue cervine
lupuli

majoranae
malvae
mandragorae
marrubii
marricariae
melissae
menthae crispae
menthae aquaticae
mercurialis
millefolii
musci cranii humani
musci quercini
myrti
nasturtii aquatici
nasturtii hiemalis
nasturtii hortensis
nepetae
nicotianae
nummulariae
ocymi
origani cretici
origani vulgaris
oxalidis
papaveris hortensis
papaveris nigri
parietariae
persicariae
petroselini
phellandri
phyllitis
pilosellae
pimpinellae
plantaginis
polii montani
polygoni
polytrichi
portulaccae
primulae veris
prunellae
pulegi
pulmonariae albae
pulmonariae maculosae
pyrolae
quercus
ribesii nigri
rorismarini
rosarum
rubi summit
rutae
rutae murariae
sabinae
salicis
salviae
saniculae
saturejae
scabiolae
scarleae
schoenanthi
scolopendrii
scordii
scorzonerae
semperviri majoris
semperviri minoris
senae
serpilli
solani
soldonellae
solidaginis
sonchi laevis
tanaceti
tapsi barbati/verbasci
taraxaci
thee chinensisum
thymi
trifolii
tussilaginis
verbasci
verbenae
veronicae
vincae pervincae
violariae
virgae aureae
urticae

FLORES
anethi
balaustia
betonicae
boraginis
buglossae
calendulae
caprifolii
caryophylleus
chamaemeli romanum
chamaemeli vulgaris
cheiri
crocus
cyani
genistae
hyperici
lavendulae
liliorum alborum
liliorum convallium
malvae arborae
meliloti
nympheae albae
paeoniae
papaver erratici
rorismarini
rosarum pallidarum
rosarum rubrarum
salviae
sambuci
schoenanthum
staechydis
tiliae
trifolii odorati
verbasci violarum

SEMINA
acetosae
agni casti
allii
altheae
amnios
amomi
anethi
anisi
antherae rosarum
apii
aquilegiae
asparagi
atriplicis
bardanae
basilicon/ocymi
berberorum
bombacis
buniadis
caepae
cannabis
cardamomi minoris
cardui benedicti
carvi
carthami

caulium
cicer rubrum
citri
citrulli
cnici
colocynthidis
coriandri
cubebe
cucumeris
cucurbitae
cumini
cydoniorum
dactylorum
dauci cretici
endiviae
ericae
fabae
foeniculi dulcis
foeniculi vulgaris
foenugraeci
fraxini
fumariae
genistae
grana paradisi
hordeum integrum
hordeum mundatum
hordeum perlatum
hyperici
lactucae
lentium
levistici
linguae avis
lini
lupini
malvae
melonum milii folis
miliifolis vulgaris
nasturtii
nigellae
nuclei cerasorum
nuclei persicor
nuclei prunor
nuclei pini
nuclei pistachior
oleris atri
orobi
oryza
paeoniae
papaver albi
papaver nigri
pastinacae
petroselini
phellandri
plantaginis
porri
portulacae
psyliii
raphani
rusci
rutae
sambuci
santonici/zedoariae
saxifragiae
scariolae
seselios maciliens
sileris montana
sinapi
sophiae
staphidis agriae
sumach
thlaspios
urticae

FRUCTUS
alkekengi
amygdalae amara
amygdale dulcia
anacardi
baccae ebuli
baccae hederae
baccae juniperi
baccae lauri
baccae mezeroei
baccae myrti
baccae sambuci
ribesiorum rubrum
ribesiorum nigri
berberorum
cacoa
capita papaver
capparis
caricae
carpobalsam
caryophylli
cassia fistula
cerasa
costi
colocynth
corni
cucumer asininum
dactyli
ficus
fraga
gallae
gariophylli/amomi
glandes
grana kermes
jujubae
mespila immatura
myrobalani bellericae
myrobalan chebulae
myrobalan citrin
myrobalan emblicae
myrobalan indicae
myrtilli
nuces avellanae
nuces cerasorum
nuces cupressi
nuces juglandium
nuces mespilor
nux moschata
nuces persicor
nuces pini
nux pistachior
nux vomica
olivae
passulae majores
passulae minores
piper album
piper brasiliense/achi
piper longum
piper nigrum
poma acida
poma aurantia
poma chinensia
poma citria
poma cydonia
poma dulcia
poma granata
poma immatura
poma limonia
mala
morum celsi
pruna brignolensia

pruna catharinae
pruna damascena
pruna gallica
pruna silvestria
rubi idaei
sebesten
siliquae dulces
tamarindum
uvae

FARINAE
amylum
fabarum
foenugraeci
hordei
lupinorum
rad.altheae
rad.consolid
sem.lini
volatilis

SUCCI LIQUIDI
acetum
afrestae
aurantiorum
berberorum
citriorum
cydoniorum
fumariae
granatorum
limonum
oleum
omphacium
rosarum pallidarum
vinum canarium
vinum gallicum
vinum hispanicum
vinum moeselanicum
vinum rhenanum

SUCCI CONDENSATI
GUMMI & RESINAE
absinthii vulgaris
acacia vera
aloe hepatica
aloe succotrina
ammoniacum
asa foetida
bals.peruvian album
bald.peruvian nigrum
bals.copaivae
bdellium
benzoinum
bitum judaicum
caphura
colophonia
elaterium
eupatrii
euphorbium
fuligo
galbanum
gluten
glycyrrhiza
gutta gamba
gum anime
gum arabicum
gum caranna
gum ceraforum
gum copal
gum elemi
gum hederae
gum juniperi
gum persicorum
gum prunorum
gum tacamahaca
hypocistidis
laccae
laudanum
liquidamber
manna
mastiche
myrrha
olibanum (thus)
opium
opobalsamum
opoponax
pix
pix liquida
resina abietina
resina citrina
resina laricae
resina pini
resina terebinth
saccharum album
saccharum rubrum
saccharum cantum album
saccharum cantum rubrum
saccharum penidium
sagapenum
sandaracha arabum
sandaracha juniperinum
sanguis draconis
sanguis in lacrym
sarcocolla
scammonium
styrax calamita/assa
styrax liquid
succinum album
succinum citrin
tartarum rhenatum
tartarum rubrum
terebinthina vulgaris
terebinth veneta
tragacanthum

ANIMALIA
adeps anatis
adeps anguillae
adeps anseris
adeps canis
adeps cervi
adeps felis
adeps gallinae
adeps hominis
adeps taxi
adeps ursi
album graecum
angues
araneae
axungia porci
bezoar occidentale
bezoar orientale
bufo
butyrum
cantharides
caseus
castoreum
cera alba
cera citrina
cochleae
conchenilia
cornu cervi
cornu rhinocerotis
cortices ovorum

cranium hominis
dens apri
ebur
fel tauri
hirci sanguis
hirudines
ichthyocolla
lac animalium
lapides asellor
lumbrici terrae
mandibulae lucii
medulla ossium
mel album
mel flavum
millepedes/aselli
moschus
mumia
oculi cancri
ossa corde cervi
ova
priapus cervi
ranae
sapo niger
sapo venetus
scincus
sepiae
serici
sevum hircinum
sevum ovinum
spermaceti
sperma ranarum
spodium
stercus capri
stercus columbi
stercus equi
stercus gallinae
stercus hominis
stercus ovini
stercus vaccae
tela aranearum
testae chamarum
testae cochlearum
testae concharum
testae ostreorum
testae tellinarum
viperae
ungula alcis
unicornu
vulpes
zibetum/civet

MINERALIA-METALLA-LAPIDES
aerugo/viride aeris
aes ustum
alumen rubrum
alumen rupeum
alumen plumeum
alumen ustum
alabastrum
antimonium
argentum foliaceum
argentum vivum/mercur vivus
arsenicum album
arsenicum rubrum/sandaracha
auripigment
aurum foliatum
bolus armenia
bolus vulgaris
bolus alba
borax
calx viva
cerussa
chalcitis
chalybs
chrysocolla
cinnabaris
creta alba
crystallus
ferrum
granatus
hyacinthus
lapis armenius
lapis calaminar
haematites
haemat judaic
haemat lazuli
haemat scissilis
haemat silicis
lithargyrium argenti
lithargyrium auri
magnes
mercurius vivus
minium
nihil album/pompholix
nitrum/salpetra
osteocolla
plumbum ustum
rubinus
rubrica
sal armoniac
sal gemmae
sal vulgare
saphirus
sardus
scoria ferri
smaragdus
sublimatum
sulphur
terra lemnia
terra sigillata
topasius
tutia
vitriolum album
vitriolum anglicum
vitriolum cyprium
vitriolum hungaricum
vitriolum romanum
vitrum antimonii

MARINA
ambra grisea
blatta byzantia
corali albi
corallina
margaritae
mater perlatum
pumex
spongia

APPENDIX II

CONTENT PHARMACOPAEA AMSTELREDAMENSIS 1686

COMPOUNDS KEPT IN APOTHECARY SHOPS

ACETA
Acetum calendulae
Acetum lavandul
Acetum rosarum
Acetum scillae

ANTIDOTA
Confectio alkermes
Confectio hyacinthorum
Diascordium fracastorii
Mithridatium Damocratis
Theriaca Andromachi
Diatessaron Mesue

AQUAE
Aq. alexipharmaca
Aq antiepileptica
Aq.antinephritica
Aq. hysterica
Aq. theriacalis
Aq. vitae compositae

AQUAE SIMPL.STILAT.
Aq. absinthii
Aq.acetosae
Aq.artemisiae
Aq. betonicae
Aq. boraginis
Aq. camomillae
Aq. caprifolii
Aq. cardui benedicti
Aq. centauri minoris
Aq. cochleariae
Aq. chelidon.majoris
Aq. cichorei
Aq. cinnamomi
Aq. cochleariae
Aq. euphrasiae
Aq. fabarum
Aq. foeniculi
Aq. flor.caryophyllorum
Aq. fumariae
Aq. graminae
Aq. hedera terr.
Aq. hyssopi
Aq. lactucae
Aq. lavendulae
Aq. liliorum alborum
Aq. liliorum convallorum
Aq. matricariae
Aq. Melissae
Aq. Mellis
Aq. Menthae
Aq. Papaveris erratici
Aq. Petroselini
Aq. Plantaginis
Aq. Paeoniae
Aq. Portulaccae
Aq. Pulegii
Aq. Rorismarini
Aq. Rosarum
Aq. Sambuci
Aq. Solatri
Aq. Spermacis ranarum
Aq. Tiliae

CERATA
santalinum
stomachicum

CONDITA
caro cydoncorum
caulus lactucae
cortices aurantiorum
cortices citri
flores aurantiorum
flores citriorum
fructus berberi
cerasa
cerasa amara
mirobalani
nuces juglandes
moschatae
ribesii
passulae purgantes
radices acori
cichorei
enulae campanae
eryngii
satyrii
scorzonerae
zingiberis

CONSERVA
absinthi vulgaris
acetosae

betonicae
boraginis
calendulae
caryophyllorum
cichorei
eupphrasiae
malvae
melissae
menthae
paeoniae
rorismarini
rosarum pallidarum
salviae
symphyti
trifolii acetosi
violarum

ELECTUARIA-SOLUTIVA
benedictum laxativum
confectio hamech
diacarthamum
diacatholicum
diaphaenicum
diaprunum solut.
hierae diacolocynthidos
hierae picrae Galeni
lenitivum
succi rosarum

EMPLASTRA
betonicae
diacalciteos
diachylum cum gummi
diachylum simplex
gratia dei
griseum (Lapis calaminaris)
meliloti
minii
mucilagin
oxycroceum
ranarum c.mercurio
ad rupturas fernellii
sparadrapum
stichticum Paracelsi

MELLITA
diamorum Nicolai
mel centauri
mercurialis
rorismarini
rosarum adstringens
rosarum solutivum
oxymel scilliticum
simplex

OLEA PER DELIQUIUM
guajaci
myrrhae
petrae naturale
plumbi
tartari

OLEA PER DESTILL.
anethi
anisi
baccae juniperi
carei
caryophyllorum
cerae
cinnamomi
corticum aurantiorum
corticum citri
foeniculi
laterum
ligni rhodii
macis
majoranae
nucis moschatae
origani cretici
rorismarini
salis
spicae
succini
sulphuris
terebinthinae
vitrioli

OLEA EXPRESS/DECOCT.
absinthiii
anethinum
capparum
castorei
chamaemelinum
crocinum
euphorbii
hyperici
irinum
keirinum
liliorum alborum
lumbricorum
majoranae
menthae crispae
mucaginum
myrtillorum
nardinum
nepetae
nymphae
rosaceum
rosaceum omphacinum
rutaceum
scorpionum
solani
trifol.odorati
violaceum
verbasci
vulpinum

OPIATA
Philonium Mesue
Requies Nicolai

PILULAE
aloephanginae
agarici
aureae
cochiae
cynoglossi
extract.catholicum
fetidae major
hierae c.agarico
lapid.lazuli
laudan.opiati
mastichinae
nitri A.Trallini
pestilentiales
sine quibus

PRAEP.SIMPLIC.
aeris ustio
aloes
calcis lota

chalybis
corallorum
cornu cervi
coriand.cumini
eboris
elaterium
esulae
hellebor.nigri
laccae
lapis alchymiae
lapidis calaminae
lapidis lazuli.
lapidum praetiosorum
margaritarum
oculor cancri
opii
plumbi
ruptorium commune
scammonii
turiae
vitrioli

PULVERES AROMATICI
aromat.rosaceus
diacalaminthes
diagalangae
diaireos simplex
dialaccae major
diamargar frigidus
diambrae mesue
dianthos Nicolai
diarrhodon abbatis
diatragacant frigidus
diatrion santalorum
liberans
nephriticus

PULV CHYMICI
cremor tartari
cristalli tartari
flores sulphur
lapis prunellae
magist corallorum
margaritarum
oculi cancri
mercurius praecip. rubeus
tartarus vitriolatum

PULV.PURGANTES
diasennae montagnanae
diaturbith c.rhabarbero
hierae simplicis Galeni

ROB
acaciae
berberorum
ribesiorum

SALES
absinthii
cardui benedicti
fabarum

SYRUPI
absinthi compositus
aceti
acetosae
agrestae
altheae fernel
betonicae
boraginis
botrios
byzantinus
capillorum veneris
cardui benedicti
cichorei simplex
cochleariae
cydoneorum
diacnicui
diacodium
fumariae
glycyrrhizae
granatorum
hyssopi
jujubinus
limonum
menthae
myrtinus
papaveris
papaveris erratici
portulacae
quinque radicum
rosarum siccartarum
rosarum solutivus
rosarum sol.c.sena
scabiosae
staechidis
symphyti fernelii
violarum compositus
simplex

TABELLAE
sacchar. altheae
sacchar. perlatum

TROCHISCI
agaricus
albi rhasis(Sief alb)
alhandal
alkekengi
bechici
capparum
cypheos
hedychroy ad theriac
myrrhae
rhabarberi
scillitici ad theriacam
terrae sigillatae
viperini

UNGUENTA
adstringens
aegyptiacum
agrippae
album camphoratum
altheae compositum
altheae simplex
apostolorum
arthanitae
aureum
basilicum
calcis
diapompholygos
enulatum c.mercurio
martiatum
nervinum
nutritum
oculare
pectorale
pomatum
populeum
refrigerans
rosaceum

Number of compound medicines: 361

Specification:

Aceta et aquae	59
Syrups and robs	50
Conserva	44
Electuaria	10
Antidota et opiata	8
Powders	28
Trochisci	13
Pills	14
Oils	73
Ointments	22
Plasters	18
Medicinal preparations	22

APPENDIX III

GLOSSARY OF SOME DRUGS AND THERAPEUTIC INDICATIONS[1]

Ammoniacum gum	Antispasmodic, heartburn
Annatto	Yellow colorant obtained from the plant Bixa orleana Inflammation, colic
Aqua alexipharmaca	Diaphoretic, spasmolytic
Aqua antiepileptica	Sudden convulsive disorders
Aqua antinephritica	Urinary calculi, local irritation
Aqua antiparalytica	Coryza, odontalgia, headache
Aqua chelidonii majoris	Sedative, irritable colon
Aqua cinnamomi	Analeptic, carminative
Aqua hysterica	Dysmenorrhea
Aqua styptica	Haemostatic, astringent
Atropine	Active principle of belladonna, jimsonweed a.o.; Antispasmodic, narcotic
Balsamum locatelli	Analgesic ointment; gout, backache, arthritis
Balsamum sulphuris anisatus	Diuretic, sudorific, urolithiasis
Bolus armena	Astringent, adsorbtive
Butyrum antimonii	Caustic, used on difficult to reach skinsites
Campeche wood	Wood of Haematoxylon campechianum Colorant, astringent
Camphora	Tonic, diuretic, cardiac stimulant
Cantharides	Brings about blisters; internal aphrodisiacum
Caranna	Resinous gum obtained from Protium species
Cascarilla	The bark of Croton eluteria. Febrifuge
Cassava	The rootstock of plants of Manihot spp., produces the staple food manioc

1 De Farvaques, R. and J. Schröder, *Medicine Pharmaceutica of Groote Schatkamer der Drogbereidende Geneeskonst.* Isaak Severinus (Leiden 1741). See also *Pharmacopaea Amstelredamensis of d'Amsterdammer Apotheek.* Jan den Hoorn (Amsterdam 1768); Sieur de Saint Hilaire, *Les rémèdes des maladies du corps humain.* Barthelemy Girin (Paris 1702) 613; Estes, J. Worth. *Dictionary of Protopharmacology. Therapeutic Practices 1700-1850.* Canton: Science History Publications, 1990.

Cinchona	Peruvian bark of Cinchona succirubra Febrifuge, malaria
Cochineal	Colorant of the dried body of an insect Anodyne and antispasmodic
Coloquinte	Fruits of Citrullus colocynthis. Tropical Africa, Arabia. Violent cathartic
Confectio alkermes	Analeptic, astringent, stops bleading; haemorrhoids
Confectio Hamech	Purgative; skin disorders, scabies, worms
Confectio hyacinthorum	Excitans, vomitif; intestinal hypermotility
Copaiba	Resin of Copaifera spp.. South America. Diuretic, anti-gonorrhoea
Cornu cervi pp.	Absorbs toxic products: flux, dysentery, worms
Cremor tartari	Mild laxative and diuretic, used in dropsy
Crocus sativus	Sedative, used in syncope, apoplexia
Diascordium Fracastorii	Heartburn, colitis
Divi divi	The pods of Caesalpinia coriaria. Curaçao. Adstringent, diarrhoea, aphthae
Electuarium diaphoenicum	Purgative; gastric hyperactivity and flatulence
Electuarium diaprunum	Biliary dyskinesia, cirrhosis
Electuarium hierapicra	Cathartic, choleretic, anthelmintic
Electuarium benedictum	Oral and in clysma as a laxative; gout, rheuma, flatulence
Electuarium diacatholicum	Purgative
Elemi	Fragrant oleoresin of Burseraceae trees, used in ointments and plasters
Emplastrum defensivum	Maturatif and desiccatif plaster; superficial wounds
Emplastrum diachylum c.gummi	Mild adstringent; ulcera, pustules, furuncles
Emplastrum diapalmae	Healing swears and wounds, promotes skingrafting
Emplastrum ad fracturas.	Healing broken bones
Emplastrum gratia Dei	Paronychial infections, callus on hands or feet
Emplastrum labdanum	Stomach plaster
Emplastrum mucilaginis	Tissue necrosis, softening hard ulcers
Emplastrum oxycroci	Promotes healing of broken legs
Emplastrum ranarum c.mercuri	Joint disease, pain, swelling, venereal ulcers
Emplastrum stichticum	Splinter ointment, neglected swears
Euphorbium	Drastic, vomitif, external tumours
Fenugreek	Powdered seed of Trigonella foenum graecum Cataplasma
Gum arabic	Gum of Acacia Senegal. Tropical Africa. Styptic, phthisis, cough
Indigo	Blue dye-stuff, Indigofera tinctoria. Bronchitis, nervous disorders
Ipecac	Roots of Psychotria ipecacuanha. S. America. Amoebic dysenteria, emetic
Jaborandi	Leafs of Pilocarpus jaborandi. Brazil. Eye affections, madness
Jalap	Roots of Ipomoea purga. Mexico, Vera Cruz. Purgative, cathartic
Lapis hematitis	Haemostatic

Laudanum opiatum	Narcotic, diaphoretic, sedative; colic, diarrhea, coughs
Logwood	Dye-wood of Haematoxylon campechianum See campechewood
Mel rosarum	Inflammatory conditions of mouth and throat; sprue
Mercurius dulcis	Purgative, sudorific; in 'curing syphilis'
Mercurius pp.rubrum	Emetic, diaphoretic; smallpox, lice-powder
Mercurius sublimatus	External: escharotic-caustic action; oral in syphilis (cave ptyalism)
Mithridatium	Same indications as theriacum, but preferred to whoman
Musk	Secretic matter of musk animal. Asia. Spasmolytic, febrifuge
Oleum absinthi	Worm infections
Oleum anisi	Aromatic carminative, expectorant
Oleum bacca juniperi	Stimulant, diaphoretic, diuretic, anticonvulsive
Oleum ligni rhodii	Analgesic, antirheumatic
Oleum terebinthinae	Diuretic, urinary calculi, phthisis, tinnitus, podagra, rheuma liniment
Oleum vitrioli	Febrifuge, cholelithiasis
Oxymel scillae	Purging, vomiting and sweat inducing; dropsy
Peruvian bark	See cinchona
Philonium	Contains hyoscyamine and opium; sedative, analgesic, febrifuge
Pilulae aloephanginae	Cathartic, intestinal disorders
Pilulae cochiae	Headache, colic, flatulence
Pilulae maioranae	Gout, colic, gastric pain, amenorrhoea
Pilulae pestilentialis communis	Infectious diseases, drastic
Pimento	The dried berries of Pimenta officinalis Stimulant, carminative
Pyrethrum	Roots of Chrysanthemum cinerariaefolium Tooth and headache
Pulvis diamargariton	Tonic, carminative
Quassia	Wood of the tree Quassia amara. Guyana, Jamaica Amarum, febrifuge
Quebracho	Bark of Aspidosperma quebracho. Argentina Amarum, antispasmodic
Radix hermodactylorum	Gout, rheuma
Requies Nicolai	Hyoscyamine and opium containing sedative, narcotic, analgesic
Sal armoniacum	Expectorant, carminative
Sal volatilae cornu cervi	Excitant; headache, swoon, stupor
Sanguis draconis	Astringens, haemostatic
Sarcocollum	Pulmonairy disease, cough
Scammonium	Drastic, emetic
Spiritus cochleariae	Carminative, antiscorbutic
Syrupus acetosa	Febrile states
Syrupus papaveris erratis	Whooping cough, fever, gastroenteritis
Syrupus rosarum	Cholagoge, laxative
Syrupus scolopendri	Liver disease, malignant growth
Syrupus violarum	Stomatitis, measles, smallpox

Tacúla	Redwood of Pterocarpus tinctorius Dye-stuff, astringent, headache
Tartras emeticus	Emetic, febrile illness, worminfections
Tartras vitriolatum	Nephrolithiasis, fevers, hydrops
Theriacum	Sudorific, antiphlogistic, antidiarrheal, dysentery, rheuma
Tinctura bezoardi	Stimulant, carminative; cachexy
Turbithum minerale	Purgative
Unguentum aegyptiacum	Skin infections, necrotic tissue, gangrene, bloody gingivae
Unguentum album camphoratum	All kinds of inflammations, burns, scabies, furuncles
Unguentum altheae	Pulmonary disorders, neuralgia
Unguentum opodeldoch	Posttraumatic neuralgia, bruise, rheuma, gout
Unguentum nervinum	Nervous disorders
Unguentum populeum	Headache, bruises, burns, haemorrhoids, sleep inducing
Unguentum rosaceum	Exanthems, erythema, mouth lesions
Unguentum ad scabiem	Scabies, scratch dermatitis

APPENDIX IV

GLOSSARY OF SOME MEDICAL TERMS

Alexipharmic	An antidote against poison or infection
Anthelmintic	Product whose action expels or destroys intestinal worms
Anti-inflammatory	Counteracting inflammation
Antispamodic	Relieves spasm
Arthritis	Inflammation of a joint
Astringent	Produce contraction of the tissues
Bilharzia	Parasitic worm infection in portal vein and lymph spaces (Schistosoma)
Bos-yaws (Forest yaws)	Leishmaniasis caused by protozoon transmitted from man to man by sand-flies.
Carminative	Relieves flatulence
Cataplasma	Poultice
Cathartic	Drastic purgative
Colitis	Inflammation of the colon (large intestine)
Diaphoretic	Increase perspiration.
Diuretic	Increase volume of urine secreted.
Dry bellyache	Painful condition due to lead poisoning
Dyspepsia	Indigestion
Dyspnoea	Difficult respiration
Electuary	Medicated sweet paste administered by smearing on the tongue.
Emetic	Agent which causes vomiting.
Emmenagogic	Promotes menstruation
Emollient	For softening or soothing the skin
Emplastrum	Plaster
Endotoxines	An intracellulair toxin.
Expectorant	Stimulates expectoration.
Febrifuge	Reduces hight temperatures of feverish conditions.
Filariasis	Infection with parasitic thread-like worm (elephantiasis).
Flux	Excessive discharge from the bowels.
Framboesia	Tropical disease resembling syphilis; see yaws.
Haemostasis	Prevention of haemorrhage (flow of blood).
Leprosy	Disease of low infectivity caused by Mycobacteriae

Lithiasis	Formation of stones
Narcotic	Produces sleep or general anaesthesia
Purgative	Produces evacuation of the bowels
Rubefacient	Mild irritant drug producing redness of the skin
Saccharomyces	A group of fungi including yeasts
Scurvy	Syndrome of extreme vitamin C deficiency
Soporific	Agent causing sleep
Spasmolytic	Relieves spasm
Stomachic	Improves digestion and appetite
Sudorific	Agent causing perspiration
Trachoma	Conjunctivitis which untreated results in blindness
Unguent	Ointment or salve
Vermifuge	Expulses intestinal worms
Yaws	Framboesia, tropical disease which resembles syphilis caused by Treponema pertenue

1 De Farvacques, R. and J. Schröder. *Medicine Pharmaceutica of Groote Schatkamer der Drogbereidende Geneeskonst.* Isaak Severinus (Leiden 1741). See also *Pharmacopaea Amstelredamensis of d'Amsterdammer Apotheek.* Jan den Hoorn, (Amsterdam 1768); Sieur de Saint Hilaire, *Les rémèdes des maladies du corps humain.* Barthelemy Girin (Paris 1702) 613; Riley, P.A. and Cunningham, P.J. *The Faber Pocket Medical Dictionary.* London: Faber and Faber, 1988.

APPENDIX V

A RANDOM SEARCH ON PLANT DRUGS SHIPPED IN THE EIGHTEENTH CENTURY TO CURAÇAO

The purpose of this list is to gain insight into both the basic core and the total number of herbals sent in 15 years to Curaçao in the 18th century. A number of 770 plants formed the baseline of the pharmacopoeial materia medica. Of these vegetable drugs 124 items made a really significant impact on Curaçaoan professional practice at the time. Only 11 of these drugs: Virginia snakeroot, copaiba, cinchona, gum anime, caranna, elemi, tacamahaca, contrayerva, ipecac, jalap and sarsaparilla can be considered to be major contributions of New World materia medica. Most important items encountered in the years covered in the list are aloe, saffron, senna, jalap, liquorice root and rhubarb (more than 90%). Individual herbals commonly prescribed at the time were camomile, camphor, meliloti, myrrh, anise and liquorice extract (70-80%). Copaiba, asa foetida, benzoin, cinnamon, lavender, rose, nutmeg, laurel, elemi, wormwood, rue, sage, manna, mastiche, frankincense, opium, marshmallow, snakeroot, contrayerva, ipecac, orris root, zedoaria, cumin and fennel represented 40-60%. Sarsaparilla was only once ordered (1775) and sassafras, guaiac and senega are absent. These four drugs, however, were most commonly prescribed at the time. They were always stocked for export in Curaçao and easy of access. Of the plants listed here about 20 items are still of importance in modern medicine

SIMPLES															
Source	1	2	3	4	5	6	7	8	9	10	11	12	13	14	15
Year	1700	01	07	09	11	15	17	22	25	35	44	51	65	75	77
Aloe	☐	☐	☐	☐		☐	☐	☐	☐	☐	☐	☐	☐	☐	☐
Asa foetida		☐	☐		☐					☐				☐	☐
Balsam.copaivae		☐	☐			☐	☐	☐		☐			☐	☐	
Bdellium			☐												
Benzoinum gum			☐	☐	☐	☐	☐	☐							
Camphora		☐	☐	☐	☐	☐	☐	☐		☐	☐	☐	☐	☐	☐
Cortex chinae peruvian.											☐				
Cortex cinnamomi			☐		☐			☐		☐	☐	☐	☐	☐	☐
Flores chamomillae romanae			☐	☐	☐	☐	☐								☐
Flores chamomillae vulgaris	☐	☐	☐	☐	☐	☐	☐	☐		☐	☐	☐			☐
Flores croci	☐	☐	☐	☐	☐	☐	☐	☐		☐	☐	☐	☐	☐	☐
Flores lavandulae	☐		☐			☐		☐		☐		☐		☐	☐
Flores meliloti	☐	☐	☐	☐	☐	☐		☐		☐		☐		☐	☐
Flores melissae															☐
Flores papaveris erratis								☐							☐
Flores rosarum rubrum	☐		☐		☐	☐		☐						☐	☐
Flores sambuci			☐		☐	☐				☐				☐	
Folia altheae			☐												☐
Folia artemisiae			☐												
Folia lauri											☐				
Folia sennae	☐		☐	☐	☐	☐	☐	☐	☐	☐	☐	☐	☐	☐	☐
Fructus baccae juniperi			☐	☐		☐	☐	☐		☐					
Fructus baccae lauri			☐	☐		☐	☐			☐	☐	☐			
Fructus caryophylli			☐		☐	☐		☐		☐				☐	
Fructus colocynthidis			☐		☐							☐			
Fructus gallae						☐									
Fructus grana kermes			☐												
Fructus myrobalani chebulae			☐		☐										
Fructus myrobalani citrini			☐		☐							☐			
Fructus nux moschata			☐		☐	☐		☐		☐	☐		☐	☐	☐
Fructus piperis albae			☐			☐				☐					
Fructus prunae sylvestris			☐												
Fungus agaricus			☐										☐	☐	
Fungus orbicularis			☐	☐	☐										
Galbanum			☐		☐						☐				
Grana Paradisi												☐		☐	
Gum ammoniacum	☐		☐							☐		☐			
Gum anime	☐		☐												
Gum arabicum			☐												
Gum caranna			☐												
Gum elemi	☐		☐		☐	☐						☐	☐		☐
Gum gamba			☐		☐	☐		☐		☐				☐	☐
Gum tacamahaca			☐												
Herba absinthii vulgaris	☐	☐	☐	☐	☐	☐	☐						☐		

SIMPLES

Source	1	2	3	4	5	6	7	8	9	10	11	12	13	14	15
Year	1700	01	07	09	11	15	17	22	25	35	44	51	65	75	77
Herba alchemillae			□												
Herba cardui benedicti					□										
Herba centauri minor		□			□										□
Herba hyssopi						□					□	□			
Herba maioranae			□											□	
Herba malvae														□	
Herba melissae			□											□	□
Herba menthae crispae			□												
Herba origani vulgaris											□				
Herba phellandri								□							
Herba rorismarini			□			□				□	□	□		□	□
Herba rutae						□		□						□	□
Herba sabinae			□			□	□			□		□			
Herba salviae			□			□	□			□	□	□		□	□
Herba saniculae			□												
Herba scordii					□	□	□	□		□			□		□
Lignum nephriticum			□												
Lignum rhodium			□		□										
Lignum santalinum album			□		□										
Lignum santalinum rubrum			□		□										
Manna	□		□	□	□	□		□		□	□			□	□
Mastiche	□		□	□	□	□	□	□				□		□	□
Myrrha		□	□	□	□	□	□	□		□			□	□	□
Olibanum	□		□	□	□	□	□	□						□	□
Opium		□	□	□	□					□		□		□	
Opoponax			□												
Radix altheae					□	□		□		□			□	□	
Radix angelicae	□		□	□	□	□		□		□	□	□			□
Radix bardanae			□				□	□							
Radix bryoniae								□							
Radix calami	□		□				□			□					
Radix chinae smilax	□	□	□	□	□			□		□	□				
Radix cichorae	□														
Radix consolidae	□		□								□			□	
Radix contrayervae			□		□					□	□	□		□	
Radix enulae					□			□		□					
Radix galangae					□					□					
Radix gentianae					□					□		□		□	□
Radix heleni			□	□											
Radix helleboris albae			□					□							
Radix ipecacuanhae								□		□	□		□	□	□
Radix iridis florentinae	□		□	□	□	□	□	□		□	□				
Radix jalappae	□		□	□	□	□	□	□	□	□	□	□	□	□	□
Radix liquiritiae		□	□	□	□	□	□	□	□	□	□	□	□	□	□

SIMPLES															
Source	1	2	3	4	5	6	7	8	9	10	11	12	13	14	15
Year	1700	01	07	09	11	15	17	22	25	35	44	51	65	75	77
Radix polypodii			□												
Radix pyrethri	□		□			□									
Radix rhabarberi	□	□	□	□	□	□	□	□	□	□	□	□	□	□	□
Radix rubiae	□		□							□					
Radix sarsaparillae														□	
Radix scorzonerae			□												
Radix serpentariae virgin.			□					□		□		□			□
Radix tormentillae	□		□		□			□		□					
Radix zedoariae	□		□	□	□			□		□		□			□
Resina jalappae				□		□		□		□	□	□	□	□	□
Resina pini			□							□	□				
Sanguis draconis			□					□							□
Ssammonium	□		□			□	□	□				□			□
Semen amomi												□		□	
Semen anisi	□	□	□	□	□	□	□	□		□	□	□		□	
Semen bardanae								□							
Semen cardamomi minor	□		□											□	
Semen carvi	□		□		□	□		□							
Semen coriandri			□								□				
Semen cubebae			□												
Semen cumini			□	□	□	□	□	□		□					
Semen cydoniorum						□	□	□							
Semen foeniculi			□	□	□	□	□	□	□		□			□	
Semen foenugraeci		□		□	□										
Semen lini		□	□	□	□										
Semen papaveris albi	□	□	□	□	□	□					□				
Semen sambuci			□												
Semen santonici	□														
Semen zedoariae	□			□	□	□	□	□		□				□	
Styrax calamita			□					□							
Succinum album	□		□	□				□							□
Succinum citrinum			□		□										
Succus liquiritiae	□	□			□	□	□	□	□	□	□	□	□	□	□
Terebinthina veneta			□	□	□	□									
Terebinthina vulgaris			□	□	□	□		□				□			
Tragacantha	□		□	□	□										

Notes

1 WIC 566 (1700) 25.
2 WIC 566 (1701) 442.
3 WIC 569 (1707) 295.
4 WIC 570 (1709) 198.
5 WIC 570 (1711) 624.
6 WIC 572 (1715) 255.
7 WIC 573 (1717) 131.
8 WIC 576 (1722) 421.
9 WIC 576 (1725) 415.
10 WIC 1155 (1735) 165.
11 WIC 591 (1744) 287.
12 WIC 598 (1751) 298.
13 WIC 604 (1765) 1373.
14 WIC 610 (1775) 117.
15 WIC 211/12 (1777) 508.

List of medicines and instruments. Guide of the Amsterdam Admiralty (1692) for the equipment of the surgeon chests including the quantaties and assortment of drugs that ships should carry in a journey of 6 months wit a crew of 100-500 heads.

L Y S T E
D E R
M E D I C A M E N T E N,
E N
I N S T R U M E N T E N,

Die de Chirurgijns ten dienſte van den Lande, op de Schepen van Oorlog, ſorteerende onder het Ed. Mog. Collegie ter Admiraliteyt tot Amſterdam, gehouden zijn mede te voeren voor een togt van ſes maenden, met

	Koppen. 100.	200.	300.	400.	500.
Emplaſtra.					
Diapalmæ - -	℔ iv	℔ vj	℔ viij	℔ ix	℔ x
Diachyli cum Gumm.	℔ j ß	℔ ij	℔ ij ß	℔ iij	℔ iij ß
Mucilagin. - -	℔ j ß	℔ ij	℔ ij ß	℔ iij	℔ iij ß
Baſilici - -	℔ j ß	℔ ij	℔ ij ß	℔ iij	℔ iij ß
Ranar. cum Mercur. 4.	℔ j	℔ j ß	℔ ij	℔ ij ß	℔ iij
Oxycrocei - -	℔ j	℔ j ß	℔ ij	℔ ij ß	℔ iij
Ladani - -	℔ ij	℔ iij	℔ iij ß	℔ iv	℔ iv ß
Defenſiv. Vigonis -	℔ ij	℔ iij	℔ iv	℔ v	℔ vj
Unguenta.					
Digeſtivi - -	℔ iij	℔ iv	℔ v	℔ vj	℔ vij
Ægyptiaci -	℔ j ß	℔ ij	℔ ij ß	℔ iij	℔ iij ß
Baſilici - -	℔ ij	℔ iij	℔ iv	℔ v	℔ vj
Albi caphurat -	℔ j	℔ j ß	℔ ij	℔ ij ß	℔ iij
Populei - -	℔ j	℔ j ß	℔ ij	℔ ij ß	℔ iij
Diapompholygos -	℔ j	℔ j ß	℔ ij	℔ ij ß	℔ iij
Martiati - -	℔ j	℔ j ß	℔ ij	℔ ij ß	℔ iij
Ceræ flavæ - -	℔ j	℔ j ß	℔ ij	℔ ij ß	℔ iij
Axungiæ porci -	℔ j ß	℔ ij	℔ ij ß	℔ iij	℔ iij ß
Olea.					
Ol. Chamæmelini -	℔ ſ	℔ j ß	℔ ij	℔ ij ß	℔ iij
Laurini - -	℔ j	℔ j ß	℔ ij	℔ ij ß	℔ iij
Therebenthin. -	℔ j	℔ j ß	℔ ij	℔ ij ß	℔ iij
Aniſi - -	℥ j	℥ j ß	℥ ij	℥ ij ß	℥ iij
Lini - -	℔ j	℔ ij	℔ iij	℔ iv	℔ v
Juniperi - -	℥ j	℥ ij	℥ iij	℥ iv	℥ v
Opiata.					
Laudani opiati -	℥ j	℥ j ß	℥ ij	℥ ij ß	℥ iij
Diaſcord. Frac. complet.	℔ j	℔ j ß	℔ ij	℔ ij ß	℔ iij
incomplet. ſine Gent. & Galb. - -	℔ j	℔ j ß	℔ ij	℔ ij ß	℔ iij
Philonii Roman. -	℔ ß	℥ x	℔ j	℥ xx	℔ j ß
Mell. Roſar. - -	℔ j	℔ ij	℔ iij	℔ iv	℔ v
Commun. -	℔ ij	℔ iij	℔ iv	℔ v	℔ vj
Conſerv. Roſar. Rubrar.	℔ j	℔ j ß	℔ ij	℔ ij ß	℔ iij
Aquæ.					
Card. Bened. - -	P. ij	P. iij	P. iv	P. iv ß	P. v
Roſar. - - -	P. j ß	P. ij	P. ij ß	P. iij	P. iij ß
Alexipharmac. -	P. ß	℥ xx	P. j	℥ xxv	P. j ß
Cinamomi - -	P. ß	P. j	P. j ß	P. ij	P. ij ß
Fæniculi - -	P. j	P. j ß	P. ij	P. ij ß	P. iij
Stypticæ - -	P. ß	P. j	P. j ß	P. ij	P. ij ß
Mercurialis - -	P. ß	P. j	P. j ß	P. ij	P. ij ß

	Koppen. 100.	200.	300.	400.	500.
Pilulæ, Trochiſc. & pulv. ppt.					
Pil. Extract. Cathol. -	℥ ij	℥ iij	℥ iv	℥ v	℥ vj
Ruffi - -	℥ ij	℥ ij ß	℥ iij	℥ iij ß	℥ iv
Reſin. Jalapp. -	℥ j	℥ j ß	℥ ij	℥ ij ß	℥ iij
Diagrid. - - -	℥ j	℥ j ß	℥ ij	℥ ij ß	℥ iij
Trochiſc. alb. rhaz. -	℥ ij	℥ ij ß	℥ iij	℥ iij ß	℥ iv
Tutiæ ppt. - -	℥ ij	℥ ij ß	℥ iij	℥ iij ß	℥ iv
Ocul. cancr. crud. ppt.	℥ iv	℥ v	℥ vj	℥ vij	℥ viij
Cantharid. - -	℥ j	℥ j ß	℥ ij	℥ ij ß	℥ iij
Chymica.					
Sal. Card. bened. -	℥ ij	℥ iij	℥ iv	℥ v	℥ vj
Cremor. tartar. - -	℥ iv	℥ vj	℥ viij	℥ x	℥ xij
Tartar. vitriol. - -	℥ j	℥ ij	℥ iij	℥ iv	℥ v
Flor. ſulph. - -	℥ iv	℥ vj	℥ viij	℥ x	℥ xij
Merc. dulc. - -	℥ j ß	℥ ij	℥ ij ß	℥ iij	℥ iij ß
Præcip. rubr. -	℥ iij	℥ iv	℥ v	℥ vj	℥ vij
Sublimat. - -	℥ ß	ʒ vj	℥ j	ʒ x	℥ j ß
Ruptor. - -	℥ j	℥ ij	℥ iij	℥ iv	℥ v
Vitri antimonii - -	℥ ß	ʒ vj	℥ j	ʒ x	℥ j ß
Alumin. uſti - -	℥ iv	℥ vj	℔ ß	℥ x	℥ xij
Lap. prunell. - -	℥ x	℔ j	℥ xx	℔ j ß	℔ ij
Capit. mort. vitriol. -	℔ j	℔ j ß	℔ ij	℔ ij ß	℔ iij
Croci Mart. reſtring. -	℥ iv	℥ vj	℔ ß	℥ x	℥ xij
Sacchari Saturni -	℥ j	℥ j ß	℥ ij	℥ ij ß	℥ iij
Sp. cochlear. - -	P. ß	P. j	P. j ß	P. ij	P. ij ß
ſal. armoniac. - -	℥ ij	℥ iv	℥ vj	℥ viij	℥ x
vitriol. - -	℥ ij	℥ iij	℥ iv	℥ v	℥ vj
Elix. propriet. ſine acid.	℥ iv	℥ vj	℥ viij	℥ x	℥ xij
Antimon. diaphoret.	℥ j	℥ ij	℥ iij	℥ iv	℥ v
Pulver. reſtring. -	℔ j	℔ ij	℔ iij	℔ iv	℔ v
Succi condenſati, gummi & Reſinæ.					
Guttæ Gambæ - -	℥ j	℥ j ß	℥ ij	℥ ij ß	℥ iij
Euphorbii - -	℥ ß	℥ j	℥ j ß	℥ ij	℥ ij ß
Aloes - - -	℥ ij	℥ iij	℥ iv	℥ v	℥ vj
G. Ammoniac - -	℥ iv	℥ vj	℥ viij	℥ x	℥ xij
G. Galban. - -	℥ iv	℥ vj	℥ viij	℥ x	℥ xij
Caphuræ - - -	℥ ij	℥ iij	℥ iv	℥ v	℥ vj
Maſtiches - -	℥ j	℥ j ß	℥ ij	℥ ij ß	℥ iij
Myrrhæ - -	℥ j	℥ ij	℥ iij	℥ iv	℥ v
Sang. dracon. -	℥ j	℥ ij	℥ iij	℥ iv	℥ v
Succ. glycyrrh. - -	℔ j	℔ j ß	℔ ij	℔ ij ß	℔ iij
Therebinth. Simpl. -	℔ j	℔ j ß	℔ ij	℔ ij ß	℔ iij
Venet. -	℔ ß	℥ xij	℔ j	℥ xx	℔ j ß
Mineralia & Marina.					
Argenti vivi -	℔ ß	℥ xij	℔ j	℥ xx	℔ j ß
Alumin. crudi . -	℔ ß	℥ xij	℔ j	℥ xx	℔ j ß
Boli Armen. - -	℔ j	℔ j ß	℔ ij	℔ ij ß	℔ iij
Ceruſſæ - - -	℔ ß	℥ xij	℔ j	℥ xx	℔ j ß

	Koppen. 100.	200.	300.	400.	500.
Lithargyr. aurei -	℔ j	℔ j ß	℔ ij	℔ ij ß	℔ iij
Vitrioli albi -	℥ iv	℥ vj	℔ ß	℥ x	℥ xij
Romani -	℥ iv	℥ vj	℔ ß	℥ x	℥ xij
Cyprii -	℥ ij	℥ iij	℥ iv	℥ vj	℔ ß
Rad. Cort. & Ligna.					
Glycyrrhizæ - -	℔ j	℔ j ß	℔ ij	℔ ij ß	℔ iij
Iridis Florentin. - -	℥ iv	℥ vj	℔ ß	℥ x	℥ xij
Bardan. - -	℔ j	℔ j ß	℔ ij	℔ ij ß	℔ iij
Tormentill. - -	℔ ß	℥ xij	℔ j	℥ xx	℔ j ß
Rhabarbar. - -	℔ ß	℥ xij	℔ j	℥ xx	℔ j ß
Jalapp. - - -	℔ ß	℥ xij	℔ j	℥ xx	℔ j ß
Cortic. granator. -	℥ iv	℥ vj	℥ viij	℥ x	℥ xij
cinamom. -	℥ ij	℥ iij	℥ iv	℥ v	℥ vj
Raſur. lign. Guajac.	℔ iv	℔ vj	℔ viij	℔ x	℔ xij
Herbæ.					
Fol. Sennæ - -	℔ ß	℥ xij	℔ j	℥ xx	℔ j ß
Herb. abſynth. vulg.	℔ j ß	℔ ij	℔ iij	℔ iv	℔ v
ſcordii - -	℔ j ß	℔ ij	℔ iij	℔ iv	℔ v
phylandrii -	℔ j ß	℔ ij	℔ iij	℔ iv	℔ v
rutæ - -	℔ j ß	℔ ij	℔ iij	℔ iv	℔ v
card. bened. -	℔ j	℔ ij	℔ iij	℔ iv	℔ v
biſmalvæ -	℔ j	℔ j ß	℔ ij	℔ ij ß	℔ iij
Orbicularis ſeu boviſt.	℥ xij	℔ j	℔ j ß	℔ ij	℔ ij ß
Flores.					
Roſar. rubrar. - -	℔ ß	℥ xij	℔ j	℥ xx	℔ j ß
Chamæmel. - -	℔ j	℔ j ß	℔ ij	℔ ij ß	℔ iij
Melilot. - -	℔ ß	℔ j	℔ j ß	℔ ij	℔ ij ß
Sambuc. - -	℔ j	℔ j ß	℔ ij	℔ ij ß	℔ iij
Croci - -	℥ j	℥ j ß	℥ ij	℥ ij ß	℥ iij
Semin. & Fructus.					
Sem. fænic. - -	℥ iv	℥ vj	℔ ß	℥ x	℥ xij
Capitum Papav. alb. -	No. 30	35	40	45	50
Tamarind. - -	℔ j ß	℔ ij	℔ ij ß	℔ iij	℔ iij ß
Inſtrumenten.					
Een Saeg met 2 bladen, &c.					
Een krom Mes en Separator.					
Een Trepaan met ſijn toebehooren.					
Een Catheter.					
Twee Sny-Tangen.					
Twee Koegel Tangen, een krumme, en een rechte.					
Twee Ravebekken.					
Een Pellikaen.					
Vier Cauteria van verſcheyde ſoorten.					
Twee clyſteer Pypen.					
Blaaſen. - - - -	12	15	20	25	30
Spongien. - - - -	1	2	3	4	5
Twee tinne Spuyten.					
Verſcheyde Spalken, &c.					
Een kopere Vyſel.					
Een Schaeltje met ſijn gewigt.					
Een kopere Pannetje.					

Aldus gearreſteert by de Ed. M. Heeren Raaden ter Admiraliteyt, reſideerende tot Amſterdam, den 1 April 1692.

Ik ondergeſchreven Mr. Opper-Chirurgijn op 't Schip onder de Hr. Capiteyn voerende Koppen, bekenne naer voorgaende viſitatie van de Medicijn Kiſte, deſelve bevonden te hebben van alles, in de bovenſtaende Lyſte vermelt, behoorlijk en na mijn genoegen voorſien: waer op de Kiſt in mijn tegenwoordigheyt is geſlooten, en de ſleutel my ter handt geſtelt.

Tot Amſterdam, By AART DIRKSZ. OOSSAAN, Ordinaris Drukker van 't Ed. Mog. Collegie ter Admiraliteyt.

BIBLIOGRAPHY

ABBREVIATIONS

WIC	Tweede West-Indische Compagnie (Second Dutch West India Company) National Archives, 's Gravenhage (ARA)
OAC	Oud Archief Curaçao (Old Archive of Curaçao) ARA
VOC	East India Company, ARA
SB	Societeit van Berbice, ARA
NAA	Notarieel Archief, Stadsarchief Amsterdam
Ph A	*Pharmacopaea Amstelredamensis* 1686

PRINTED MATERIALS

Anon, *De Curaçaosc Courant*, Willemstad:Drukkerij de Weduwe William Lee, 1820, 1828.

Archivo General de Indias, *Legajo 3249 f.31-32, libros de armada, Agosto de 1495*. Sevilla: Casa de Contratación.

Bajon, Bertrand, 'Mémoires sur le pian (framboesia)'. *Archives Académie Royale de Chirurgie*, 1774.

Bankroft, E.van. *Beschrijving van Guiana en een bericht van de rivieren en plantagien in Berbice, Essequebo en Demerary*. Amsterdam: Roos, 1794.

Basilius Valentinus. *The Triumphal Chariot of Antimony*. London: Vincent Stuart Publishers, 1962.

Bauer, C. 'Conrad Peutingers Gutachten zur Monopolfrage'. *Archiv für Reformationsgeschichte*, vol. 45 (1954).

Bénézet, J.P. 'Pharmacie et découverte de l'Amérique'. *Revue d'Histoire de la Pharmacie*, vol. 85 (1997).

Benjamin, M. 'Medicine, mortality and the politics of Berkeley's tar water'. In: Andrew Cunningham and Roger French, *The Medical Enlightenment of the eighteenth century*. Cambridge: Cambridge University Press, 1990.

Benjamins, H.D. and J.F. Snelleman, ed. *Encyclopaedie van Nederlandsch West-Indië*. Amsterdam: Emmering, 1981.

Bloom, H.I. *The Economic Activities of the Jews of Amsterdam in the 17th and 18th Centuries*. Washington NY, 1937.

Bosman, Willem. *A New and Accurate Description of the Coast of Guinea*. London: Frank Cass & Co., 1967.

Bosman, L. *Nieuw Amsterdam in Berbice*. Hilversum: Verloren, 1994.

Broeders, A.N. *Handleiding tot het gebruik van inheemse en ingevoerde planten op Aruba, Bonaire en Curaçao*. Willemstad: Augustinus, 1967.

Brun, Samuel. *Schiffarten, Welche er in etliche newe laender und insulen zu fünff unterschiedlichen malen mit Gottes hülff gethan etc.* Basel: Genaths, 1624.

Buchan, W. *Huislyke geneeskunde of verhandeling over de verhoeding en genezing van ziekten etc.* 2 vols. Haarlem: Tetmans, 1791.

Butterfield, H. *The Whig Interpretation of History*. New York: AMS Press, 1978.

Caspary, W.F. *Saccharomyces species*. Deutsche Apotheker Zeitung, vol. 134 (1994).

Catalan, R., et al. Cent cinquantenaire de l'abolition de l'esclavage – Concours de l'historien de demain – Ali Shandora, emir de Trarza et la Compagnie du Sénégal en 1723. www.fwinetwork.com/abolition/alishandora.html 1998.

Cau, C. ed. 'Ordre van Regieringe soo in Policie als Justicie in de Plaetsen verovert en te veroveren in West Indien', *Groot Placaetboeck*. Vol. 2. The Hague: Van Wouw, 1797.

Chaucer, Geoffrey. Daniel Woodward and Martin Stevens ed. *The Canterbury Tales*. San Marino CA: Huntington Library Press, 1995.

Chevalier, A. *Dictionaire des altérations et falsifications des substances alimentaires, medicamenteuses et commerciales*. Paris, 1850.

Clayton, E.G. *A Memoir of the late Dr. A.H. Hassal. The Genesis of the Adulteration Acts*. London: Bailliere, 1908.

Correia da Silva, A.C. et al. *Catálogo de Exposição de Obras Antigas e Revistas Portuguesas de Farmácia*. Lisbon: Congresso Internacional de Ciências Farmacêuticas, 1972.

Cowen, David L. 'The impact of the Materia Medica of the North American Indians on Professional Practice'. In: Wolfgang-Hagen Hein ed. *Botanical Drugs of the Americas in the Old and New Worlds*. Stuttgart:Wissenschaftliche Verlagsgesellschaft, 1984.

Cowen, David L. and William H. Helfand. *Pharmacy, An Illustrated History*. New York: Abrams Publishers, 1990.

Cowen, David L. *The Colonial and Revolutionary Heritage of Pharmacy in America*. Wisconsin: American Institute of the History of Pharmacy, 1976.

Coxe, J. Redman. *The American Dispensatory*. Philadelphia: Carey, 1827.

Craton, Michael. *Searching for the Invisible Man. Slaves and plantation life in Jamaica* London: Harvard University Press, 1978.

Craton, Michael. *Testing the chains:resistance to slavery in the British West Indies*. Ithaca: Cornell University Press, 1982.

Craton, Michael. 'Reshiffling the pack: the transformation from slavery to other forms of labor in the British Caribbean'. *Nieuwe West-Indische Gids*, vol. 68 (1994).

Crosby, A.W. *The Columbian Exchange.Biological and Cultural Consequences of 1492*. Connecticut: Greenwood Press, 1983.

Cruickshank, Brodie. *Achttien Jaren aan de Goudkust*. Amsterdam (1853) 1953.

Curtin, Philip D. *Africa Remembered*. Madison:University of Wisconsin Press, 1968.

Curtin, Philip D. *The Atlantic Slave Trade: A Census*. Madison:University of Wisconsin Press, 1969.

Curtin, Philip D. 'The White Man's Grave: Image and Reality, 1780-1830' *Journal of British Studies*, vol. 1 (1961)

Daems, W.F. and L.J. Vandewiele, *Noord- en Zuidnederlandse Stedelijke Pharmacopeeën*. Mortsel en Joppe, 1955.

Dalziel, J.M. *The Useful Plants of West Tropical Africa*. London: Crown Agents, 1936.

Dapper, Olfert. *Naukeurige Beschryvinge der Afrikaansche Gewesten*. Amsterdam: Van Meurs, 1668.

D'Arcy, P.F. and D.W.G. Harron (ed). *Tropical diseases, a therapeutic update*. Den Haag: FIP Publications, 1987.

De Farvacques, R. *Medicina pharmaceutica*. Leiden: Isaak Severinus, 1741.

De Jonge, J.K.J. *De opkomst van het Nederlands gezag in Oost-Indië*. The Hague: Nijhoff, 1862.

De Haan, J.C. and P.C. van Winter. *Nederlanders over de Zeeën*. Utrecht: De Haan, 1940.

De Knecht van Eekelen, A. 'Tropische geneeskunde in Nederland en koloniale geneeskunde in Nederlands Indië'. *Tijdschrift voor Geschiedenis*, vol. 105 (1992).

De Laet, Joannes. *Iaerlyck Verhael van de Verrichtinghen der Geoctroyeerde West-Indische Compagnie* (1644) S.P. l'Honoré Faber (ed). The Hague: Nijhoff, 1931-34.

De Marees, P. *Beschrijvinghe ende historische verhael van het Groot Koninckrijk van Gunea, 1602*. Linschoten Vereeniging. The Hague: Nijhoff, 1912.

De Oviedo, Gonzalo Fernandez. *Natural History of the West Indies*. Translated and edited by S.A. Stoudemire. Chapel Hill: University of North Carolina, 1959.

De Pina, Luis, 'A cura dos nautos Portuguesas em Goa no Século XVI'. *Boletim Geral das Colónias*, vol. 18 (1944).

De Pina, Luis, 'Notas para a medicina indígena Angolense no século XVIII'. *Boletim Geral das Colónias*, vol. 12 (1938).

De Villiers, J.A.J. *Storm van 's Gravesande, zijn werk en zijn leven*. The Hague: Nijhoff, 1920.

Den Heijer, Henk J. *De geschiedenis van de WIC*. Zutphen: De Walburg Pers, 1994.

Den Heijer, Henk J. *Goud, ivoor en slaven. Scheepvaart en handel van de Tweede Westindische Compagnie op Afrika 1674-1740*. Zutphen: De Walburg Pers, 1997.

Doerffel, Carel. 'Berichten en aanmerkingen over de in Curaçao van tyd tot tyd in zwanggaande ziekten'. *Verhandelingen uitgegeven door de Hollandsche Maatschappye der Wetenschappen*. Haarlem: J. Bosch, 1758.

Dragendorff, G. *Die Heilpflanzen der Verschiedene Völker und Zeiten*. München: Fritsch, 1967.

Emboden, William. *Narcotic Plants*. London: Studio Vista, 1972.

Emmanuel, I.S. and S.A. Emmanuel. *History of the Jews of the Netherlands Antilles*. Cincinnati: American Jewish Archives, 1970.

Emmanuel, I.S. *Precious Stones of the Jews of Curaçao. Curaçaoan Jewry 1656-1957*. New York: Bloch Publishing, 1957.

Emmer, Pieter C. *Engeland, Nederland, Afrika en de Slavenhandel in de Negentiende Eeuw*. Leiden: Brill, 1974.

Emmer, Pieter C. 'Suiker, goud en slaven; de Republiek in West Afrika en West Indië 1674-1800'. In: E. van den Boogaart (ed). *Overzee; Nederlandse Koloniale Geschiedenis, 1590-1975*. Haarlem: Van Dishoeck, 1982.

Emmer, Pieter C. 'The History of the Dutch Slave Trade; A Bibliographical Survey'. *Journal of Economic History*, vol. 32 (1972).

Emmer, Pieter C. 'The West India Company, 1621-1791', In: L. Blusse and F. Gaastra (eds), *Companies and Trade*. Leiden: University Press, 1981.

Emmer, Pieter C. *The Dutch in the Atlantic Economy 1580-1880*. Hampshire: Ashgate Publishing Ltd., 1998.

Emmer, Pieter C. and W.W. Klooster. 'The Dutch Atlantic, 1600-1800. Expansion without Empire'. *Itinerario* vol. 23 (1999).

Emmer, Pieter C. and F. Gaastra, *The Organization of Interoceanic Trade in European Expansion, 1450-1800*. Hampshire: Ashgate Publishing Ltd., 1996.

Enserink, M. 'Can Placebo be the cure?' *Science* vol. 284 (1999)

Essers, S. *Removal of cyanogens from cassava roots*. Wageningen: Landbouw Universiteit, 1995.

Estes, J. Worth, *Dictionary of Protopharmacology. Therapeutic Practices 1700-1850*. Canton: Science History Publications, 1990.

Estes, J. Worth, *Naval Surgeon. Life and Death at Sea in the Age of Sail.* Canton: Mass.: Science History Publications, 1998.

Feinberg, Harvey M. 'New Data on European Mortality in West Africa: The Dutch on the Gold Coast, 1719-1760', *Journal of African History*, vol. 15 (1973).

Fordyce, George, *A third dissertation on fever.* Part II, London 1799.

Franck, I.M. and D.M. Brownstone. *Trade and Travel Routes. From Gibraltar to the Ganges.* New York: Facts on File, 1990.

Friedländer, I. *Sittengeschichte Roms.* Stuttgart: Parkland Verlag, 1934.

Gennaro, A.R. ed. *Remington's Pharmaceutical Sciences.* Pennsylvania: Mach Publishing Co., 1990.

Githens, Th.S. *Drug plants of Africa.* Philadelphia:University of Pennsylvania Press, 1949.

Godschalck van Focquenbroch, W. *Afrikaense Thalia.* Amsterdam: Jan ten Hoorn, 1678.

Gordon, M.B., *Naval and Maritime Medicine During the American Revolution.* Ventnor: Ventnor Publications, 1978.

Goslinga, Cornelis Ch. *A Short History of the Netherlands Antilles and Surinam.* The Hague: Nijhoff, 1979.

Goslinga, Cornelis Ch. *The Dutch in the Caribbean and in the Guianas*, 1680-1791. Assen: Van Gorcum, 1985.

Gramberg, J.S.G. *Schetsen van Afrika's Westkust.* Amsterdam: Weijting & Brave, 1861.

Griebel, C. 'Über zwei Afrikanische Ersatzpfefferarten: Paradies körner und Mohrenpfeffer (Kani)' *Zeitschrift für Untersuchung der Lebensmittel*, vol. 85 (1943).

Guillemin, J.A., S. Perrottet and A. Richard. *Florae Senegambiae regionibus.* Paris: Treuttel & Würtz, 1830-1833,

Haeser, H. *Leerboek van de geschiedenis der geneeskunde.* Reprint 1859. Amsterdam: Meesters, 1980.

Hair, P.E.H., A. Jones and R. Taw ed. *Barbot on Guinea.The writings of Jean Barbot on West Africa.* 2 vols. London: Hakluyt Society, 1992.

Handler, J.S. and J.A. Jacoby. 'Slave medicine and plant use in Barbados'. *Journal of Barbados Museum and Historical Society*, vol. 41 (1993).

Harris, C.A. and J.A.J. de Villiers. *Storm van 's Gravesande. The Rise of British Guiana.* London: Hakluyt Society, 1911.

Harrison, M. *Mountain and Plain. From the Lycian Coast to the Physical Plateau in the late Roman and early Byzantine Period.* Michigan: University Press, 1999.

Hartog, J. *Geschiedenis van de Nederlandse Antillen. Dl. 3 Curaçao – Van kolonie tot autonomie.* Aruba: De Wit, 1961.

Hartog J., *De Bovenwindse Eilanden.* Aruba: De Wit, 1964.

Hartsinck, J.J. *Beschrijving van Guiana of de Wilde Kust van Zuid Amerika...*, 1770. 2 vols. Amsterdam: Emmering, 1974.

Haver Droeze, J.J. *Het Collegium Medicum Amstelaedamense 1637-1798.* Haarlem: Bohn, 1921.

Helps, A. *The Spanish Conquest in America and its Relation to the History of Slavery and to the Government of Colonies.* Vol.1. London: Parker, 1857.

Hering, J.H. *Beschrijving van het eiland Curaçao en de daaronder hoorende eilanden 1779.* Aruba: De Wit, 1969.

Hünerfeldt, P. *Korte geschiedenis der geneeskunde.* Utrecht: Spectrum, 1960.

Huntingford, G.W.B. *The Periplus of the Erythraean Sea.* London: The Hakluyt Society, 1980.

Instructie voor de schippers in den dienst van de Geoctroyeerde West-Indische Compagnie op den slaefhandel varende. (*Instruction for the Skippers in the Service of the West India Company sailing in the Slave Trade*). Middelburg: De Later, 1675.

Isert, Paul E. *Voyages en Guinée et dans l'Iles Caraibes en Amérique.* Paris: Karthala, 1989.

Israel, Jonathan I., 'The Phasis of the Dutch *Straatvaart* 1590-1713. A chapter in the Economic History of the Mediterranean'. In: Emmer, P.C. and F. Gaastra (ed.), *The Organization of Interoceanic Trade in European Expansion 1450-1800*. Hampshire: Ashgate Publishing, 1996.

Israel, Jonathan I. *Dutch Primacy in World Trade 1585-1740*. Oxford: Clarendon Press, 1989.

Israel, Jonathan I. *Empires and Entrepots. The Dutch, the Spanish Monarchy and the Jews, 1585-1713*. London: Hambledon, 1989.

Jaspersen-Schib, R. 'Phytotherapie'. *Deutsche Apotheker Zeitung*, vol.132 (1992).

Jourdan, A.J.L., *Pharmacopée universelle ou Conspectus des Pharmacopées*. Tome 2. Paris: Baillière, 1828

Kesler, C.K. 'Een Duits medicus in Essequebo in de laatste jaren der 18e eeuw'. *De West-Indische Gids*, vol.11, (1929).

Kiple, Kenneth F. *The Caribbean Slave: A Biological History*. New York: Cambridge University Press, 1984.

Klooster, W.W. *Illicit Riches. The Dutch trade in the Caribbean*. Dissertation Leiden University, *1995*.

Kolodziej, H. 'Phytoalexine – Chemische Abwehrstoffe Höhere Pflanzen'. *Deutsche Apotheker Zeitung*, vol. 129 (1989)

Kunst, A.J.M. *Recht, Commercie en Kolonisatie in West-Indië*. Zutphen: Walburg Pers, 1981.

Labat, J.B. *Nouveau voyage aux îles de Amérique etc.* (1742). Fort de France: Editions des Horizons Caraibes, vol.2 (1972).

LaWall, Charles H. *Four thousand years of Pharmacy*. London: Lippincott, 1927.

Lawrence,W. 'Some source books for West African History'. *The Journal of African History*, vol. 2 (1961).

Lemery, N. *Pharmacopée universelle*. Paris: d'Houry, 1761.

Lewin, I. *Die Gifte in der Weltgeschichte*. Hildesheim:Gerstenberg Verlag, 1984.

Leuftink, A.E. *De geneeskunde bij 's Lands Oorlogsvloot in de 17e eeuw*. Assen: Van Gorcum,1953.

Lötschert, W. and G. Beese, *Elseviers Gids van Tropische Planten*. Amsterdam: Elsevier, 1982

Lutz, E. *Die Rechtliche Struktur Süddeutscher Handelsgesellschaften in der Zeit der Fugger*. Tübingen: Mohr, 1976.

Lijste der medicamenten en instrumenten. Amsterdam: Aart Dirksz. Oossaan, 1692.

Lijste der medicamenten na dewelke de Chirurgijns der Schepen van Oorloge ten dienste der Ed: Mog: Heeren Raden ter Admiraliteit op de Maze resideerende tot Rotterdam, haar zullen hebben te reguleren in het voorzien harer kisten, voor een zomertocht of den tijd van zes maanden. Rotterdam: 14 februarij 1691.

Maier, D. 'Nineteenth Century Asante Medical Practises'. *International Quarterly – Society for the Comparative Study of Society and History*, 1979.

Matthews, L.G. *History of Pharmacy in Britain*. London: Livingstone Ltd. 1962.

Meilink-Roelofsz, M.A.P. *Dutch authors of West Indian History*. The Hague: Nijhoff, 1982.

Meredith, H. *An account of the Gold Coast of Africa*. London, 1812.

Morton, Julia F. *Atlas of Medicinal Plants of Middle America, Bahamas to Yucatan*. Springfield: Thomas, 1981.

Müller, M. *Die Afrikanische auf der Guinesischen Goldküste gelegen Landschafft Fetu*. Hamburg: Born, 1676.

National Institute for Occupational Safety and Health. *Hazard Control of Wood Dust* HC10, March 2, 1998. Publication no.96-127.

Nederlandse Pharmacopee, (*Dutch pharmacopoea*) vierde uitgave. Amsterdam: J.H. de Bussy, 1905.

Netscher, P.M. *Geschiedenis van de Coloniën Essequebo, Demerary en Berbice*. The Hague: Nijhoff, 1888.

Neuburger, M. *Geschichte der Medizin* II Band, erster Teil. Stuttgart, 1911.

Oostindie, G. *Het paradijs overzee. De Nederlandse Caraiben en Nederland.* Amsterdam: Bakker, 1997.

Parry, J.H. and Philip M.Sherlock. A Short History of the West Indies. London: The Macmillan Press, 1978.

Parry, J.H. *Trade and Dominion. The European Oversea Empires in the 18th century.* London: Cardinal, 1974.

Parry, J.W. *The Story of Spices.* Brooklyn: Chemical Publishing Co., 1969.

Pharmacopaea Amstelredamensis of d'Amsterdammer Apotheek (1686). Facsimile Tilburg: Peters, 1986.

Pereira, J. *Beginselen der materia medica en der therapie.* Dl.2. Amersfoort: Van Bommel van Vloten, 1849.

Piso, Willem. *Historia Natural do Brasil Ilustrada.* Tradução Alexandre Correira.São Paolo, 1948.

Pop, G.F. *De geneeskunde bij het Nederlandse Zeewezen.* Weltevreden-Batavia: Kolff & Cie., 1922.

Postma, Johannes M. *The Dutch in the Atlantic Slave Trade 1600-1815.* Cambridge: Cambridge University Press, 1990.

Postma, Johannes M. 'West African exports and the Dutch West India Company 1675-1731'. *Economisch en Sociaal Historisch Jaarboek*, vol. 36 (1973).

Quincy, John, *Pharmacopoeia officinalis extemporanea or a complete English dispensatory in four parts.* 10th ed. London: Longman, 1736.

Ransford, O. *The Slave Trade. The Story of Transatlantic Slavery.* London: Murray, 1971.

Ratelband, K. (ed.) *Vijf Dagregisters van het Kasteel São Jorge da Mina aan de Goudkust 1645-1647.* The Hague: Nijhoff, 1953.

Riley, P.A., and Cunnigham, P.J., *The Faber Pocket Medical Dictionary.* London: Faber and Faber, 1988.

Roberts, W.I., 'Samuel Storke: an Eighteenth Century London Merchant Trading to the American Colonies', *Business History Review*, vol. 39 (1965).

Rogge, J. *Het handelshuis Van Eeghen.* Amsterdam: Van Ditmar, 1949.

Romieux, Y. 'Les coffres de mer de la Compagnie des Indes Hollandaise suivant le tarif de 1739'. *Revue d'Histoire de la Pharmacie*, vol. 40 (1993).

Roy, A.K., K.K. Sinka and H.K. Chourana. 'Aflatoxin contamination of some common drug plants'. *Applied Environ Microbiology*, vol. 54 (1988).

Rushton, J.Ph. *Race, Evolution and Behaviour. A Life History Perspective.* London: Transaction Publishers, 1995.

Rutten, Alphons M.G. *Apothekers en Chirurgijns. Gezondheidszorg op de Benedenwindse Eilanden van de Nederlandse Antillen in de 19e eeuw.* Dissertation Leiden University. Assen: Van Gorcum, 1989.

Rutten, Alphons M.G. 'Ziekten en geneesmiddelen op Curaçao in de tweede helft van de achttiende eeuw'. *Pharmaceutisch Weekblad*, vol. 125 (1990).

Rutten, Alphons M.G. 'Farmaceutische prijsgeschiedenis van de West-Indische Compagnie'. *Pharmaceutisch Weekblad*, vol. 127 (1992).

Rutten, Alphons M.G. 'Slavenhandel, ziekten en mortaliteit in de Curaçaose medisch-farmaceutische geschiedenis'. *Pharmaceutisch Weekblad*, vol. 127 (1992).

Rutten, Alphons M.G. 'Geneesmiddelen leveranciers van de Tweede West Indische Compagnie' *Pharmaceutisch Weekblad*, vol. 127 (1992).

Rutten, Alphons M.G. 'In het voetspoor van een indigo maker. Farmaceutische aspecten van het plantagebedrijf op Curaçao en aan de Goudkust'. *Bulletin Cercle Benelux d'Histoire de la Pharmacie*, vol. 42 (1993).

Rutten, Alphons M.G. 'Geneesmiddel voorziening op de Nederlandse Goudkust in de eerste helft van de 18e eeuw'. *Pharmaceutisch Weekblad*, vol. 129 (1994).

Rutten, Alphons M.G. Een medicijnkist voor Pomeroon in 1686. *Bulletin Cercle Benelux d'Histoire de la Pharmacie*, vol. 43 (1994).

Rutten, Alphons M.G. 'Geneesmiddelen voor de Traan- en Zouthandel in de 17e eeuw'. *Geschiedenis der Geneeskunde*, vol. 2 (1995).

Rutten, Alphons M.G. 'Het Zwarte Gat in de Historisch Medisch-Farmaceutische Informatie'. *Pharmaceutisch Weekblad*, vol. 130 (1995).

Rutten, Alphons M.G. 'Jacques Cassard et la Pharmacie militaire à l'Ile de Curaçao en 1713'. *Revue d' Histoire de la Pharmacie*, vol. 84 (1996)

Rutten, Alphons M.G. *Ondergang in bedwelming – Drugs en giften in het West Romeinse Rijk*. Rotterdam: Erasmus Publishing, 1997.

Rutten, Alphons M.G. 'Drinkbaar goud voor zwarte slaven. De geneesmiddel-fabricatie op Curaçao in 1707 en de Hallese piëtisten'. *Gewina*, vol. 21 (1998).

Rutten, Alphons M.G. 'Storm van 's Gravesande en de geneeskruiden van het 18e eeuwse Guiana'. *Farmaceutisch Tijdschrift voor België*, vol.73 (1996).

Rutten, Alphons M.G. and Pieter C. Emmer, 'Harmful silica fibres and slave demography', *Itinerario* (Leiden University) vol. 23 (1999).

Sabieraj, J. 'Hemmstoffe der Leukotrien-biosynthese'. *Deutsche Apotheker Zeitung*, vol. 132 (1992).

Scagiola, R. *Les apothecaires de Paris et les distillateurs*. Clermont: De Bussac, 1943.

Schmitz, R. *Geschichte der Pharmazie*. Eschborn: Govi Verlag, 1998.

Schomburgk, R.H. *A Description of British Guiana*. New York: Kelley, 1970.

Segersz van der Brugge, J. *Twee journalen neder gehouden by seven matroosen in haer overwinteren op Spitsbergen, gelegen in Groenlant....* Amsterdam: Gillis Joosten Zaagman, 1668.

Sesseler, W.M. and W. Spoon. 'Over het gebruik van wilde salie op de Benedenwindse Eilanden'. *De West-Indische Gids*, vol. 33 (1952).

Sheridan,Richard B. *Doctors and Slaves. A medical and demographic history of slavery in the British West Indies 1680-1834*. Cambridge:Cambridge University Press, 1985.

Sieur de Saint Hilaire. *Les rémèdes des maladies du corps humain*. Paris: Barthelemy Girin, 1702.

Sigerist, Henry E. *History of Medicine*. Vol. 1 New York: Oxford University Press, 1951.

Sonnedecker, Glenn, *Kremers and Urdang's History of Pharmacy*. Wisconsin: American Institute of the History of Pharmacy, 1976.

Stander, S., 'Transatlantic trade in pharmaceuticals during the industrial revolution', *Bulletin History of Medicine*, vol. 43 (1969).

Steele, I.K. *The English Atlantic 1675-1760. An exploration of communication and community*. New York, 1986.

Steele, I.K., *Atlantic Merchant-Apothecary Joseph Cruttenden 1710-1717*. Toronto: University of Toronto Press, 1977.

Stirrett, A.P. *Medical book for the treatment of diseases in West Africa, also pharmacy, notes, dispensary, recipes and health hints*. Nigeria: Sudan Interior Mission, 1931.

Stoll,U. and B.Müller. 'Alte Rezepte Modern betrachtet'. *Geschichte der Pharmazie*, vol. 42 (1990).

Stothers, R.B. and M.R. Rampino. 'Volcanic eruptions in the Mediterranean before AD 630'. *Journal of Geophysical Research*, vol. 88 (1983).

Swaluwe. E.B. *De daden der Zeeuwen gedurende den opstand tegen Spanje*. Amsterdam, 1846.

Symon, D.E. and L.A.R. Haegi. 'Datura is a New World Genus'. In: J.G. Hawkes (ed.) *Solanaceae III Taxonomy, Chemistry, Evolution*. London: Royal Botanic Gardens Kew, 1991.

Taffin, D. *Maladies et médécine à la Guadeloupe au XIXe siècle*. Thèse. Paris: Ecole de Chartres, 1985.

Taffin, D. 'Calamités, catastrophes naturelles et maladies'. In: *Voyage aux Iles d'Amérique*. Exposition Archives de France. Paris: Archives Nationales, 1992.

Teuscher. E. and U. Lindequist. *Biogene Gifte*. Stuttgart: Fischer, 1994.

Teuscher, E. 'Biogene Gifte'. *Deutsche Apotheker Zeitung*. vol. 132 (1992).

Thompson, R. Campbell. *Assyrian Medical Texts from the Originals in the British Museum*. Osnabruck: Zeller, 1983.

Thorwald, J. *Heelmeesters – Macht en Geheimen in de Oude Geneeskunst*. The Hague: Gaade, 1962.

Tschirch, A., *Handbuch der Pharmakognosie*. Bd.1-3. Leipzig: Tauchnitz, 1909-1927.

Unger, W.S. 'Bijdragen tot de geschiedenis van de Nederlandse slavenhandel'. *Economisch Historisch Jaarboek*, vol. 26 (1956).

Van Berkel, A. *Amerikaansche voyagien, behelzende een reis na Rio de Berbice etc.* Amsterdam: Ten Hoorn, 1695.

Van den Boogaart, E. and P.C. Emmer. 'The Dutch Participation in the Atlantic Slave Trade, 1596-1650', In: Henry A. Gemery and Jan S. Hogendorn, eds. *The Uncommon Market*, New York: Academic Press, 1979.

Van der Aa, Robidé. *Afrikaansche Studien. Koloniaal bezit en partikuliere handel op Afrika's Westkust*. The Hague: Nijhoff,1871.

Vandewiele, L.J. *De Grabadin van Pseudo-Mesues en zijn invloed op de ontwikkeling van de farmacie in de Zuidelijke Nederlanden*. Dissertation University of Ghent, 1962.

Van Goor, J. *De Nederlandse koloniën.Geschiedenis van de Nederlandse expansie 1600-1975*. The Hague: SDU, 1994.

Van Harten, A.M. 'Melegueta Pepper'. *Economic Botany*, vol. 24 (1970).

Van Zanen, G.E. *David Ricardo Capriles*. Assen: Van Gorcum, 1969.

Vieyra, M. 'Lijst van geneesmiddelen op koopvaardij schepen'. *Nederlands Tijdschrift voor Geneeskunde*, vol. 80 (1935).

Ward, J.R. *British West Indian Slavery 1750-1834. The Process of Amelioration*. Oxford: Clarendon Press, 1988.

Weatherall, D.E. et al. *Oxford Textbook of Medicine*.Vol. 1. Oxford: Oxford University Press, 1988.

Wichtl, M. *Teedrogen*. Stuttgart: Wissenschaftliche Verlagsgesellschaft, 1989.

Williams, E. *Capitalism and Slavery*. Chapel Hill: University of North Carolina Press, 1995.

Wilson, A.M. 'The logwood trade in the 17th and 18th centuries'. In: Douglas McKay ed. *Essays in the history of Modern Europe*. New York, 1936.

Wilson, Renate. 'The traffic in Halle Orphanage Medications:Medicinals, Philanthropy and Colonial Mission'. *Caduceus*, vol. 13 (1997).

Wilson, Renate. 'Pietist universal reform and care of the sick and the poor. The Medical Institutions of the Francke Foundations and their Social Context'. In: Norbert Finzsch and Robert Jütte, ed. *Institutions of confinement, hospitals, asylums and prisons in Western Europe and North America 1500-1950*. Cambridge: Cambridge University Press, 1996.

Wright, C.W. *Economic History of the United States*. New York: McGraw-Hill Book Company, 1941.

TABLES FIGURES AND MAPS

TABLES

FIGURES

MAPS

INDEX OF NAMES

INDEX OF SUBJECTS

Tables, Maps and Figures are not included